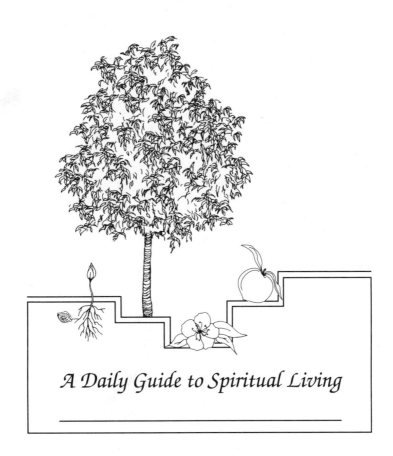

A Daily Guide to Spiritual Living

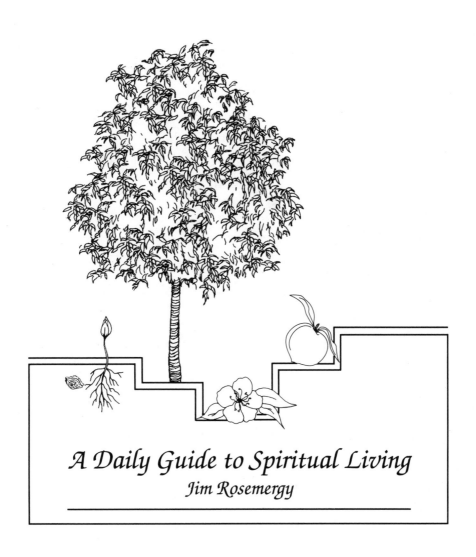

A Daily Guide to Spiritual Living
Jim Rosemergy

Unity Books
Unity Village, MO 64065 USA

Endorsed by the Unity Movement Advisory Council,
a joint committee of the
Association of Unity Churches and Unity School of Christianity
Unity Village, MO 64065

Text and cover designed by Linda Gates

This book is printed on recycled paper.

Dedicated to the Sacred Human,
whose inner journey
reveals its spiritual nature and God mission.

Table of Contents

Section Two: The Inner Journey

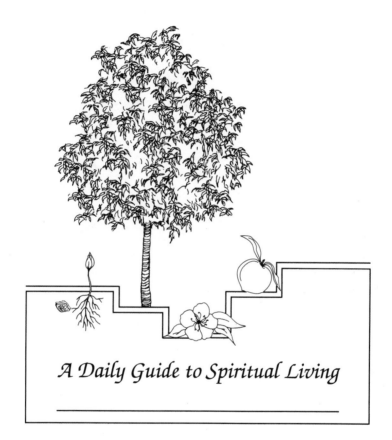

A Daily Guide to Spiritual Living

Preface

As we develop on our life's journey toward wholeness, every human being feels a yearning inside for freedom and fulfillment. Initially, each of us yearns to live life free from worldly concerns. Next, we seek the respect and love of family members and associates. Then we begin to think of making a contribution to the world. These urges compel us to seek their fulfillment, and on occasion, we succeed. However, there is a greater desire, the desire for a life that includes love of others, service, and freedom from worldly concern. It is a desire to live a spiritual life, a life centered in God.

Some of us may have attempted to live this life and thought we had failed. We may have put aside for a time this "absurd" notion of a life whose center is God, but then the urge returns, as if to say that what we yearn for can be realized.

A Daily Guide to Spiritual Living provides daily encouragement to the person who has allowed this divine desire to become life's motivating force. This guidebook is more than words to read; it is a companion for the journey. It is designed to be used for one full year, but it can be utilized over and over again. As the daily lessons are practiced, know that you are not alone. Many people around the world are united in the desire to live a spiritual life and in the study and practice of the lessons of *A Daily Guide to Spiritual Living*.

Introduction

A Daily Guide to Spiritual Living is divided into four sections of thirteen weeks each. Each week addresses a central theme, and the seven days of that week contain ideas that complement and expand upon the weekly thought or concept. These daily lessons are not just to be read, but experienced, for they ask your persistent participation. At times you are requested to express a thought or to share a feeling. On other occasions, you may be enjoined to repeat a thought silently, to pause for a few moments throughout the day, or to record in the guidebook an impression or a dream.

These lessons invite your daily attention. This is helpful, for a spiritual life requires commitment and daily practice. From your persistence will come fulfillment stretching far beyond human imagining, because God has prepared for you peace passing understanding, a joy that is full, and an everlasting love.

As you work with *A Daily Guide to Spiritual Living*, set aside twenty minutes each day so you can gain the maximum benefit from its use. Some lessons call for an action to occur early in the day, so you may wish to set your regular study time shortly after rising or to scan the next day's lesson the night before.

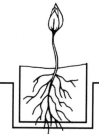

Section One
The Sacred Human

Week One
Divine Discontent

Innate to all men and women is the spiritual search. Discontent first mounts this expedition and makes us seekers, but there will be other leaders on the journey of life. Just as hunger and thirst are the body's first prodding to care for itself, so discontent is the soul's first desire to know itself. Early in the search this discontent will motivate us, but one day it will become fulfillment and contentment.

Take a moment to be still and become aware of your divine discontent. Today it may seem unsettling, but before the search progresses far you will bless this feeling.

What areas of your life seem incomplete? Use the shortest description you can to indicate these areas of daily living, but be sure that what you write brings to mind easily and quickly the area or areas that seem lacking.

List any areas of your life that seem incomplete:

After you have briefly described the area(s) of your life in which you feel discontent, proceed to *Week 1, Day 1.*

Discontent is evidence that a greater good is knocking at life's door.

The spiritual journey, like all journeys, begins with a single step. Oddly, that which leads to the highest and most fulfilling life often begins with discontent. We know that life can be more than it seems to be; therefore, we are motivated, but often not to live a spiritual life. Our initial motivation is to dispel pain. If the pain subsides, we breathe a sigh of relief and forget the spiritual search, but in a short period of time the discontent returns, and we seek again.

Today, let us acknowledge our discontent and this helpful insight. Unhappiness is evidence that a greater good is available to us. For instance, assume you are sitting on the back porch of your home reading the evening newspaper. Someone comes and tells you that there is a visitor at the front door who wants to talk to you. The knock on the door may be perceived as an intrusion, but what if the person at the door is delivering a gift? Discontent is the person calling us to rise, open the door, and receive the gift.

If you experience feelings of discontent today, refuse to consider them a curse. Instead, declare: *Discontent calls me to rise and open the door to a greater good.*

"I will not let you go, unless you bless me."

In the thirty-second chapter of Genesis, there is a story from the life of Jacob. Jacob was the biblical character who deceived his brother, Esau, and his father, Isaac. The deception resulted in Jacob receiving the birthright as the head of the family and Isaac's blessing, which was to be bestowed upon the firstborn, Esau. Although Jacob was officially the head of the family, he feared his brother's wrath and fled to another land.

Years later Jacob and his family returned home, and they learned that Esau was coming to "greet" them with four hundred men. Needless to say, Jacob was troubled, and while the family camped at Jabbok Ford, Jacob crossed the river alone and wrestled with a man until daybreak. As the man (some think the "man" is Jacob, wrestling with himself and his feelings of guilt) attempted to flee, Jacob said, "I will not let you go, unless you bless me" (Gen. 32:26).

This famous verse of Scripture is the theme for the day. There is a blessing in each of life's circumstances. It is experienced by first refusing to avoid the problem or the feelings that accompany it. The human tendency is to want to avoid problems and mental or emotional pain, but the spiritual life requires personal integrity and a willingness to experience life to the fullest.

During this day, whenever a thought of a negative circumstance, feeling of discontent, or challenging event occurs, remember to pause and silently declare: *"I will not let you go, unless you bless me."*

I acknowledge what I once believed would bring me joy.

There are at least two kinds of discontent. Human discontent promises that we will feel better when changes take place in our outer world. Divine discontent causes us to want to change the way we think, act, and live. It calls for inner change.

Human discontent is as much a part of life as divine discontent. It is a "town" we travel through on our way to the final destination. Today, we acknowledge what we once believed would banish discontent and bring us joy.

In the space below, list a few of the outer changes that you once believed were the answers to your problems:

I admit I do not know how to find contentment.

We once thought we knew how to find contentment. Like the horse with the carrot dangling on the string before it, we were compelled. We knew, or so we thought, what would bring us peace and joy. One of two things eventually happened.

One possibility is that we continued to see the carrot, or held the firm conviction that we knew the answer to our problem. We simply did not know how to achieve it. We went from person to person, book to book, church to church, looking for the how, but we never found it. The other possibility is that we finally got the carrot—acquired the job, found our perfect soul mate—but the discontent remained.

Now we admit we do not know what will grant us contentment. We are willing to start again in a new way.

Three times today, once at each meal, pause and silently declare: *I admit I do not know what will grant me contentment.*

Today I do not need to know
how to find joy.

A spiritual life is a life of mystery, faith, and letting. Today provides us with an opportunity to continue to admit we do not know the answer. May we find contentment in the mystery.

This is necessary if we are to live a spiritual life, for God is mystery. If God is to be a part of our lives, mystery must be a part of us. There is no need to know all the answers. Today our greatest need is to begin to find contentment within mystery.

Become like a child and briefly describe from your perspective the four most mysterious things in the universe or in your life:

1.

2.

3.

4.

My discontent is a step I took long ago
in search of joy and purpose.

Part of the spiritual life is vision—the ability to see events, thoughts, and feelings, and their relationship to our unfoldment. Before a peach tree bears fruit, it grows through many stages. First the pit crumbles on the ground. Then the seed reaches into the earth, establishing its roots so it can begin to reach for the light. Next, a delicate, green blade emerges from the darkness of the earth. The tree begins to form, and leaves shade the ground beneath the tree. Blossoms send their fragrance into the air and attract bees to aid in pollination. Finally, the fruit is formed. How helpful it is to see the greater picture and to know that time spent in darkness is just as important as time spent growing in the light.

Discontent is the sprouting of the seed.

In the space provided, describe the stages of your growth:

The seed

The green blade

The tree and leaves

The blossom

The fruit

You may need to return to this day in the future as you continue to grow, for at this time there may be stages of your unfoldment that you have not reached.

15

Contentment, joy, and purpose are
my destiny.

We now know that our discontent is an important part of our spiritual journey. We accept our feelings of unhappiness with the realization that they are not our destiny. We are destined to be fruitful.

The previous days have been a healthy look back at our discontent. Now we no longer look behind us, but forward to a life of contentment, joy, and purpose.

Three times during the day, pause and silently affirm: *Contentment, joy, and purpose are my destiny.* Begin to establish order in your life and the ability to follow through on your commitments by writing the time of day in which you paused to declare your destiny.

First time: _____

Second time: _____

Third time: _____

Week Two

Hope Springs Eternal

Divine discontent and our dissatisfaction with our lives cause hope to spring eternal. None of us can exist for long unless there is at least a belief that things can be different than they are at present. For some people, hope sustains them and allows them to endure the negative cycles of life. They may fantasize about the way things can be or grasp at every "opportunity" which presents itself, but the dreams seldom come true.

A Dream You Have Dreamed

In the space below, outline your hope for a new life. Perhaps it is a marriage you anticipate, a particular job you would like, or an honor to be bestowed upon you.

Dreams That Have Come True

List four "things" you have hoped for that have manifested themselves in your life:

1.

2.

3.

4.

There are times when dreams are fulfilled, and other instances when they are not realized and despair sets in. Hope is suppressed temporarily, but it rises again. Yet, limitation continues. Hope keeps us going, but it never gets us there.

Hope is not to be the center of our lives. It is not an end in itself; it is a stepping-stone to the way life can be. Divine discontent is the first step taken in search of a spiritual life, and hope is the second step. Let the hope that springs eternal in us do more than enable us to cope with limitation and problems. Let it empower us to step forward into a new life free of restriction and chronic challenges.

Hope is the conviction that

there is an answer.

Hope springs from within us with amazing swiftness. It only takes a positive word of encouragement or the prospect of constructive change, and we are hopeful again. This positive surge of thinking is a prelude to the as yet unspoken promise of a brighter future.

Hope does not require that we know what the future holds. The prospect of a better tomorrow calls forth positive thoughts and the willingness to experience life anew.

There once was a counselor who listened intently as people shared their problems and concerns. Often the counselor would be as confused as the client. He had to choose between entering into despair with the person or pointing the way to a new life. The favorite phrase of this helper was, "There is an answer." He would continue, "I am as confused as you are, but I know there is an answer." These simple statements quickened hope.

The initial emphasis of this book has been upon you, the reader. Now for a brief time, attention shifts to other people. The new direction will not only help others, but you too.

As you move through the day, remain sensitive to the people around you and any problems they are having. Your contribution to the world today is to be willing to say, "There is an answer."

Without vision, I perish.

Yesterday's exercise brings to mind the uplifting nature of hope and how quickly hope can become a part of life when we look constructively to the future. In Proverbs 29:18 (AV) we read, "Where there is no vision, the people perish." Perhaps it could be stated, "Where there is no vision, hope fades, and then the people perish."

No one knows what the future holds. This vision is not vivid like a city skyline on a sunny, clear day. It is not exact and specific. This vision is the soul's willingness to experience a new life. This vision does not know what lies ahead, but it knows there is an answer.

This knowing is enough to cause hope's birth in us, for nothing is born as quickly as hope. Faith takes months, even years to grow to maturity, but hope is born in a day, in an instant. This is the day hope is born in you.

Please write today's date: _____

Through hope, I envision a new life.

We do not know what lies ahead, but we can sense a greater good unfolding in our lives.

Today's activity is destined to bear great fruit, but it requires an extended time of quiet and stillness. Find a place where you will not be disturbed. Let your mind roam freely for awhile, and then declare: *Through hope, I envision a new life.* Then rest, and allow the sense of the greater good to emerge from within you.

In the space below, write any thoughts, feelings, or images that enter your mind. You may not think they are important, but record them anyway. These thoughts, feelings, and images are the beginning of a vision, not only for your life, but for your life's purpose. At another time, greater attention will be given to purpose.

Hope keeps me going,
but it never gets me there.

Hope is an important part of the spiritual journey, but it is only part of the whole, one step on the path. Refuse to allow hope to become fantasy and daydreams about the future. Occasionally, a person will live in this imagined world, and because it is more peaceful and harmonious than the earthly experience, the fantasy becomes the person's reality. Admittedly, this is an extreme of human behavior, but it points out a nonconstructive dimension of hope.

Today, consider your past behavior and determine whether fantasy and daydreaming have sustained you. There is no condemnation if this has occurred.

If you have engaged in fantasy and unwholesome daydreaming, describe the fantasy or daydream. This is done so you can be aware of the tendency to fantasize.

Now, and at any time hope tends to become fantasy, remind yourself:
Hope keeps me going, but it never gets me there.

I refuse to allow hope to cause me to accept limitation.

We now see hopefulness as a *human* paradise, for it brings us joy today and promises us a brighter tomorrow. However, there is another paradise, not conceived of by the human mind, that awaits us. Hopefulness can be a barrier to this paradise, which is our destiny.

By hoping for a better tomorrow, it is possible to accept the limitation of today. This we do not want to do. Limitation is not our destiny; it is not our way of life.

Hope resides within us and opens our souls to new possibilities, but it does not bring the possibilities into being. Remember that hope keeps us going, but it never gets us there. *Faith* gets us there. Faith extends far beyond the soul, for it helps bring possibilities into our world. Faith calls for action, for without action even faith is dead. Hope is a call for faith.

Please indicate what you think are your limitations:

In the space below, write: *I do not allow hope for a brighter tomorrow to cause me to accept these perceived limitations.*

My destiny is not limitation.

Your destiny is not limitation. Your hope for the future is not primarily for a better human experience: more wealth, esteem, or recognition. People have thrived and expressed a remarkable compassion and spirituality while physical limitation was a part of their lives. Victor Frankl, while in a Nazi concentration camp, was able to give his attention to a flower blooming in a prison courtyard. The apostle Paul, while in prison in Rome, found an inner peace that moved him to declare: "For I have learned, in whatever state I am, to be content" (Phil. 4:11).

It is not enough to say our destiny is not limitation. We sense there is a part of us that cannot be limited. Victor Frankl and Paul demonstrated that this is true. The body may be housed, but not the mind or spirit.

This day is destined to include extended times of reflection and inner listening. At least three times during the day, dedicate yourself to experiencing the unlimited truth of your being. Envision the most unlimited, freeing, and creative environment you can imagine, place yourself in the midst of it, and declare: *Let that which I am be revealed.*

Have no expectations as to what may be revealed.

Hope wed to action gives birth to faith.

The Bible declares, "Faith apart from works is dead" (Jas. 2:26). Perhaps it is true to say that faith without works is hope. Hope keeps us going, but it never gets us there. Hope is quickened in us, and we give thanks that it has brought us this far on our spiritual journey. But to hope we now add action, a special kind of action that brings us one step closer to a faith-filled life.

Choice is a powerful action of the soul. By choice, we consent to limitation. By choice, we decide to overcome the law of inertia and move forward in life. Science discovered this law, which states that an object at rest tends to remain at rest; an object in motion tends to remain in motion. Trying to push a stalled car is an excellent example of inertia. At first, great effort is expended in an attempt to get the car moving; however, after it begins to roll, pushing gets easier. A person who is limited and mired in negativity experiences the same law.

Write a statement that illustrates your willingness to move from hope to faith:

Week Three

The Power of Choice

Human beings are granted many powers, and the first is the power of choice. We are not pawns tossed by the sea of circumstance or the winds of turmoil. We have been given power and dominion not only over the birds of the air and the fish of the sea, but over our own lives as well. Through choice we may consent to defeat or triumph.

Consider for a few moments choices you have made that have altered your life. First, briefly describe a situation in which your "choice" was to allow another person to determine the course of your life:

Second, list three examples of choices you made that affected your life positively:

1.

2.

3.

Finally, list three examples of choices you made that affected your life adversely:

1.

2.

3.

The choices you make determine the direction and quality of your life experience. In the space below, write a statement that expresses your willingness not only to make wise choices, but to consciously acknowledge the influence of the power of choice in your life.

Choice is a gift given to me.

Some gifts are limited editions, for only a few people on earth will receive certain gifts. For example, only a few people on earth have owned the Hope Diamond. But there is a gift given to everyone. It is unique to each person and more valuable than precious gems. It is the gift of choice!

No one and no thing can determine our choices. We have been given the power to determine what we think, how we feel, what we do, and how we respond or react to people and the world. You are not powerless; you are not a vessel driven by wind or storm. Through the power of choice, your life becomes a thing of beauty and a blessing to the world. Spend today in joy and in giving thanks for the gift of choice. It is a gift that can never be taken from you.

Today is a Conscious Day! As the minutes and hours of this day are lived, simply be conscious of the choices that you make. Perhaps an item is purchased or a date for an outing is set. Maybe the choice is made to have lunch with a friend or to return to school for your degree. The possibilities are infinite.

In the space provided, indicate ten choices you made during this Conscious Day.

1. _____

2. _____

3. _____

4. _____

5. _____

Week 3
Day 15
continued

6. _____

7. _____

8. _____

9. _____

10. _____

No longer do I allow other people
to make choices for me.

We are capable. We come complete with instructions. In us there is a direct line to wisdom. There is no need to depend upon other people to make decisions for us. Even when we have depended upon others for wisdom, we still made the decision to do so. It was a choice we made.

Give one example of a time when you gave another person dominion over your life:

What were the results of the other person's choice?

Give the most recent example in which you allowed another person to choose for you:

Declare: *No longer do I allow others to make choices for me. I have been given the gift of choice. I will not give away that gift.*

Doing nothing is a choice I make.

There are times when the wisest decision is to do nothing. There are other times when failing to act is a choice to live in limitation.

One of the primary reasons we struggle when faced with a difficult decision is that we are afraid we will make the wrong choice. During times like these, it is important to remember that we can always choose again. Life is a perpetual stream of choices. In nearly every moment of every day, a choice is enacted. Much of life is trial and error. Through this much-used process, we move forward to a greater good.

Today, choose not to hesitate in decision making. There will be times when you choose to do nothing, but it will not be because of fear. It will be because inaction is the appropriate choice at the time.

Indecision, on the other hand, is your choice to feel anxiety and to let fear dominate your life. The choice to act is your decision to discover that you have the inner resources to move through any circumstance.

Periodically throughout the day and just before going to bed, affirm: *I live this day in the realization that doing nothing is a choice I make.*

I use the gift of choice wisely.

Today acknowledge that you did not realize the impact of the power of choice in your life. Choice is the fountainhead from which the river of life flows. For earthly rivers, the fountainhead is usually pure, but there have been times when a choice we made was inconsistent with a spiritual life. The power of choice was not used wisely.

If you are to use the gift of choice wisely, decisions made must allow wisdom to escape from within you. It begins with humility and acknowledging that apart from God, you do not know what to do. Next, declare that you are willing to act upon the light that shines from within. Third, rest quietly and let the light shine. Perhaps it will be helpful to say out loud, "Let the light shine." Finally, when the choice is revealed, take action. You have discovered that a wise choice is an expression of an inner wisdom.

In your own words outline the four steps to the wise use of the gift of choice, and use them whenever you are faced with a decision:

1.

2.

3.

4.

I no longer choose . . .

Making wise choices requires that we do certain things. It also means that we cease doing other things. Today's focus is upon the things and actions that you need to release from your life.

A choice of words has been made in order to stress the fact that what is to be released was once chosen. It is time to choose again.

In the space provided, complete the following sentence. Then act out the words in daily living. Complete this sentence in as many ways as necessary in order to discover the choices which no longer need to be made:

I no longer choose to:

I no longer choose to:

I no longer choose to:

I no longer choose to:

I no longer choose to:

I choose . . .

Today, exercise your God-given power of choice. In the course of a day, many choices are made. Many of these decisions are made easily and, in some cases, unconsciously. Today, make a conscious choice. Respond to the question: What choice can I make today that will have the greatest impact on my spiritual life?

I choose:

Choices encourage change.

During the course of *Week 3* you have become aware of the idea that choices impact your life. You may have assumed much, but no mention has been made of the nature of the impact on you. Before you proceed to *Week 4*, know that choice encourages change.

This book is a call for change. You should not expect to pursue a spiritual life and remain the same. All people sense this truth. It is fundamental. A spiritual life is different from our ordinary, human experience and expression.

Pause now and verbally declare: *Choice encourages change.* Say this three times. The third time you speak, note how it feels to make this statement. Ask yourself the question, "Am I willing to change?" Notice that there is no reference to the world's changing. It is you who must change. If the answer is yes, rest this evening in preparation for *Week 4*, which considers the only constant—change.

Week Four
The Only Constant

When you acknowledge the power of choice, you invite change. Know today that change is the only constant on your spiritual journey. God and your spiritual essence are changeless, but your awareness of Spirit and your spiritual identity are perpetually changing. All of creation is in a state of change. Everything is either growing or deteriorating.

Most people know of the two types of change, but not everyone is aware that life is change. Change is something we cannot avoid; it is our destiny. We can choose not to grow, but then we experience the form of change called deterioration. The question is whether we will choose transformation or deterioration.

Therefore, let today be a day not only of change, but of choice!

Pause for five minutes and consider the idea that change is the only constant in life. If you believe this statement is true, make a conscious choice by writing on the line below either "I choose transformation" or "I choose deterioration."

_____

_____

Signature

I choose transformation.

Some choices are obvious. Who would consciously choose deterioration and limitation? No one, yet the human tendency is to want to run from difficulties. Such a choice only leads to hardship, limitation, and deterioration. Today, choose transformation.

A traveler who was journeying to a promised land of plenty encountered a mammoth mountain on the path. Inquiries with the people who lived at the foot of the mountain revealed that no one had ever found a way around the mountain. There was only one way to the other side—over the top. Of course, thought the traveler, there is only one way beyond a difficulty, and that is to rise above it.

Precious metals and other treasures are found by some who climb mountains, but the true treasure is a traveler's discovery of his or her innate capacities. This is transformation.

If there is a mountain before you now, climb higher. No difficulty is put behind you until you have changed and been transformed.

Only through change may I experience my destiny.

Eye has not seen nor ear heard what God has prepared for us. Our destiny is beyond words. The peace and joy offered to humankind is boundless. It is no wonder that we push onward to this greater good.

Today is the day to affirm that only by changing may you experience your destiny. You cannot remain a child and become an adult. You must put aside your childhood and become who you are. Your destiny lies before you.

For too long, you have avoided change and thus avoided your destiny. Your method of achieving the greater good may have been to demand that other people and the world change. To demand that another person change is to refuse to accept the greater good.

List the people and conditions you have asked to change:

Now declare: *I no longer refuse my destiny by demanding that the above changes be made. Only one change is required.* What is that change?

Change is a call for faith.

Change is a call for faith, for only with faith can we face the unknown. Change brings us face-to-face with that which is uncertain and mysterious. Even when we sense a greater good, there is often trepidation, for we do not know what lies ahead. If we only knew that the greatest mystery of life is God!

If you are to be transformed and fulfill your purpose, change must become your way of life. The fear of the unknown, the fear of change, is rooted in the realization that all change requires the death of the old and a letting go of what was once of value. Usually, there is a brief time when the soul releases the old and has not yet taken hold of the new. Some experience this as fear, others know it as faith.

Today, begin to change by facing the unknown in a casual way. Before this day ends, do two of the following things:

1. Drive home a new way from work or play.

2. Go to a place you have never gone before.

3. Eat a kind of food you have never eaten before.

4. Talk to a stranger.

5. Read a magazine you have never read before.

May this simple exercise be the beginning of the revelation that this is a friendly universe whose unknown is a greater good.

To change is to grow.

To grow is to be.

The oldest living creatures on earth are trees. There are olive trees in the Garden of Gethsemane that were seedlings when Jesus wept on the mountainside. It seems appropriate that the oldest living creatures are some of the wisest living things on earth. Trees "know" that in order to live they must grow. If for one season a tree ceases to grow, its deterioration has begun.

Only through growth will you fulfill your destiny. Only through change will you grow. The great tragedy of life is to remain the same year after year. Nations have attempted to isolate themselves from other countries, so they might remain the same. In every instance, the nations began to deteriorate, for nothing can remain the same and fulfill its destiny.

In what area of your life do you feel stagnant?

What change is necessary if you are to grow?

What must you let go of in order to come alive?

Change carries me into the unknown.

We allow ourselves to be carried by the natural forces of the universe into the unknown and beyond, to our reason for being. Imagine the transformation that the larvae experiences as it is wrapped in a cocoon, only to emerge many days later as a butterfly. There is no greater example of change in nature than the larvae's transformation into a butterfly. The tiny worm allows itself to be shaped by the natural forces of the universe. First, it is wrapped in a cocoon of darkness, and then its sinuous body becomes a winged creation able to soar above the ground it once crawled upon. There is a metamorphosis more marvelous awaiting us as we allow spiritual forces to carry us into the unknown.

From the mundane changes of yesterday comes a look into an unknown region of your soul. Consider a possible area in your life into which you have been reluctant to venture, and indicate it in the space below. (Some possibilities are: low self-esteem, suppressed memories, poor health, troubled relationships, and chronic unemployment.)

Now declare: *I allow myself to be carried into this unknown area of my life.*

I am willing to change.

Nothing is more natural than change and yet, from the perspective of human consciousness, nothing is more unsettling. It is said that public speaking is the number one fear among human beings. It is not so. Change is our greatest fear. It is strange that what holds the greatest promise is also the most persistent barrier to that promise.

If we inquired at the home of one who had accepted the great promise and asked, "What is change's first commandment?" this would be the answer: Change asks that we let go of what we think we are, so we can discover who we are. The worm destined to become a butterfly sheds the cocoon, and then it flies and flutters from flower to flower.

Silently declare: *Not only am I willing to change, I am willing to adhere to change's first commandment—to let go of who I think I am.*

Obviously, before you can let go of who you think you are, this false one must be uncovered. In the space provided, write four descriptions of who you think you are:

1.

2.

3.

4.

No matter how accurate these descriptions may seem, there is more. As precious as these words may be, they must be released. Perhaps you are now discovering how difficult change can be. Nothing is sacred when it enters the realm of change.

Life is change.

We are most alive when we are changing, for the change that is transformation allows us to discover our inner resources. Change's first commandment is to let go, but its first gift is life.

Look around you today and examine the trees, flowers, or plants in your world. Remember that they live because they grow and change. They do not change for change's sake. They change because life is change.

Today's work is simple. Spend at least twelve minutes pondering a tree, flower, or plant. Carefully study this living creature, and write a reminder to yourself to return to it in seven days to witness its growth and its enduring message that life is change.

Beginning Anew

There are two ways to begin. We can begin *again* and potentially repeat the same mistakes, or we can begin *anew*. Many people begin again, but the ones who live a spiritual life have learned to start over in a new way. Obviously, this must occur, for a fresh start with an old, unsuccessful method produces after its kind.

In gaining self-knowledge, there are penetrating questions to ask. Are there any unproductive, limiting experiences in your life that can be labeled cycles? For instance, do hurtful human relationships continue to hamper you? Do you meander from job to job, never seeming to find your direction or perfect place?

Can you identify any limiting cycles in your life? What disturbing happening is present today that has been present in the past?

If you are aware of an unproductive cycle, there is a need to begin *anew*. If you have described it in the space above, you are beginning anew. As you continue with *Week 5*, you will receive additional ideas that support your new start.

Week 5
Day 29

Today I do a new thing.

This week is not a week to learn new ideas from reading. It is a week of action. Did Jesus not say that we are to be doers of the word as well as hearers? Children can read about playing baseball or tennis, and even watch a game others are playing, but the true experience is in playing the game. Since the conception of the written word and its spread into the household, there has been a tendency to be "overread and underdone." Not this week. "Do it now" is the consistent admonition of change.

Today do a new thing, and write below what it was and how it felt:

Today I say a new thing.

Today choose a new word you have never uttered before and use it in conversation. Write the word below:

Also, choose a positive, uplifting phrase you have never uttered before and use it in conversation. Let these words which affirm life be a constant companion of your self-talk today. A good example might be: *Yes, I can.* Please write the phrase in the space below:

Today I journey to a new place.

Today begin anew by going to a place you have never gone before. In a previous lesson a similar suggestion was made, but the new place could have been a store or some other busy place. Today's assignment is to be in a new place where you can sit and ponder new beginnings. In fact, you may want to come to this place any time it is necessary to consider beginning anew. This place is to be remembered as a starting line. Call it your Alpha Place.

Please describe your Alpha Place and reveal in a few words any insights that came to you there:

Today I hear a new sound.

The world is alive with sound, as is the soul. Those who have heard the still small voice have discovered that attunement and sensitivity to the world of sound are helpful in developing the skill of listening.

Today, listen for a new sound. The possibility of hearing a new sound lies in several areas of life. You can hear someone say something you have never heard before. Perhaps you can hear what your friend or spouse or child is really asking of you. You can hear the voice of God in stillness. You can hear a new song or the sounds that are around your home each day, but which you have not heard.

No matter what the new sound, please describe it and the circumstances that allowed you to hear it:

Today I respond in a new way.

Today's "doing" is a challenge, for it calls for a new response to a person or situation. This day we do not run on automatic, relying on instinctive reactions that repeat themselves again and again. Remember, this week is dedicated to beginning *anew*. It is possible that this exercise may take several days to complete.

Become aware of a reactive response you have repeated again and again. Describe this reaction:

Next, describe the situation, event, or whatever is prelude to your instinctive reaction. Perhaps it is a phone call from your previous spouse or something that your child or a parent consistently does. Please indicate the situation:

Finally, describe the response you want to make:

All that remains is for you to respond anew!

Today I am new.

Yesterday's work was a demand for much more than a new response to a person or situation. We do not do a new thing or respond in a new way unless we are new. Life is not a matter of doing. Life requires being.

Today rejoice, for you are a new being. Three times throughout this day, take time to be still and rest quietly. Be sure that no one is nearby, for you will be speaking out loud. Speak these words from the stillness of these moments: *Today I am new.*

A new heaven, a new earth

There is no other creation that seems newer or more filled with possibilities than a newborn child, and yet the babe is not any newer than we are!

In Revelation 21:1 it is written, "Then I saw a new heaven and a new earth." Most people are familiar with the idea of a new earth, but most think of heaven as remaining constant. Is there not perfection in heaven? Many believe earth will pass away, but not heaven, yet Jesus said, "Heaven and earth will pass away, but my words will not pass away" (Mt. 24:35).

Further along in this book we will consider in detail the nature of heaven, but a seed will be planted today. The heaven that will pass away is the perception of life which we once believed was true. From the new heaven that rises, a new earth or earthly experience will be made manifest.

This has been a great week. There is a new heaven and a new earth. You have no assignment for today, but remember to return to *Week 4, Day 28* to complete that lesson. Relax and enjoy the new you which you have become!

Week Six
The Sacred Human

The fact that we are human is evident for all to see. There is the vicious human who commits atrocities, who feels hurt so deeply that it attempts to hurt others. The vicious human finds itself behind bars and in the most debilitating circumstances. This one is easy to identify.

Let us also have the courage to witness the sacred human. The sacred human feels joy when the world conforms to its expectations, and is the one who hurts not only physically but emotionally, who feels guilt and remorse, and who cries and expresses sadness. In general, the sacred human does not consciously and maliciously strike out at other people. It wants peace, but does not know how to achieve it. People who are counselors have seen the sacred human, and they have grown to love it. Some people bury this precious side of themselves in an attempt to hide it from others and from themselves. They think that by burying the hurt inside it will not affect their lives, and they will not experience the pain. But they do. Sometimes the body becomes ill and reflects what is housed within. At other times, depression comes and robs a person of peace and joy.

Now is the time to accept, honor, and love the sacred human. Only by accepting this part of your human self will you find and express your spiritual self.

Write a one-word description of your sacred human:

There is no need to be ashamed of this part of yourself. Through the power of choice, you can accept, honor, and love the sacred human in yourself and others. On the following page, write a brief statement that expresses your decision to face and embrace your sacred human:

Week 6
continued

Sacred human,

come stand in the light with me.

Today, acknowledge that there is a part of you that you have shunned. This one feels hurt and is looking for love, but searching in inappropriate ways. There are times when you think this part of you must always remain hidden. How happy you could be, you think; but then, when you least expect it, the hidden part of you is not hidden any more. You are out of control and acting in ways that you know are not for your highest good. You are like the apostle Paul, who said, "For I do not do what I want, but I do the very thing I hate" (Rom. 7:15).

This sacred human is to be ignored no longer. Today acknowledge a hidden part of you, a part of you that you have shunned. Your spiritual journey cannot continue until you come to know the sacred human and discover who it is and what it wants.

In the space below, write a brief apology to your sacred human. Be sure to include the following things:

1. An acknowledgment of the presence of the hidden part of you.

2. A reference to the hidden part of yourself as the sacred human.

3. An acknowledgment of your fear of facing your sacred human.

4. The reason you have shunned the sacred human. If you do not know the reason, include this fact in your apology.

I am willing
to face the sacred human.

Once you have apologized to your sacred human, ask this one to stand in the light and tell you of its conception and what it desires from you and the world. You do not know this part of yourself you have shunned, but it is time for your orphaned self to come home. You may suspect this hidden part of yourself is not God's creation. It is more likely that this is something you have created. Be willing to face your sacred human self.

It is evident that this part of you does not want to remain hidden. It rises when you least expect its appearance. Now make the call, "Come stand in the light and let yourself be seen. Tell me of your conception and what you want from me and the world."

It is likely that when called to stand in the light, the sacred human will be shy and retiring; therefore, persistence is necessary as you continue in your willingness to face your human self. The sign of the coming of the sacred human will most likely be a feeling. Often throughout this day, pause and say to the sacred human, "Come stand in the light. Tell me of your conception and what you want from me and the world." Then rest and wait for the feeling that announces the coming of this hidden part of you.

When the sacred human "appears," do not turn away, but listen as a mother listens to a child whom she has not seen for many years.

When the sacred human "appears," there is often a tendency to want to turn away, or, if this is resisted, to believe that one meeting is sufficient. This is not true. There is much to be revealed. We are destined to know all things about ourselves—the human and the divine. Hiding does not permit discovery, and without discovery peace and joy will remain forever a dream.

Return to yesterday's activity and repeat it. To your previous invitation now add the statement, "There is nothing that needs to remain hidden. I am willing to see all things."

Remember, there is nothing that is unbearable when you willingly face it. In fact, getting to know your sacred human is destined to be a precious part of your spiritual journey.

The sacred human means no harm.

The primary desire of the sacred human is to be loved. However, when one has been hurt often, along with the cry for love is an attempt to be protected from pain. The exterior is sometimes harsh, and there is seemingly no desire for friendship or love, but this is not true.

No matter what the antics of the sacred human, know that the one thing it desires is acceptance and love. The sacred human means no harm, but neither does it want to be hurt. Sometimes the desire to avoid hurt is greater than the desire to be loved. By being gentle with the sacred human, you will find it will slowly but steadily lower the defenses and become like a child.

Continue with yesterday's exercise, with the added realization that the sacred human means you no harm. The reason the acceptance of the sacred human is stressed so thoroughly is that unless you are willing to face, honor, accept, and love your creation, you will not be able to look with greater vision to discover who you really are. Always remember, the sacred human is your creation and is not to be shunned.

I call forth the sacred human.

The most common experience of our sacred human is like that of a small child who has been hurt and wants to be loved. Perhaps this little one was abused by a parent or someone who was supposed to protect and respect it. At the moment of trauma, the sacred human was born. It was not conceived in love as was the image of God, but in pain. Is it any wonder that adults act as children long after their years of infancy?

Now it is time for this little one to understand. For years it has wanted to be loved, and now the most loving act is to help the child understand how it came to be. The sacred human is now developed enough to understand what it could not understand so many years ago. For instance, in the distant past a child could not understand why an adult would abuse it. It never occurred to the little one that the parent was sick, but had not asked for help.

Truth will set the sacred human free. Truth will allow it to accept itself. The hurt self does not need to be hurt. Like a small child, it needs to be loved, to be told that all things can be healed, and to learn the truth of its conception.

Today's exercise is the first of a number of imaginings which you will be asked to experience as you utilize this book. Before beginning, read the following exercise thoroughly so that you will not have to refer to it as you take today's action step.

In your mind's eye either see or sense the presence of a small child which you know to be yourself during a time of hurt. You, the caring adult, are the only one with this sacred human. Open your arms to this little one, and invite the child to sit on your lap. Do not be surprised if at first there is reluctance, but remember that this child wants to be loved; it wants to understand. Watch as the child comes before you and crawls onto your lap. There may be tears. They will be your tears. Rest in silence for a time, and

61

Week 6
Day 40
continued

then tell your sacred human of your love and of the truth that will set it free. At the completion of sharing, hold each other close, and let the two of you become one.

I love and honor the sacred human.

Read the following statements seven times throughout this day:

"I love and honor my sacred human. In fact, I love being human. This is a specialness I do not want to lose. God has honored me with the ability to create according to my vision. It may not be accurate, but it is still my creation and is not to be shunned.

"A child's first attempts at art are not masterpieces, but they are precious to the child and to the parent. My creation does not even approach the truth of being, but it is my first encounter with the creative process. It is the first step of a child who will one day run. Once the sacred human is accepted, loved, and honored, the time draws near when God's creation can emerge."

I accept the sacred human.

This week is crucial as you continue your quest to live a spiritual life. Obviously, the living of this special way of life requires transformation. Specifically, you must be transformed. Often you may have thought others needed to change or that the world had to be different if your life was to be all that it could be.

The oddity is that before there can be transformation, there must first be acceptance. We might think that if we accept something it will never change, but the dynamics of change reveal that once we bring what is hidden into the light and accept it, then it can be released. *Week 6* has been a time to stand with the sacred human and accept it as it is. No change is required, only acceptance. This acceptance is the beginning of transformation.

This has been a good week. But remember, the sacred human has a tendency to shy away from the light. It and its thoughts and emotions must be called to stand in the light again and again so that the thoughts and emotions from the past can feel your acceptance.

Your task today is a simple one, but one that is to be remembered. Be willing to call the sacred human forth every day, if necessary, and to accept its thoughts and emotions just the way they are.

Let the transformation begin!

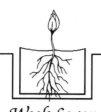

Week Seven
Be Transformed

The beginning of our new life is like the coming of spring. The air is fresh and the seeds begin to sprout and grow. In fact, spring is the outpicturing of a law: "For whatever a man sows, that he will also reap" (Gal. 6:7). The harvest of spring is the result of planting seeds. There are seeds of numerous varieties, and they account for the plentiful colors that come when the sun warms the earth and the seeds sprout. Not many people know that the seeds which bear fruit as our lives are thoughts.

Ancient wisdom declares, "Be transformed by the renewal of your mind" (Rom. 12:2), and "For as he thinketh in his heart, so is he" (Prov. 23:7 AV). People who have practiced this way of life affirm: *Thoughts held in mind produce after their kind.* The key to new life is in understanding the constructive and nonconstructive nature of thought. Let us exercise our power of choice by beginning to choose thoughts that, when they produce after their kind, yield a harvest of beauty, peace, love, and joy.

People whose lives change always change their thoughts and viewpoints of themselves, others, and the world. Write a statement below that expresses your willingness to change the way you think:

Thoughts are things.

We are destined to be transformed, but it is we who must unlock the door to this new life. We no longer have to wonder what to do. A key to change is given to us—THOUGHTS ARE THINGS. These three words reveal a great truth that every person will eventually understand: our life experience flows from the thoughts which we hold in mind. Thoughts actually manifest themselves in our lives.

Do happy people think negatively? Those who think life is a struggle have much they can point to which justifies their belief. Before a miserable life is lived, there are always thoughts of misery. Before we rise from despair, there must always be thoughts of hope.

There once was a man who was attending his brother's funeral. Before the service the man talked with the minister, who shared an interesting story with the man. The minister said, "Your brother came to me several months ago in perfect health. He insisted on making his funeral arrangements because he said that he was going to die soon. He said, 'Men in my family always die around their sixtieth birthday, and mine is just around the corner.' When your brother died shortly after his sixtieth year, I remembered what he had said to me."

The brother replied, "Several men in our family have died around their sixtieth birthday, but not everyone; I am in my seventies. And by the way, there is something my brother did not know. He was adopted."

Our thoughts and beliefs have a powerful impact on our lives. When we are not conscious of this, transformation is difficult, if not impossible. However, today is a day for rejoicing, for you now know that thoughts, attitudes, and beliefs beget what you experience on earth.

Now you have the key to changing and beginning anew. Your daily lessons have helped you live in this way, but more is necessary.

There must be transformation.

Today's assignment is to list four significant happenings in your life. These can be wondrous things or things you wish had not occurred.

1.

2.

3.

4.

Next, consider the idea that your thoughts, rather than other people, luck, or circumstance, were the cause of these happenings.

Because thoughts are things,
I am responsible for my life.

Because thoughts are things, we are not helpless or out of control. People, luck, and circumstance need not determine what we think. Thoughts enter our minds by our choice, not the dictation of another person. Nor can conditions determine what we think, for they do not determine our reactions or our life experience.

We now understand the implications of the Bible verse that states, "Let them have dominion over the fish of the sea, and over the birds of the air, and over the cattle, and over all the earth" (Gen. 1:26). Dominion over circumstance is possible because we have been given the ability to determine our thoughts, attitudes, and beliefs.

This realization brings us face-to-face with something we have wanted to avoid for much of our lives—responsibility. When we were pawns and helpless to determine the course of our lives, we believed other people and circumstances were responsible for the way we were and the situations of our lives. The truth is: we were responsible.

With this understanding there often comes a sense of guilt. Let it pass away, for you have the keys to transformation. If our lives are in shambles, it is true that we are responsible for the mess, but we can also be responsible for our new lives. The same principle—"thoughts are things"—which brought us to our knees will soon lift us to new heights.

If you are currently in the midst of a difficult time in your life, pause throughout this day and silently declare twenty times: *I am responsible for this problem, or my response to it, and I can be responsible for its solution.*

If this is currently a time of peace in your life, pause throughout this day and silently declare twenty times: *Because I am responsible for my life and I am willing to accept this responsibility, this peace need never leave me.*

I choose to think constructive thoughts.

You are responsible for your life, and through choosing constructive thoughts, you will build a creative life of love, peace, and joy. Notice that the call is not for positive thoughts, but for constructive thoughts. The truth is, all thinking is positive. For instance, negative-thinkers are actually positive people—they are positive they will lose their jobs, positive that life is a struggle, positive that others are out to get them, positive that they will become sick at certain times of the year, positive that something is wrong with them.

Today, let your thinking be constructive. Paul declared, "Whatever is true, whatever is honorable, whatever is just, whatever is pure, whatever is lovely, whatever is gracious, if there is any excellence, if there is anything worthy of praise, think about these things" (Phil. 4:8). By thinking constructively, life is built up rather than torn down.

For each of the following situations, please give an example of constructive thoughts you would like to hold in mind:

1. You have just experienced the disapproval of someone.

2. You have just learned that you must have an operation.

3. You have just learned that for the fourth time you came in second in the running for the job for which you applied.

4. You have been told that a relationship is over.

5. You have lost your car keys.

Thoughts, attitudes, and beliefs are part of your interior world. Some of them move deep within you and are, therefore, difficult to identify. However, your words are windows into the depths of you. Your words reveal the nature of your thoughts.

Today listen to your words. Do not attempt to hold your tongue or to think before you speak. It is best that you simply speak and listen. This day will be no different from any other day, except for the fact that you will listen to what you say with the knowledge that your words reveal your thoughts, attitudes, and beliefs.

There is an episode in Jesus' life that is helpful in understanding the power of words and the consciousness out of which the words come. Jesus was walking down a road and went to a roadside fig tree to obtain a few figs to eat. The tree was bare, and Jesus said, "May no fruit ever come from you again!" (Mt. 21:19) The tree withered at once. Jesus may have done this to illustrate the negative impact of our words. There are many examples of the constructive use of words in Jesus' life, but this one example alerts us to the impact of nonconstructive thinking and speaking.

Write down any key phrases that give you insight into your inner self. Pay particular attention to words that are not constructive. Let there be no attempt to change the words at this time. This is a day of observation.

Today I speak only positive words about myself and others.

Today begins a process that will be part of your life for years to come. It is the conscious attempt to speak only positive words about yourself and others. At first these words may be contrary to the thoughts that move deep within you, but the words are a beginning.

Thoughts, attitudes, and beliefs will not change as easily as words, but with persistence and adherence to principle, the changes will occur. Words are the choice we make today.

As the day progresses, do not be discouraged to discover that old patterns of thought are expressed in familiar phrases that seem like old friends. This is normal. When this happens, acknowledge that the words spoken are not constructive and declare what is "lovely, pure, and just."

As you make positive statements about yourself and others, write the constructive phrases in the space below. Don't concern yourself with the nonconstructive words. Record only that which is constructive.

There are laws and principles that govern all areas of life. For instance, there are traffic laws that assist us as we drive from place to place. Scientists discover laws that have been operating eternally in our universe. Although known for centuries, only recently have many people begun to find that there are principles which govern our interior life. One important law is the Law of Mind Action: Thoughts held in mind produce after their kind.

This law is the heart of mental science. The premise is that thoughts are like seeds, for they bear fruit. The principle each person must discover and work with is the idea that there is a direct relationship between the thoughts we *hold* in mind and what happens to us. This concept is in concert with the idea that we are all responsible for our lives.

This affirmative approach to life is often focused on specific life issues. For instance, we might declare: *The power of love is healing my hurt feelings toward* _____. Or we might affirm: *I am healed and restored to perfect health.*

Allow yourself to experience this approach to living. Choose a statement that is constructive and aligned to one of your heartfelt desires, and repeat the affirmation at least one hundred times throughout this day. Write the statement you chose in the space below:

If this approach to living is new to you, you will want to practice it until your affirmations begin to bear fruit. It is appropriate that everyone experience the planting of seeds in this way. Tomorrow's idea will help us understand how the subconscious is actually changed.

I am thinking God-thoughts.

Yesterday's ideas grew out of the Law of Mind Action that states: Thoughts held in mind produce after their kind. Today's insight reveals the way in which this law actually works. The previous lesson said that thoughts are *held* in mind through repetition. This approach is consistent with the idea that the mind (the subconscious mind) must be taught the truth. This is sometimes called conditioning the mind or "programming" the mind. But Truth is already within us.

In the Bible this is expressed in this way: "I will put my law within them, and I will write it upon their hearts" (Jer. 31:33). If this premise is true, then there is no need to fill the mind with what is already present. Instead, the truth is to be released from within you!

Remember Paul's incredible insight that we have the mind of Christ. The purpose of "thoughts held in mind" is to allow the Christ mind to do its sacred work.

When we "hold" thoughts in mind instead of programming the mind, we allow certain thoughts to rest within the mind. They are not held captive through repetition, but remain in us as a friend would remain with us during a time of sharing. Perhaps the same affirmation or statement of truth is used. We speak the truth, but then we rest with this statement until the mind drifts. Then we think or speak the statement again. This process of speaking or thinking the truth and waiting is repeated again and again.

The result of this process is that thoughts and insights rise from within. Charles Fillmore called the place from which they arise the superconscious. We have the experience of the German astronomer Johannes Kepler who spontaneously prayed, "O God, I am thinking Thy thoughts after Thee." This process of speaking the truth and waiting expresses a cooperative relationship between us and God. It calls forth a wisdom that is innate to the

Christ mind. We might think of this process as priming the pump. A little water is poured in, so the wellspring below (or within, in this case) can rise to the surface.

Practice this method today. It is challenging, for the human mind has a tendency to wander. Remember your acceptance of and love for the sacred human. On other days, we will explore this way of life in more detail, and you will be given helpful ideas for dealing with the wandering mind. In the meantime, please realize that you have the mind of the Christ and that the normal state of a creative human being is to have the wellspring of wisdom surface and touch daily life in practical and wondrous ways.

Week Eight
Feelings

Our thoughts are seeds which produce after their kind. Life's circumstances and experiences originate in the mind. However, life is not all circumstances and experiences. In fact, much of what we call life is made up of feelings. An emotion is actually the first fruit of the seed which we plant in the field of the mind. In general, positive feelings tell us that the seeds are wholesome and productive. Negative feelings reveal to us the need to sow new seeds.

Remember this idea: The first fruits of the seed thoughts you plant are feelings. Feelings tell you the nature of the seeds you have planted or the thoughts you are thinking.

As you move through your day, be sensitive to your feelings. Picture in your mind a stroll through an orchard where you pause from time to time to examine the fruit of the trees. You are simply noting the emotions you are having at certain times throughout the day.

How much of the time from morning to noon was your thinking constructive? _____

How much of the time from noon to 6 p.m. was your thinking constructive? _____

How much of the time from 6 p.m. to the time you retire for the evening was your thinking constructive? _____

I allow myself to feel
the emotions present in me today.

The spiritual journey, like all journeys, begins with a single step. Oddly, that which leads to the highest and most fulfilling life begins with discontent. First we are motivated, but usually it is not to live a spiritual life. Our initial purpose is to dispel pain. If the pain subsides we breathe a sigh of relief and forget the spiritual search, but in a short time, the discontent returns, and we seek again.

If we no longer want anguish—physical or otherwise—to be our experience, a principle must be realized. *The first step to banishing pain is to experience what we feel.* The avoidance of hurt only gives it a hiding place from which it ambushes us.

Therefore, give attention this day to what you feel. Pause during the day to feel and to note what you are feeling.

Feelings can be expressed in one word. There are three basic categories of emotion: sad, mad, and glad. Counselors notice that people often give a sentence or even a paragraph when asked what they are feeling. Many times, not a single feeling is included in what they say.

Always express how you feel in one word. Here are some one-word feelings: guilty, happy, frustrated, angry, glad, sad, fearful, frightened, exuberant, defeated, joyful, hateful, loving, belonging, alone, worthless, worthy, accepted, peaceful.

Feelings experienced today:

My feelings are acceptable,
no matter what they are.

We have told ourselves a lie: Some feelings are acceptable and others are not. *Ought* and *should* are watchwords we have erroneously declared for ourselves. "We *should* be feeling love. We *ought* to be at peace. We *should* be experiencing anger." The watchwords *should* and *ought* are not in the vocabulary of one who feels what is present to be felt.

No matter what emerges from within you today, allow yourself to experience it. In feeling fully, you are totally alive. You discover that the power of a negative feeling is not in feeling it, but in its threat to rule your life. As you experience your feelings, do not call some acceptable and some abhorrent. No longer is your quest to feel certain feelings and shun others. Desire to live life fully. Feel what emerges from within you.

Feelings experienced today:

Is there a difference between the intensity of the feelings you felt today and the intensity of the emotions of yesterday? Use the space on the following page to comment on this question. You will find that when you accept feelings, their intensity eventually lessens.

Week 8
Day 51
continued

Today I do not label my feelings good or bad.

You have learned the necessity of feeling what emerges from within you, and today you take another step on the spiritual path. As a feeling is felt, do not label it good or bad.

Instead declare: *I refuse to call my feelings bad or good. It (the feeling) simply is.* For instance: *I refuse to call anger good or bad. Anger simply is.*

Today, give careful attention to your tendency to label what you are feeling as good or bad. Realize that your need is to acknowledge what you are feeling, rather than to label it.

There is only one door.

Throughout your life you may have thought there were two doors to your feelings. One door, which you desired to open, led to feelings of joy, peace, and love. The other door, which you tried to lock from the outside, led to hurtful emotions. But no matter what you did, the feelings "locked" behind the door escaped. They overwhelmed you at times, although you tried to keep them safely secured behind the second door.

Now because of simple observation, you know there are not two doors. There is only one door. Near the entrance lie the lame and crippled negative emotions waiting to escape. As you allow these feelings their expression, they are seen to be powerless, and you are free. Then feelings of joy, peace, and love can course through your being.

Indicate the feelings that you have tried to keep hidden:

Feelings are my first alert.

In the past you may have felt that feelings betrayed you, and at other times you believed them to be king, for their impact was so strong they ruled you. Now you know that feelings are your first alert. They are like messengers of a king allowing you to know the inner state of the kingdom. On future days you will delve deeper into yourself, but for today, listen to your feelings. They declare your inner state of mind. As before, refrain from labeling the feelings, but hear their message. When you feel ill at ease you may believe some lie, but a truth is yet to be known. When you feel at ease you are expressing your true nature.

Today it is not necessary to know the truth, only to hear the message, for feelings are your first alert. Throughout the day experience your emotions with the understanding that they alert you to the state of the inner kingdom of your soul.

How many times throughout this day did you allow your feelings to alert you to your state of mind? _____

By remaining sensitive to your feelings, you will be able to know whether your thinking is constructive or in some way limiting.

Note: Read tomorrow's lesson first thing in the morning.

Feelings are the prelude to sensitivity and intuitiveness.

Do you wonder why so much attention is being given to feelings? Today's lesson reveals the importance of this week's work. Feelings provide an avenue through which Spirit can express itself. When you do not allow yourself to feel, a conduit of divine expression is denied access to the world. Obviously, there will be divine discontent until this channel of Spirit is opened wide.

As you progress with the lessons, this portal between the kingdom of God and the kingdom on earth widens, and sensitivity and intuitiveness become a natural part of daily living. The more you feel, the more you experience flashes of insight and hunches that bear fruit.

There are two things to do today. First, pause and read today's lesson in the morning, in the middle of the day, and in the evening. This reading is simply a reminder that feeling is the beginning of sensitivity and intuitiveness. Second, note if there is a tendency to hide or disallow emotions. There is no condemnation if this happens, only the understanding that the flow of Spirit is restricted.

My feelings help me
live in the here and now.

Week 8
Day 56

It is our inability to live in the present moment that leaves us with a sense of powerlessness. Concern for the past or future places us out of touch with the power residing in the present moment. By giving attention to what we are feeling, we are able to dwell in the here and now. It is not necessary that we label the current moment pleasant. Instead, we understand the need to experience the feelings and thus the power of the moment.

Three times during this day, remind yourself to be aware of your feelings, for this awareness is the prelude to knowing the power that innately resides in the here and now.

Once you have completed *Week 8*, finish the following sentence:

The dominant feeling I experienced during the week was _____
_____ .

Remember: Whatever the feeling is, it is acceptable.

Week Nine

Stand Still

Trying to live a spiritual life does not ensure that we will never have problems. There will be challenges because we are growing and dynamic beings; however, because we strive to live a life centered in spirit, we are becoming aware of principles that enable us to move through and beyond any problem.

The first step in moving beyond a challenge is to stand still. When there is some difficulty, the normal human tendency is to act. Everyone knows that doing nothing produces nothing. "Give it the college try," we say. The "can-do" attitude is what we need. This seems to be a wise approach, but there are millions of people who try, only to find that their actions make the problem worse. They have not learned the value of standing still.

Moses, trapped between the Red Sea and the approaching Egyptian army, said to the people, "Stand still, and see the salvation of Jehovah, which he will work for you today" (Ex. 14:13 ASV). Spirit must be allowed to do its sacred work. Premature actions rising from the same attitudes and beliefs which helped create the problem are a barrier to Spirit-directed activity. Therefore, the first step in conquering a problem is to stand still. The reason is simple: *We cannot face the problem on the level of the problem.* Memorize this statement. It is a worthy companion for the spiritual journey.

My problem appears to be . . .

Problems are not what they appear to be. When people are in conflict, the problem seems to be the other person. If she would only act the way we want her to act, there would be no problem. When there is disease, the answer is considered to be a healed and restored body. The cancer must be rooted out or the broken arm healed. A new job or a better boss may seem to be the answer to our financial needs. Winning a state lottery has been considered the solution to many a problem. It has been said, "I don't have any problems a million dollars wouldn't cure."

In a previous week, you began to consider the idea that there is a relationship between your thoughts and your life experience (the things that happen to you). You considered the idea that inner changes are required if your experience is to be different. This is the truth, but you are not to ignore problems either. In fact, it may be important to outline what you think the problem is from the human perspective. There are things you can learn about yourself by doing this.

In the space below, complete the following sentence from the human viewpoint:

My problem appears *to be*

I cannot face the problem on its level.

I cannot face the problem on its level is one of the first insights that brings us new life. Many self-defeating and limiting cycles of behavior and experience are repeated because the problem is faced on its level. Sometimes we try harder, but the result is always the same. We may even utilize a new technique, but unless we are different the cycle will continue.

Describe below any unhealthy cycles that have been part of your life. Indicate the month and the year in which the cycle repeated itself. For instance, perhaps a failed relationship occurred in June 1987 and again in February 1988, or maybe you have changed jobs on a regular, three-year basis.

In each instance indicate the "method" you used which you thought would stop the unhealthy cycle:

This problem is an opportunity.

Each problem is an opportunity to grow and change. In fact, each problem is actually a challenge to come up higher and be a different person. The Chinese are a wise people. As their language developed, two Chinese symbols were combined to form the word for crisis. One of the symbols meant danger and the other meant opportunity. These two markings provide us with a choice. We can sense danger and be fearful, or we can look for and find the opportunity.

Opportunity is the focus of any person interested in living a spiritual life. Time and time again in history, problems have challenged us not so much with the need for a solution, but with the task of discovering something about ourselves. David faced Goliath and did much more than defeat the giant. He found in himself resources that would enable him to lead his people. Through his lion's den experience, Daniel found that a consciousness of God is all the protection anyone really needs.

Today choose whether you will give attention to a perceived danger or will consider the discovery of something about yourself you have not known before. Whenever your problem comes to mind, remind yourself: *This problem is an opportunity.*

Also, as the thought of a problem enters your mind, complete the following statement:

My opportunity is

My first step is to stand still.

Let us give thanks that the first step in solving any problem is to stand still. The human tendency is to act. Actions yield results, we are told, but while actions yield results, they do not always yield solutions. Sometimes things get worse. Sometimes we become exhausted. Sometimes we generate unhealthy cycles of life. It is no wonder that the first step is to stand still and do nothing. Remember, the happenings in life originate within us, and unless we become a different person, the feelings and experience will be the same no matter what we do. This is a particularly difficult lesson for those who have accomplished much in the world through their own effort. In the earthly sense, actions seem productive, but remember that we are pursuing not just a better human existence, but a spiritual life.

Today cease doing anything you think will solve the problem. Instead, prepare yourself to grow and change. Are you willing to be a person who has harmonious human relationships? who is not sick? who enjoys stable, creative employment? Today, do nothing to solve your problem. Instead, answer these questions again and again.

A cycle is broken.

By standing still, a cycle is broken. Have we ever thought that a new life could begin with inaction? Actually, we are probably aware that standing still is not the easiest thing to do. But standing still is the way of Spirit.

When challenged in life, attempt to stand still as soon as you can. In general, life is structured in such a way that you may not be able to stop what you are doing for a couple of hours. But when you are able, be still. You see, standing still is not inactivity; it is the first step of a spiritual approach to facing challenges.

If a crisis came up, how long a period of time would pass before you could stop what you were doing and sit down? Is your schedule so hectic that you could not begin the process of inner growth and change for a long time?

When you believe that inner change is required before the gift of a problem is revealed, then you will develop a way of life that allows, even demands, time for standing still.

Now the burden becomes a bridge.

There once was an ant who was carrying a piece of straw. When he came to a crevice in the earth, he scurried along its edge, looking for a way around. However, the crack in the earth was longer than the ant was willing to walk. Suddenly, the ant took the straw he was carrying, placed it across the crevice, and walked to the other side. Then he picked up his burden and went on his way. The ant's burden had become a bridge.

Any burden we carry can be a bridge to some greater good. Actually, the first transformation is of ourselves. The burden causes us to think in a new way, to uncover previously hidden inner resources, and to become a new person. This "newborn" will act differently and see problems differently. Also, solutions will be forthcoming which transcend anything the "old us" could envision.

Today if a challenge comes to mind, remind yourself: *A burden can become a bridge not only to a new life, but to a new me.*

*I am prepared and eager to cross over
to a new approach to problem-solving.*

There is a way to solve any problem. There is always an answer; however, it is necessary to be aligned with the principles that govern the universe and our lives. Answers do not come because we want them to come or because we work hard. Solutions are realized because we give allegiance to spiritual laws and principles.

In learning how to face life, a human being moves through a rite of passage. The first step is usually not productive because it is problem-oriented. We dwell upon the difficulty and give more energy to the problem than to finding a solution. This state is marked by negative thinking—"it can't be done"—and is often accompanied by feelings of despair and hopelessness. In addition, because we fail to discover our inner resources, the problem leaves us with a feeling of being less than we are.

Next we become solution-oriented. We feel that there is hope, and we try to solve the problem. We solicit the help of others and even ask God to get us out of the jam. Bargaining with the Almighty marks this stage of our growth. "God, if you get me out of this one, I'll _____ for you." Viable solutions come to mind when we are solution-oriented. In fact, perhaps the thing we are going to do has been tried before, and it has worked for others. The additional dilemma is that often it does not work for us, or the challenge retreats for a while only to return again. Negative cycles enter our experience and can continue to plague us for years. There is the necessity of entering the next part of this rite of passage. It is to be God-oriented.

The challenges and difficulties of life are greater than they seem. This does not mean we are to magnify them, but that we are to realize they are a bridge to something greater. The true "solution" to any problem is a deepened awareness of God and who we are in relation to God.

Identify your current position in this rite of passage—from being problem-oriented, to solution-oriented, to God-oriented. In the space below, indicate where you are in your approach to human challenges:

Describe the feelings and thoughts you have when you are living life in this way:

Week Ten
Label Not

It is written that the first mistake made by humankind was to eat of "the tree of the knowledge of good and evil." Botanists have never discovered a tree that bears such fruit. The reason is simple; a literal tree of the knowledge of good and evil does not exist. However, the message is clear.

We are not to have knowledge of, or believe that something is, either good or evil. "Label not" is the commandment. Shakespeare wrote, "There is nothing either good or bad, but thinking makes it so."

To cease labeling "things" good or bad does not mean we cease evaluating our life condition. A sense of value and good judgment should always be part of our approach to daily life. However, ceasing to call something good or evil is a step we take toward freeing ourselves from total dependence on human knowledge, and this takes us a step closer to understanding ourselves to be greater than any circumstance. Eventually we place our experiences in God's sphere of meaning—in the context of the whole. Through this practice of detachment, we move beyond the limitations of human judgment and invite God's wisdom as we evaluate our life circumstances.

This important idea is introduced now, but it is so challenging that it will be addressed again in a later section of this book. Try not to contend with what is being shared at this time. Work with the next two weeks' ideas before you determine the validity of this concept. Yearning to live a spiritual life brings us face-to-face with ideas that the sacred human knows little about or fails to understand.

It is not so important at this time that you understand or believe what is read. Instead, live a week of your eternal life striving to not label conditions, people, thoughts, or feelings either good or bad. Not labeling brings a special insight into daily living.

I label not.

Be aware that we are not what happens to us. We are not events or circumstances. This is nonattachment to the world. Was this not Jesus' stance: "Be of good cheer, I have overcome the world"? (Jn. 16:33) We often say, "I am in the world, but not of it."

A life of loving nonattachment to the world begins by ceasing to label. Begin this important week by becoming aware of the many labels you place upon people, yourself, and things. Notice that these labels sometimes group together a whole country and its people. Often we make blatant statements about ourselves that are obviously not true. For instance, we might declare that we always make mistakes or that we are stupid. We make mistakes, but not all the time. We may do or say things that we are quick to label stupid, but we are not stupid.

Today begin the process of becoming aware of the labels you place upon yourself, others, and things. List these words and phrases not only today, but whenever you become aware of "eating of the tree of the knowledge of good and evil."

List of label words and phrases:

This is a Turn Page Day. Please turn down the corner of the page. This will remind you to return to this exercise during the week so that you can add to your list as you become aware of other labels you use.

It is.

———

Whenever we become aware that we "have knowledge" of someone or something as good or bad, let us quickly declare: *It is not good or bad; it is.* Our individual perspective makes all the difference. Rain on the day of a picnic may seem bad, but for the farmer it may seem good. Many people consider jam on toast good, but jam on the rug is usually considered bad.

There is an interesting story that illustrates the "it is" principle. There was a man who gave his son a horse for his birthday. This was labeled good. The son fell off the horse and broke his leg. This was labeled bad. A day later the king's men were coming through the village in search of young men, for the king was preparing for war. In the eyes of the boy's mother, the broken leg was good. On and on it goes. It is evident that a horse or a broken leg is not good or bad. It simply is. Although this concept is more challenging when something seemingly bad happens in our life, it remains true.

Today, become aware of three people or conditions that you have labeled *either* good or bad. Say of each one: *It is.* List below the three people or conditions that you now realize are neither good nor bad:

1. _____

2. _____

3. _____

Today I do not label people good or bad.

This is our first attempt at living a twenty-four-hour period of time without "eating of the tree of the knowledge of good and evil." Today the focus is upon our thoughts about people. It is a time to observe our interior life. People are not good or bad. People are.

Silently say to each person you meet: *I do not see you or label you good or bad. I am, and you are.* Remember, there is no failure regardless of whether you find yourself labeling people good or bad. This is the beginning of a special approval to living.

Some of the people you refused to label good or bad are:

Today I do not label conditions good or bad.

On this day the focus is upon your thoughts about situations. It is a time to observe your interior life. Conditions are not good or bad. Conditions are.

Silently declare for each condition you encounter: *I do not see or label this condition good or bad. It is.*

Some of the conditions you refused to label good or bad are:

Note: Read tomorrow's lesson first thing in the morning.

Today I do not label myself good or bad.

This day the focus is upon our thoughts about ourselves. It is a time to observe our interior life. We are not good or bad. We are.

Let there be two 20-minute times throughout this day when you rest and give your attention to the two words *I am*. Begin each of these times of quiet reflection by first declaring what you are not. For instance, "I am not what I think. I am not what I feel. I am not what happens to my body," and so on. Silently declare as many things as come to mind.

Then speak out loud the words *I am*. If you are familiar with the tune of "Amazing Grace," you might softly sing *I am* to this tune. Then rest in a state of patience, acceptance, and expectancy. If your mind drifts, move through the process again, then rest again. Do this twice during the day. It is best that this be done in the morning when you first rise and in the evening before you go to bed.

Today I do not label my thoughts or feelings good or bad.

On this day the focus is upon the thoughts and feelings that course through our beings. There is a tendency to label each thought or feeling. If we label a feeling bad, we try to push it away. If a thought is called bad, it may cause us to think of ourselves as bad also. By working with today's affirmation, we are moving closer to the causative side of life's experiences. It is important to begin the process of realizing that thoughts and feelings are neither good nor bad; they simply are.

Today list the thoughts and feelings that you are tempted to label good or bad. Work with the suggested process below. It will help you cease eating from the tree of the knowledge of good and evil.

List of feelings and constructive truths (the first line is an example):

Anger   Anger is not good or bad. It is.

_____ _____

_____ _____

_____ _____

_____ _____

List of thoughts and constructive truths (the first line is an example):

I cannot do this.   The thought "I cannot do this" is not good or bad. It is.

_____

_____

_____

_____

It is; I am.

Today we combine two great truths from last week: "it is" and "I am." "It is" declares the basic truth about any condition or happening. "I am" is the simple truth about ourselves. As we move deeper into this book, the implications of this simple truth will be explored. But for now, let us experience the mystery of these words.

Let the seed be planted today which gently compels us to face life's challenges by knowing, it is and I am. Once the initial shock of a situation passes, we will rest quietly and return to these two basic truths: it is; I am.

Let these words become companions and, eventually, dear friends for the journey. This is a Turn Page Day. Bend the corner of this page, for you will want to return to it again and again. As things and people challenge you to live a spiritual life, return and commune with these two truths: it is; I am. Be sure to list the people and situations that challenge you to know these two truths. Do not curse these things and people. They are a blessing.

List the people and conditions that help you remember it is; I am:

Date   Person or Situation _____

_____   _____

_____   _____

_____   _____

_____   _____

_____   _____

_____   _____

Week Eleven

Resist Not

If the only thing we did was label things good or bad, God would never have decreed that we not eat of the tree of the knowledge of good and evil. However, we do not stop with labeling. We "progress" to resistance. All the great spiritual teachers have told their followers to resist not evil. For the most part, human beings have ignored this advice. Grand campaigns are mounted to rid the world of some evil menace, but only the form of the negativity changes. The evil often remains and sometimes seems to grow. We are told that eventually good will triumph over evil, but this is not God's way. Spirit's way is to *resist not evil*.

When we resist some circumstance, we are facing the problem on the level of the problem. There is no change in us, and therefore the condition will remain. A change in consciousness is required before there can be outer change. The world is transformed because the inner being is transformed. This is a grand truth that cannot be ignored.

Name three situations in your life that you have tried to change, but which thus far remain the same. For example, perhaps you are still looking for the perfect soul mate or job or are struggling with the same disease.

1.

2.

3.

How have you tried to change your world and your life?

Please memorize this definition of resistance: *To resist is to attempt to change some person or condition without a corresponding inner change in myself.*

It is not my purpose to change the world.

It is not our purpose to change the world by outward, purely human means. If there is a mission, it is to be a part of the raising of the consciousness of the world. Today we acknowledge that it is our thoughts, attitudes, and beliefs that must be raised.

We must not resist people and things, for this is a focus upon the world instead of ourselves. Certainly there are better ways for us to interact with one another and care for our planet, but the focus must not be upon the problem. If our energies are an attempt to change the outer world, we are expending energy in a nonconstructive way, despite the fact that our motives might be pure. Is it not evident that humankind has been struggling against certain evils for thousands of years? The evils remain not because they have a foundation in Spirit, but because they find life through our resistance. They are like a parasite that needs a host in order to live.

What conditions have you sustained through your resistance?

If you are tempted to try to change outer conditions and people today, silently deny this need by stating: *It is not my purpose to change the world.*

*It is my purpose
to allow myself to be changed.*

Yesterday's lesson stressed the idea that it is not our purpose to change the world by outer means before attempting to change our consciousness. Undoubtedly, some of the people who try to change the world are simply avoiding the inevitable—that they must be changed.

Again and again our purpose is brought to mind: It is our purpose to allow ourselves to be changed. Although we can be changed in the twinkling of an eye, the process of inner transformation does not happen as quickly as we might wish. Usually, there is something which must be released before the true person can be expressed.

This calls for responsibility. No longer can we point a finger at conditions or people. When they govern our lives, we are powerless and there is nothing we can do to change our lives. Life ceases to have meaning.

In today's statement there is a key word—*allow*. Once we realize the importance of inner change, or the lifting of consciousness, the typical human being moves forward to bring about the change. Through our efforts, we believe the change will take place. This may seem to occur, but the revelation of who we are and the life that can be is not brought about by human effort. We must *let* it happen.

Three times today, rest silently for at least twenty minutes and reflect upon today's affirmation: *It is my purpose to allow myself to be changed.*

This is a Turn Page Day. If in the weeks to come there is a tendency to try first to change the world without the corresponding inner change, return to this exercise and do it again.

First me, then the world

The character of our world is slowly changing. "Personal freedom and opportunity!" is becoming the cry of the people in countries around the world. In some of these countries, the freedom cry has been suppressed for a long time, but now it is beginning to be heard. The pattern of change is that usually a bold few rise up and plant a seed of desire for freedom and self-expression in the minds of thousands. Next, the government crushes these leaders, little realizing that the idea of freedom is becoming the topic of conversation among the people. Eventually the majority believe opportunity and self-expression are their right. The next step is revolution. In the past, freedom rose up through bloodshed. Perhaps we are now evolving beyond armed conflict.

And how did all of this come to be? Someone realized: *First me, then the world.* People who truly understand this principle do not resist. Gandhi is one who knew that the hearts and minds of the people were the birthplace of freedom. He expected the British empire to vacate India without violence. This is not what happened literally, but there was no war. The people found freedom in themselves, and their country was freed.

One day a woman who had been caught in the act of adultery was brought to Jesus. The men who brought the woman knew that Jewish law demanded she be put to death, and they were prepared to carry out the sentence. Jesus knelt down, humbling himself, and said, "Let him who is without sin among you be the first to throw a stone at her" (Jn. 8:7). The men dropped their stones and slowly, one by one, walked away. Then Jesus spoke to the woman. His final words were: "Go, and do not sin again" (Jn. 8:11).

Jesus was doing more than asking the woman to cease her previous self-debilitating behavior. The woman's life could not change until she was changed inside. Then, being a different person, she would sin no more.

Always, it is necessary that we become a new creation. We become different and then, naturally, we see a different world.

This does not mean that we sit idle until we are changed, but that we remember that authentic actions proceed out of spiritual consciousness.

Please memorize today's affirmation: *First me, then the world.*

Throughout the ages the guidance continues: resist not evil. If there is any wisdom humankind has ignored it is this insight.

Pretend you are with Jesus, and you hear Him say, "Resist not evil" (Mt. 5:39 AV). Do not reject the words immediately. Instead, ask two questions: What does this mean? What am I to do?

Do not ask anyone to answer these questions for you. Instead, close your eyes and form an image in your mind of an ancient temple in which there is a room filled with light. See yourself entering this room, sitting on the floor, and resting in the light. Then ask the two questions and listen for the answer. You may have to do this exercise each day during the week. Record any insights you receive.

Good does not triumph over evil.

Humankind is captivated by the struggle between good and evil. It fancies itself the good soldier resisting the onslaught of evil. Drama, art, poetry, and literature have addressed the war which rages on our planet and within us.

There are some who dare to believe and declare that good will not triumph over evil. Does this mean we are doomed? Far from it. It means the struggle is over. No longer do we need to try to light the cave when we can stand in the light.

Does the light resist the darkness, or is it simply true to its nature? Does the light even know of the presence of the dark? Does darkness have presence, or is it the absence of something? These are questions that are to be answered in the ancient temple and its room of light.

Late this evening after the sun has set, go into a lighted room and turn off the light. Turn it on again, sit in the light, and answer the question: Where does the darkness go when the light is turned on?

I resist not . . .

By now, any confusion about this week's theme of resist not evil is probably lessening, and you are looking forward to a life without resistance. Remember, life is not a continuous attempt to light the cave. Life is standing in the light.

Hopefully, these recent days of reflection and pondering have revealed that darkness is a "no thing." It is not a presence. It has no presence. It does not go anywhere when the light is turned on, nor does it return when the light is turned off. This is an important insight. Darkness, of course, has many names. It has been called lack, sickness, death, and sin. We are not to resist these imperfections of humankind. This does not mean that they are to be our companions forever. They are not. However, our work is not to resist them or struggle with them. This has been tried and has always met with failure.

On the other hand, we are not going to remain idle. There is work to be done. We are a full-time project. We are not going to contend with the darkness. We are dedicated to discovering the light.

Today's work is to reread the current lesson three different times during this day.

There is no evil in God.

It is because of this truth that a "resist not evil" life is possible. Clergy and religious leaders have promised us that the kingdom of heaven is free from sin, sickness, lack, and death. We have also been told that we can enter this kingdom after death if our life on this planet is filled with goodness and good deeds. This is but half the truth.

God's kingdom, the kingdom of heaven, is without sin, sickness, lack, or death, but it is not a place we go after a godly life on earth. The kingdom of heaven (which we will consider in greater detail in the next section of this book) is a consciousness of God. God is here now. The great spiritual leaders of our world have all said the same thing: What we seek is here; it is within us. "In him we live and move and have our being" (Acts 17:28).

The question is: Will we allow ourselves to become aware or conscious of the Presence? If we allow this revelation to dawn in us, we will see ourselves and others differently. This is what intrigues people when they are in the presence of a person attuned to Spirit. The spiritually minded individual seems to see things about us that we do not see. Obviously, this requires that they look beyond appearances. This vision is possible because there is no attempt to change or resist what they see.

Consider a more accurate way of stating today's affirmation. Here are a few examples: *There is no evil in God consciousness. When I am aware of God, I see no evil.*

Week Twelve
Promises

A promise is given. "Ask, and it will be given you; seek, and you will find; knock, and it will be opened to you" (Mt. 7:7). We often doubt the validity of this promise, because from our perspective we have asked, sought, and knocked, and there was no answer. However, usually we seek something in the world which we value, believe other people value, or feel will bring us happiness. Can we consider the idea that the world does not contain what we want?

A spiritual life by its nature is not of the world. The fruits of Spirit do not reside in the world. They are not held in human hands, protected by our vaults, or passed from one human being to another. The promise is true and is fulfilled when we elevate our asking.

Nothing is being withheld from us. "It is your Father's good pleasure to give you the kingdom" (Lk. 12:32). When we ask for that which Spirit can give us, we will be satisfied in all areas of life.

Please indicate three "items" you have asked for, but have not received:

1. _____

2. _____

3. _____

Are you now willing to consider the idea that what you seek is not in the world? If your answer is yes, write below: *What I seek is not of the earth!*

_____

I admit that
my desires have not been fulfilled.

It is easy for some people to admit that their desires have not been met. They have wanted a good job, and they struggle to make ends meet. They have wanted a wonderful marriage, and they are still single. They desire healing, but the pain continues. Perhaps this is the way you feel, and therefore it is simple to say: "I admit that my desires have not been fulfilled."

There is another kind of person to whom the issue of desire is more subtle. This individual has a good job, a wonderful marriage, and perfect health. There is no logical reason for this person to feel unfulfilled, but there is no contentment.

One of the numerous human challenges is a situation in which a person has a job, but it is not satisfying. When asked about the job, the individual will admit that the employment has many desirable qualities. There is freedom of expression, good pay, and travel, for instance. When asked what they are looking for from the job, some answer, "respect," "recognition," or "peace."

Now is the time for honesty. Actually, more than honesty is required. Honesty is telling others the truth. Integrity requires being honest with ourselves. Today's question is: Are your desires really being fulfilled?

Circle either *Yes* or *No*.

Today I look carefully at my desires.

Today look carefully at your desires. Begin with a brief examination of the word *desire*. It comes from two roots. *De* has a Latin root meaning "from." *Sire* likewise has a Latin root and means "stars" or "above." Literally, the word *desire* means "from the stars" or "from above." *Sire* also means "father." As we contemplate these insights into the roots of the word *desire*, an important point is revealed. In the ideal our desires are from the stars, or from above, or from the Father.

Most people look at a desire and conclude that something is missing. Thus desire appears to be evidence of lack. This is not a healthy beginning for the achievement of any aspiration. Actually our desires are the movement of Spirit. They are not evidence of lack; they are evidence that something is present and can be made manifest. Emilie Cady eloquently expresses this idea in her book *Lessons in Truth*: "Desire in the heart is always God tapping at the door of your consciousness with His infinite supply."

At the deepest level, a desire is from God. As this gift of God rises from within and moves through our consciousness, it can become tainted and deformed. For instance, a person can experience love rising from within and interpret it as lust. Our yearning to be married is the soul's willingness to experience divine love. A person can desire security and interpret the desire as an impulse to steal from others. Our envy of a neighbor's new house or automobile is "God tapping at the door of our consciousness with His infinite supply." At the deepest level of desire, Spirit is offering itself to us, but unless we understand the implication of what is happening in us, we think the desire is for something of the world.

Take a careful look at your desires today. First, notice the way you have initially interpreted what you have felt. Then, in the light of the root meaning of the word *desire*, trace your urge to the movement of Spirit. What is it that you truly desire? Indicate your true desires on the next page.

117

My true desire is _____

_____ .

My true desire is _____

_____ .

My true desire is _____

_____ .

My true desire is _____

_____ .

My hunger and thirst are for God.

Hunger is the body's desire for nourishment; mystics have likened this to the soul's desire for God. Just as food and drink are necessary for physical existence, so the fulfillment of the soul's desire is necessary for the fulfillment of life's purpose. In all ways the soul yearns for God. This union has been called a mystical marriage, and the spiritual seeker can be just as driven by the desire for union as newlyweds are desirous of each other.

One of Jesus' beatitudes expresses the soul's desire. "Blessed are those who hunger and thirst for righteousness, for they shall be satisfied" (Mt. 5:6). Also, while Jesus was on the Cross He said, "I thirst" (Jn. 19:28). The guards thought He wanted something to drink, and so they offered Him vinegar. This is not what Jesus wanted. His thirsting, just as it is with us, was for God.

Let this be the moment our desire is elevated. Only God can fulfill our yearning. It is difficult for a human being to allow the desire from "above" to be the compelling force of life, but eventually it must come to be. In this way our desire, or will, is aligned with Spirit. It is God's desire that we awaken to the Presence and bear witness to the truth of who and what we are. When we desire to know God, we are attuned to the Infinite. No longer do we march out of step with the spiritual laws and principles that govern our lives. There is unity, and life begins anew.

Perhaps you would like to rewrite your deepest desires from the last exercise, with the new insight that it is God you desire.

My true desire is to know God as _____.

My true desire is to know God as _____.

My true desire is to know God as _____.

My true desire is to know God as _____.

Now I know what to ask for.

Now it is possible to return to the promise, "Ask, and it will be given you; seek, and you will find; knock, and it will be opened to you" (Mt. 7:7). For nearly two thousand years, people have hoped this promise was true. They have asked and asked, but on most occasions the asking was for something of the earth, something which could be seen or touched. Although there are times when such things come to be, many such desires have gone unrealized. But the hunger and thirst remain. The reason is simple.

We did not know what to ask for. Now we know.

What can we ask for that fulfills the promise?

My desire is for Spirit.

Our desire is for Spirit. We want to know God as wisdom, for from this comes clear thinking and wise decisions. We want to know God as life, so death will no longer be an enemy. Health and vitality will be ours. We want to know God as source, for from this comes security, well-being, and a giving spirit. We want to know God as love, for then there will be friendship and the powerful union of souls. We want to know God as peace; then no outer condition will bring us anxiety.

In the space below, begin to pour out your soul. Let the desires that have been locked inside for ages be released. Begin by writing: *My desire is for Spirit*, and then allow the words to flow as they express the hunger and thirst of your soul.

Now I can be fulfilled.

Now you can be fulfilled. You are asking for what you really want. In truth what you desire has been offered to you, but you have rejected it. You have not lived, and moved, and had your being in God. You have been a fish, desiring water. Now you can be fulfilled.

There is not much else that needs to be said today. This has been a powerful week, a week to remember. God is willing. The promise is so simple, but it is necessary to ask for or be willing to receive what is offered. One cannot go into a Chinese restaurant and expect to be served lasagna. You can now be fulfilled, for you know your deepest desire.

There is no task today other than to experience the joy of knowing you can be fulfilled.

As the week concludes, it is necessary to reinforce the idea that only God can fulfill our desires. Jesus shared the above promise, and it has been utilized by people for many years. As it is with most spiritual principles, there are levels of understanding. For many people the above verse is the foundation of affirmative prayer and positive statements that we speak and write.

The key word in the promise is the word *it*. What is the *it* that we desire? In years past, or perhaps only a few days ago, the *it* might have been something of the earth. Maybe we were convinced it was a job we needed, someone to love us, and so on. Perhaps we declared: *My perfect place of employment is made available to me now, and I am thankful*, or *I am a center of divine love, mighty to attract my perfect soul mate*. These affirmative statements and others have been uttered for years, and they are acceptable, for they are part of a rite of passage. But let us now realize that the same process can be joined to our desire to know God. The *it* is not just something of the earth, not something we can hold in our hands or touch. It is God we desire.

Our desire is now purified and elevated. We ask, believing that Spirit is ours and we are Spirit's.

Using this formula for affirmative prayer and statements, write several sentences which declare your belief that you and God are one:

Week Thirteen

Summary

Essentially, a spiritual life begins with discontent and continues as hope springs eternal in the human heart. We make a choice to begin anew, little realizing that this step requires change. Of course, we want our outer world to change, but we do not yet understand that life's circumstances are mothered by the thoughts we think. Our feelings are the first fruits of our thoughts. This awareness of an interior life reveals the sacred human which is to be honored, accepted, and loved.

Our newfound insight into life's processes causes us to want to forge ahead to transform our lives, but we must not do this. Our next step is to stand still, for we cannot face a problem on the level of the problem. Nor are we to label ourselves, others, or conditions bad or good. This only leads to resistance or an attempt to change the outer world without the necessary work of interior change. Life can change drastically at this point. Values shift, our purpose for being is questioned, and we begin to ask, "What do I really desire?" This leads us to the next section of this book— *"The Inner Journey."*

Return to any day or combination of days that you have not understood or which you think need more work or review. Repeat the lesson(s) as *Week 13*'s work.

Resist the temptation to skip the review and continue on with *"The Inner Journey."* In many instances, the exploration of your interior life has not begun. This expedition can wait one more week.

In the spaces on the next page write the lessons which you chose to review:

Week 13
Days 85-91
continued

Day 85　*Week* _____
　　　　 Day _____

Day 86　*Week* _____
　　　　 Day _____

Day 87　*Week* _____
　　　　 Day _____

Day 88　*Week* _____
　　　　 Day _____

Day 89　*Week* _____
　　　　 Day _____

Day 90　*Week* _____
　　　　 Day _____

Day 91　*Week* _____
　　　　 Day _____

Section Two

The Inner Journey

Week Fourteen

The Good News

Let the inner journey begin! The world is filled with activity and wonders beyond belief, but it is the kingdom of heaven which holds the greatest promise. Some disciplines and religions tell humankind that the promise of heaven comes after an earthly life of goodness and a step into eternity through death. Those who truly know the kingdom of heaven know that it is at hand. This is the good news!

When Jesus began His ministry, the first words He uttered were, "The kingdom of heaven is at hand" (Mt. 4:17). This declaration must be the heart and core of the teaching of the Rabbi of Nazareth. Remember, the people were yearning for the kingdom of heaven. They believed long ago, as many do today, that it is the fulfillment of humankind's desire.

Personalize Jesus' statement, "The kingdom of heaven is at hand," and hear the words in your inner ear. Consider that the time of fulfillment is now upon you. Something wonderful is going to happen!

"The kingdom of heaven is at hand."

For something to be at hand, it must be within our grasp. A storm once swept through an area off the coast of North Carolina, and inlets of swiftly flowing water cut the narrow island into several pieces. A family was riding in a jeep along the sands near the ocean side of the island and the driver, caught up in conversation, failed to see an inlet in front of him. The car plunged into the water. The family grabbed their belongings and jumped into the shallow but swiftly moving stream. One person frantically looked for his shoes. They were on his feet! What he searched for was close at hand.

If heaven represents the fulfillment of our desires and heaven is at hand, then all that we seek is right here. We have only to awaken to its presence. Contentment, joy, peace, love, and their companions stand far from us when we believe they are not present. But these qualities are not oddities of life. They are our nature and essence. They are not *coming*. They are *here*, closer than hands and feet and breathing.

For too long we have dreamed of experiencing these qualities of life. Perhaps this is our problem. We sleep; therefore, we dream. Today we awaken to the understanding that all we desire is present now.

Have you ever temporarily lost some object—a set of car keys, for instance—and then found it close by? This recurring human experience is similar to what happens when we find that what we really want is close at hand.

As you move through this week, do so with a greater eye to your sur-roundings. Pause three times each day and look at the objects and people nearby. Be aware of what is physically "at hand." This will help you even-tually discern other "things" that are within your grasp.

Because the kingdom of heaven is at hand,
I cease my seeking.

Much of life has been a treasure hunt for us. What we want seems always to be just beyond the horizon. Beginning today, remember: The kingdom of heaven is at hand. With this realization comes a feeling of anticipation. You may not know what to expect specifically, but if it is of God, it leads to radiant living.

Because the kingdom of heaven is at hand, we cease our seeking. This idea makes today a day of rest. Breathe in the moment and all it offers. You are beginning anew.

An image of the spiritual life is helpful. You are in a garden with a white dove. You desire to hold this bird and move toward it. As you approach the dove, it hops away from you. When you move quickly it spreads its wings, flies, perches upon a branch, and watches you. The bird is beyond your grasp, but when you close your eyes and rest quietly, the bird comes to you and sits upon your shoulder.

During this day, pause three times and recall this simple image. May it remind you to cease seeking, for the kingdom of heaven is at hand.

I find no true fulfillment in the world.

Please note your surroundings. Are there items you have never consciously seen before, although they have always been present? List two of these articles:

_____

_____

If there are objects you are not aware of, undoubtedly there are also qualities and aspects of your being unknown to you.

We know that our surroundings extend far beyond the things we see and the sounds we hear. People are part of our lives too. However, when we believe fulfillment depends upon people, their actions, or worldly conditions, we are deceived. What we desire is not perceived through our five senses.

We have been looking in a place where what we seek cannot be found. All the many treks and treasure hunts have not yielded fulfillment. The good news is that joy is not found in the world.

Once during each waking hour, look around you, become conscious of what is at hand, and then remind yourself: *I find no true fulfillment in the world.* This important point will be stressed many times in this book.

I look for contentment in another place,
a place I have not looked before.

Here is a paradox. Contentment is not in the world nor discerned through the five senses, but it is within your grasp. There must be another "place" to look. If this is true, the pilgrimage is renewed.

But there is no place to physically visit and no new sight to see. Instead, there is another way of looking. Consider the many people you know, realizing that they have varied viewpoints. One sees a person's actions as hurtful while another person perceives a cry for love.

There are two awakenings for you today. First, there is no thing and no relationship in the world that can bring happiness. Secondly, you can now realize the possibility of seeing life in a new way. All you desire is at hand. It is not what is present that you first desire. It is the vision to see what is at hand.

Today is a day of realization. No exercise is given. At this point it is not helpful to look in another "place" for contentment. Simply experience the day, knowing that you have not yet looked in the place where contentment can be found. When you do look in this place, you will find happiness.

Week 14
Day 96

I am reminded that other people have found the kingdom which is at hand.

Realizing that the kingdom of heaven is at hand is exciting, but when we do not discover the kingdom, the realization can intensify our feeling of inadequacy. During such times, it is advantageous to remember that other people have felt this way. We are not alone in our anguish, just as we are not alone in seeking the kingdom.

Pause for a moment and think of those individuals you know whom you believe have found contentment. Please list their names:

Today I observe the people around me.

As we begin our day, we remind ourselves that we, too, can live a life of peace, love, and joy. Our actions and responses can be peaceful and loving. Other people are living life in this way. Today we remove our attention from ourselves and observe the people around us. We are going to pay particular attention to those people we believe are at peace. We observe their approach to life, knowing we can live life in a similar manner. Today we will allow these people to teach and inspire us.

We do not try to be like them. This is an observation day. We are the watcher and the listener. When we see individuals reacting angrily, we simply observe. Where we note peace expressed, we simply observe. It is important that we discover that there are examples of contentment and peace close at hand.

Bring to mind one occurrence in which peace and contentment were observed during the day. Give a brief account of the situation and how the person responded.

Today I ask a peaceful person how he or she found contentment.

It is important to let the freeing truth come easily to us. For too many years, we have tried too hard. We have functioned as though our good was far from us and an expedition had to be mounted to reach it. As this week ends, we understand better that the contentment and joy we seek is at hand. We have seen it in the lives of some people around us. Now we know we, too, can live life in a poised manner.

In an effort to understand the spiritual life, ask someone whom you believe has found the kingdom how he or she discovered contentment and joy. Listen intently and give thanks for these insights into the contented life.

Remarks shared by a contented person:

Week Fifteen

The Kingdom of Heaven Is Within Me

When searching for anything, it is helpful to look in the proper place.

We seek many things: love, security, peace, wisdom, wholeness, and much more. We may feel compelled to search the world for these qualities, but to do so is of no avail. What we seek may be close at hand, but it is not in the world.

There is an ancient Hindu legend which says that the gods wanted to hide humankind's divinity. The gods gathered and discussed where this "priceless jewel" might be hidden. One god suggested the highest peak, but it was determined that someone would find it there. Another god suggested the depths of the sea, but it was also concluded that this place would eventually be explored. Finally, it was decided that our divinity would be placed where we would not think to search for it: within us. This, the legend says, was done.

A spiritual life begins in earnest when the inner journey begins. For human beings who have always thought the world contained the treasures which fulfill, the idea of the inner journey may seem odd; however, simple logic tells us that we must search where the "thing" can be found.

Look around you and declare: *Nothing I see can fulfill me, for the kingdom of heaven is within me.*

There is a need to explore my inmost self.

We do not know, but we can sense, the magnitude and majesty of life; we feel an impulse to explore the kingdom of heaven. This inner urge is felt by all people and is the motivating factor which causes humankind to venture into outer space, to climb mountains, to sail the oceans, and to journey to lands called sacred.

However, we now know that we have projected this divine impulse upon the earth and left unexplored our own being. We sense a vastness in us, but we do not know the path leading into our depths. Nevertheless, we are committed to the inner journey.

Pause three times today—in the morning, at noon, and before retiring in the evening—and ask to be shown the trailhead of the path that marks the inner journey. The dedication to explore your inner self is the first step of the journey.

My true essence is unknown to me.

For most of our lives, we have been strangers to ourselves. We have been the great, unexplored territory. We have tried to know the world, but we have ignored ourselves. After a day of pausing and asking to be shown the way leading deep within us, we are aware that our true essence is unknown to us.

This realization is not a barrier to exploration and eventual discovery of the kingdom. It is a bridge. "Know thyself" is the philosopher's call, but it is also the soul calling to itself.

On ten separate occasions during the day, write: *My true essence is unknown to me.* Please know that everyone who has answered the call "know thyself" first concluded: *My true essence is unknown to me.*

All I have sought is within me.

As we go about our daily activities, there are many things we think we need. We want love, joy, peace, wisdom, security, and other qualities of Spirit. Now we acknowledge that these treasures are in the kingdom within us. No longer will we look outside ourselves for these fruits. No person and no thing can give us what is already a part of us.

Throughout this day whenever you feel the need for love, joy, peace, wisdom, or security, pause and declare: *All I seek is within me.* It is not necessary that you feel their presence or even find the "place" within the soul where these qualities reside. Today it is important only to acknowledge that they are within you.

My need is to discover the trailhead
leading to the kingdom within me.

Today our great need is not to experience love, peace, joy, wisdom, and security. It is important only that we be shown the trailhead leading into the kingdom of heaven within us.

Picture in your mind's eye an obscure path ascending a high mountain. Three times during the day, rest and allow the image of this little-known path to form in your mind. Observe this path for a few minutes.

By committing yourself to this simple exercise three times, you are asking to be shown the trailhead leading to the kingdom. Have no preconceived notions as to the nature of this path, for it is not a path you can find; it must be revealed to you.

Through stillness,
I invite the coming of the kingdom.

Today is a wondrous day, for we have realized that the trailhead to the kingdom of heaven is not like any other. It is stillness. At this trailhead, we do not draw near to God, but when we are still, God seems to draw near to us.

It is like trying to approach the beautiful, white dove. Whenever we move forward, the bird hops away from us, but when we are peaceful and still, the dove descends upon us. Obviously, the kingdom of heaven is akin to stillness, and if we are to know this vast realm, we must be still.

Record the number of times during the day that you are silent and able to pause for at least one minute: _____

Think of the dove and silently declare: *Through stillness, I invite the coming of the kingdom.*

Note: In a coming week, we will give special attention to the art of becoming still.

By being present,
I invite the coming of the kingdom.

If the kingdom of heaven is present here and now, then we must also be present. Too often we are not here. Our thoughts dwell upon the future, and the wonder of the moment is lost. Our focus lies in the past, and the healing power of the present is not experienced. Contentment is not tomorrow's gift to us. Joy cannot be resurrected from the past. Thoughts of yesterday and tomorrow declare the kingdom will never come.

By being present, we invite the coming of the kingdom. It does not matter whether the present moment is filled with joy or anguish. If we are here, the kingdom is near.

By experiencing my current feelings, I invite the kingdom.

By seeing what is at hand, I invite the kingdom.

By hearing the sounds of the moment, I invite the kingdom.

By feeling the ground beneath me, I invite the kingdom.

Pause each hour and note the following things. What are you feeling? (The feelings need not be positive.)

List five things that are close by:

List five distinct sounds you hear:

Feel the floor beneath you!

By letting go,
I invite the coming of the kingdom.

It is said that a sculptor sees within the stone a masterpiece, and through the process of letting go, the work of art is revealed. Not even a fleck of stone is added to the figure that is created. The kingdom is within us, and therefore nothing needs to be added unto us. The beauty is revealed by letting go; by subtraction, not addition.

When we attempt to add to ourselves, we turn from contentment. When we let go, the kingdom is revealed.

Make a list of what needs to be released from your life:

Week Sixteen

Shake the Dust From Your Feet

There is a reason why we are not happy. There is a reason why we do not experience the kingdom of heaven. It is simple; we hold ill feelings toward ourselves or at least one other human being. Forgiveness is the beginning of the revelation of God's love.

We must shake the dust from our feet, just as Jesus instructed His disciples to do as He sent them forth into the world. He said that they were to bless the people they met as they traveled the world. If the people received the blessings, then all was well. If they refused to accept the blessings, then the disciples were not to hold resentments and anger toward the people. Instead, the disciples were to shake the dust from their feet.

Look at your feet. Are they dusty? Search your soul. Is it filled with anger or resentment? The dust on your feet, the anger in the soul, only serve to cloud your vision and hide from you what is present within you.

Before continuing on to the first day of *Week 16*, make a list, in the space below, of those people against whom you hold ill feelings. After completing the list, enter into the activities of this coming week of forgiveness. It is a week of great importance on the inner journey.

Forgive me my debts,
as I have forgiven my debtors.

In "The Lord's Prayer," we read, "Forgive us our debts, as we also have forgiven our debtors" (Mt. 6:12). On the surface, it appears that if we fail to forgive the people in our lives, God will not forgive us. This is not true. God is love; Spirit cannot withhold love from us. In truth, we are made in love's image. Divine love enfolds us and is our nature. When we understand this principle, we wonder why we do not feel the everlasting love of God.

The answer is simple. We withhold love from others. When we fail to forgive others and hold ill feelings toward them, God still loves us, and we are still made in love's image. However, our unforgiveness shields us from feeling the everlasting love and knowing our true nature.

Consider today the fact that there is no real justification for unforgiveness. Memorize the following statement: *My unforgiveness does not allow me to experience divine love.*

Forgiveness is for me, not the other person.

Now we are beginning to understand. Forgiveness is not for the other person; it is for us. Forgiveness helps us remember who we are, and it helps us remember that our destiny is to love. How often have we felt justified in holding ill feelings and anger? After all, that person did us wrong.

From the human perspective, this feeling of self-righteousness lifts us up, but it is only so we can fall from a greater height. Our anger has a devastating effect upon us, and in fact it may not affect the other person at all.

It is time for us to be free. No one finds contentment without releasing the burden of anger and resentment. If it were not for unforgiveness, many of us would experience the wonders of divine love.

Corrie Ten Boom survived a Nazi concentration camp. After the war, she traveled and was a voice of love and forgiveness to a nation stricken with grief. One evening while lecturing, Corrie saw in the audience the prison guard who had brutalized her and her sister. This man was indirectly responsible for her sister's death. After the presentation, the man came through the crowd, held out his hand to Corrie, and said, "Isn't the forgiving love of Jesus Christ wonderful?" Corrie's hand would not move. She had just spoken of forgiveness, and now she could not respond to this man's open hand. She asked God for help, and suddenly her hand moved. She had broken through and experienced forgiveness.

On the lines provided below, complete the sentence by writing the names of the individuals you need to forgive. Do this as many times as necessary.

I am willing to forgive _____.

I am willing to forgive _____.

I am willing to forgive _____.

I am willing to forgive _____.

I am willing to forgive _____.

I am willing to forgive _____.

I am willing to forgive _____.

I am willing to forgive _____.

I am willing to forgive _____.

I am willing to forgive _____.

I am willing to forgive _____.

I am willing to forgive _____.

I remove the log from my own eye.

"Why do you see the speck that is in your brother's eye, but do not notice the log that is in your own eye? Or how can you say to your brother, 'Let me take the speck out of your eye,' when there is the log in your own eye? You hypocrite, first take the log out of your own eye, and then you will see clearly to take the speck out of your brother's eye" (Mt. 7:3-5).

Jesus expressed a principle which we sometimes wish were not true, for He told us something about ourselves that we do not always want to know. In psychological terms, He spoke of projection. He said that what we find disturbing in another person is within us. Likewise, He stressed that we, not the one whom we dislike, need to perform the work.

It is disturbing to realize that other people are mirrors of ourselves. However, this principle can allow us to catch a glimpse of what is within us. Such knowledge is part of the inner journey.

Make a list of the things about other people that disturb you:

Now complete the process by writing the following statement in your own handwriting: *That which I dislike about others is part of me.*

I behold the Christ in you.

We are never upset with the creations of God. We can find no fault with an image that Spirit has created. If there is animosity, the feeling is directed toward something we have created. We have formed a concept or belief about another person that is inconsistent with the truth of his or her being.

We have been told not to judge by appearances. Let us heed this call, for it is naturally a part of the inner journey. Remember the woman caught in the act of adultery who was brought before Jesus? When Jesus looked at the sobbing form huddled at His feet, what did He see? Was it a prostitute? Did He see a worthless human being? No. Jesus saw the image of God—the Christ within the woman.

One of the young nuns of Mother Teresa's order came to the Mother and informed her that she had been attending the Christ throughout the day. If you had been at this young woman's side, you would have seen that she had bathed and nurtured a dying beggar. Yet, the nun did not judge by appearances. When asked about this, Mother Teresa said with a twinkle in her eye that the beggar was the Christ in one of His disguises.

Each of us is the Christ in disguise, for we are made in God's image. To love is to behold the Christ, as did the young nun. When this vision is ours, the process of forgiveness is complete, for we have seen the truth of being.

Form the most glorious image you can of the Christ. Please realize that no human image even approximates the image of God, but the image you form will help you "see the Christ in disguise." Then allow a picture of someone you need to forgive to form in your mind. See this person and allow yourself to feel whatever feelings emerge. Then slowly let this earthly form fade and be replaced by the glorious image. Say to this one: *I behold the Christ in you.*

I bless those who persecute me.

When we behold the Christ in other people or see the truth of their beings, we cannot return evil for evil. Love is the response we make to the other person's antics or angry behavior. This is consistent with the wisdom of those who have best loved the human family. Both Jesus and Paul enjoined us to bless those who persecute us. We have learned that this is not for the other person; it is for us.

In addition, our refusal to respond in a like manner gives our "persecutor" the opportunity to do or say something constructive. Jesus suggested that when someone strikes us on one cheek, we turn the other cheek. Of course, the individual can strike us again, but because we have not made an angry gesture, the person can choose to do a new thing. We are presented with this same choice when someone chooses to bless instead of persecute us. Today let us turn the other cheek. Let us live boldly and bless those who challenge us.

There once were two ministerial students who did not like each other. One man went to a woman for whom he held much respect and asked her what he should do. She told him to find something about the man that he liked and return to her. The student examined his nemesis and returned to the woman, informing her that there was nothing about the other man that he liked. She replied that there had to be something and urged him to look a little closer.

Finally, he found something that he liked and returned once again to his friend, telling her, "I like the man's tie."

The woman said, "Now go and tell him." The student carried out her request and, to his surprise, the man took off his tie and gave it to him. And so, a friendship began.

Think about a person who challenges you, determine one thing that you

153

Week 16
Day 110
continued

like about that person, and then tell him or her. In the space below, write the person's name and what you like.

Because I love much

A woman lay dying in the hospital. She spoke with her minister of her impending death and her regrets. They also spoke of the purpose of life. Jointly, they concluded that it was to express love.

This minister carried in his pocket little red paper hearts. He usually gave them to children, but sometimes adults needed them too. He gave the woman in the hospital at least one hundred hearts. He asked her to be about God's business during her remaining days. Each person who entered her room was to receive a heart. She did this and died in peace, true to her purpose and her nature.

From this experience the minister has expanded the distribution of the tiny red hearts. Sometimes he leaves them at the table at restaurants along with the tip. Love can be shared in wondrous ways.

In Jesus' life, there was a time when He was invited to a Pharisee's house. After entering the home, a woman of the city, most likely a prostitute, sat near Jesus and began to wet His feet with her tears and dry them with her hair. She also anointed His feet with a precious oil. The Pharisee was thinking that if Jesus was really a prophet He would know what kind of woman this was and not allow her to touch Him.

Jesus knew the man's mind and told him a little parable that illustrated the man's lack of understanding. Then Jesus said, "Her sins, which are many, are forgiven, for she loved much" (Lk. 7:47). These last three words express the way of forgiveness. We are forgiven; we experience divine love when we express it. There is no completion to forgiveness until we love much.

Seventy times seven

Paul advised, "Do not let the sun go down on your anger" (Eph. 4:26). It is human to be angry at times, and these feelings are not to be denied or suppressed. It is best that any anger we feel be dealt with quickly before it disrupts our lives. However, it can take awhile before we are free of feelings of resentment or rejection. We can kid ourselves into thinking we have forgiven when we have not.

The wonderful thing is that, given time and the living of life, we will discover whether the forgiveness process is complete. If we are unable to love, we have not yet forgiven others. If we are unwilling to receive love, we have not yet forgiven ourselves.

There are many people who know that the kingdom of God is within them. They have the intellectual knowledge, but the kingdom is not their experience. A central reason for this is unforgiveness. Let us forgive until it is done, seventy times seven. Remember, forgiveness is not for the other person. It is for us, so we might discover who and what we are.

Like the child learning to write the alphabet, let us write the words: *There is no forgiveness without love.* This childlike exercise is not to be done at one sitting, for forgiveness is often not completed all at once. In a symbolic gesture, use the space on the following pages to write the statement seven times each day for the next seven days. Write a little in the morning, some during the day, and complete the seven at the end of the day. This sequence will allow you to experience the process of forgiveness. It takes daily practice until it is done!

Day One

_____

_____

_____

_____

_____

_____

_____

Day Two

_____

_____

_____

_____

_____

_____

_____

Day Three

_____

_____

_____

_____

_____

_____

_____

Day Four

_____

_____

_____

_____

_____

_____

_____

Day Five

_____

_____

_____

_____

_____

_____

_____

Day Six

_____

_____

_____

_____

_____

_____

_____

Week 16
Day 112
continued

Day Seven

_____

_____

_____

_____

_____

_____

_____

Week Seventeen
The Unforgivable Sin

It is written that there is a sin that can never be forgiven. "But whoever blasphemes against the Holy Spirit never has forgiveness, but is guilty of an eternal sin" (Mk. 3:29). This mistake grows out of our God-given freedom of choice. There is a "naysaying" power of the mind. Ideally, we say no to lies and falsehoods, but like any principle, this one can be misused. How often have we said no to God and Truth?

Can you think of several times in your life when you said no to your good, to God, or to Truth? Please write a brief description of the events:

Saying no to God is an unforgivable sin in that as long as we refuse our good, Spirit must honor our choice. Spirit does not force itself upon us. We say no, but God patiently waits for us to change our minds and say yes. Saying no to God does not ensure eternal pain and our demise. It simply means that we are limited and will not express our full potential until, through choice, we say yes!

161

I admit I have said no to God.

The kingdom of heaven is within, and the goodness of God and wonders beyond belief are destined to pour from within us. Yet there is no fountain of good until we begin to let go of what seems so precious. Remember, the spiritual life is not addition. We are made in God's image and after God's likeness. What must be added to us? Instead, we are like the masterpiece encased in stone. Tiny pieces of stone are chipped away; the masterpiece comes into manifestation because of subtraction.

How like children we have been. Our parents want to give us swimming lessons so we can enjoy the water, but we say no. In fact, as with the little one, "no" becomes our favorite word. This is an unforgivable sin in that as long as we refuse to cooperate with the swim instructor, we will not learn to swim. But the day will come when the lure of the water and its fun will be too great, and we will say yes.

Admit that you have said no to God. Perhaps you can remember a particular instance when you refused your good. Of course, you did not realize this at the beginning, but later the truth was revealed. If such occurrences are not part of your conscious mind, then you can turn to a principle. If life is not all it can be, then you have said no to God. Where there is a yes, there is an overflowing cup of peace, love, and joy.

Today simply admit that you have said no to God and ask, "Why?" Write down any thoughts that come to mind.

I say no to God because
I believe I am undeserving.

A question is asked: If God is the air, what is the wind? The answer is: The wind is the activity or movement of the air. The Holy Spirit is the activity or movement of God in our lives and upon our planet.

Who would say no to the activity of God? No one would consciously do such a thing, but in subtle ways we say no to Spirit. Healing is always offered, but not always accepted. Love enfolds us, but is not always felt. Guidance shines upon us, but we wander aimlessly. Security is provided, but refused. God does not withhold anything from us. In the foreword of his book *Prosperity*, Charles Fillmore states, "It is perfectly logical to assume that a wise and competent Creator would provide for the needs of His creatures in their various stages of growth."

All that we need is available. The supply equals the demand, but we say no. We say no because we do not feel deserving. We believe ourselves undeserving because authority figures from our past said we would never amount to anything. We believe ourselves undeserving because we think we have not worked hard enough; we feel we have not earned what is offered.

Consider your own life and complete the following sentence as many times as it is helpful to you:

I believe myself undeserving because

*I say no to God because
I believe I am guilty.*

In our society if we are guilty of a crime, we are punished. Sometimes we make mistakes, but they are not punishable by law. We still feel guilty, however, and often consciously or unconsciously punish ourselves. For instance, we may be close to success with some project, but we find a way to fail.

There was a woman who was in nursing school. She was doing well and knew the information necessary for her to make outstanding test scores. There was no way she could fail aside from refusing to take the exams. Because she felt guilty over a mistake in the past, she did not take one of her final examinations. This was the only way she could fail.

Guilt leaves us with a sense of unworthiness, and we are unwilling to experience the kingdom of heaven and all its joys.

In the story of Cain and Abel, we uncover Spirit's viewpoint of its creation. Cain slew his brother Abel and was banished to wander in distant lands. He was concerned for his life, afraid that someone would kill him as he had killed his brother. God responded by placing a mark upon him, so he would not be injured by others. There are undoubtedly many interpretations of this story and the mark, but one perspective may be of benefit to those who possess a deep sense of guilt. Could it be that the mark of Cain declares the truth that Cain was precious in God's sight?

The truth is we are all precious in God's sight. Punishment is not necessary, but illumination is. There are times when we "punish" our children (at least that is the way they look at it), but it is not to make them miserable. It is so they might learn values and self-discipline.

As you move through your day, do so with the awareness that the mark of Cain is upon you. It declares not the deed you did or what you left undone. It says to all the world that you are precious in God's sight.

God says yes to me.

We ask for healing and remain sick. We want secure, prospering employment and can't find it. We desire love more than anything, but find rejection. We are convinced the reason our dreams are not fulfilled is because God has said no. And when God says no, what can we do?

Let us remember that it is humankind which says no to its good. God always says yes. However, the affirmation Spirit declares is not of earthly things. Our God says yes to us, to who we are and to our innate capacities. The Creator is like the loving parent who strives to teach the children so they can discover their potential and be all they can be.

God says yes to us. In fact, the universe has been devised in a way that calls for us to express all that is within. We have been engineered for success. However, God's yes is not enough. There must be another. We must say yes to the challenges of life, yes to who we are, yes to the possibilities, yes to life itself, and yes to God.

Today carry with you the word yes. For too long, you have said no to the possibilities of your life. You have God's yes; let God have your yes. Listen to yourself and others today, and note how many times you hear the word yes.

Week 17
Day 117

I want to say yes
to God and Truth.

Just because we have carried the word yes in our minds does not mean we have said yes to God and Truth, but our preparation for this grand moment is underway. First there is desire, and then there is action. We want to say yes to God and Truth with more than our words. Spirit does not demand words. If yes is to be declared, it must be declared in silence.

Consider today how you can silently, through action, say yes to God. Actions are not called for today, only a realization of what you must do. In the space below, write what you have decided to do in order to say yes to God and Truth. If you find this exercise difficult, you will want to return to *Week 11, Day 74* and repeat that day's activity, for it is designed to be of help with a question like today's.

166

I say yes to God.

We have been building toward this day. Words will cease and actions begin, for the task is to do the things we listed in yesterday's exercise. There is no greater affirmation than action. Words mark the path, but we still must walk it.

When we say yes to God, we are in concert with the universe. Spirit always says yes to us, but before the wonder of the kingdom is expressed, we must say yes. Spirit does not force its will upon us. However, in all ways God says yes to us. If this yes were an audible sound, it would be a constant chorus played within us. If the music of the spheres had lyrics, again and again the word yes would resound throughout the universe.

As you say yes today through your actions, be aware of a process that begins. There are many wonderful things you have wanted to do in your life. There are nonconstructive habits you wish to stop. In fact, there have been times when you have done the positive things you have wanted to do, but after a brief time, the old way of doing things returned.

An act of will is the beginning of most change, but it will not sustain you. A state of mind must be built up, and then the constructive actions are not a struggle, they are natural. Begin today, even if your beginning is an act of will. Later, a state of consciousness will become part of you, and your yes to God will be complete.

The unforgivable sin is forgiven.

The unforgivable sin is forgiven. No longer are we saying no to God. When asked if we are willing to experience the fullness of life, we answer, "Yes." In the past, the answer was no, and God respected our choice. The no was unforgivable in that as long as we continued to say no to God, the flow of joy, peace, and love from within was not allowed an outlet.

For thousands of years, humankind has believed that an unforgivable sin could be committed, and with it came certain doom. When Spirit says yes to its creation, there is no doom.

Twice throughout this day, pause for twelve minutes to "listen" for the divine yes. If you do not "hear" this yes, let your heart and mind say to God, "I say yes to You; are You saying yes to me?" and then listen . . .

Week Eighteen
"I and the Father Are One"

We are as close to God as we are going to be. Then why don't we feel this closeness? Because while oneness with God is the truth of being, it is also a matter of awareness. Consider a rite of passage in which a young American Indian is to spend a night alone in the forest with his bow and one arrow. The beasts of the night might stalk this easy prey. From the perspective of the young boy, he is alone and in danger. But close at hand his father is watching over him and is prepared to assist him if necessary.

The consistent message of Spirit is that we are not alone. We are not forsaken and will never be forgotten. However, like the boy in the forest, we may not be aware of our Father. Much of humankind maintains a sense of separation between the Creator and its creation. This need not be. Spirit is not only Creator, but Sustainer of the creation. Jesus brought a stunning truth to the people. "I and the Father are one" (Jn. 10:30). So foreign was this possibility to the minds of the people that when they heard Jesus speak of His oneness with God, they took up stones to kill Him.

Three times each day throughout *Week 18*, pause and affirm: *"I and the Father are one."* Write down any happenings, thoughts, or images that reflect the truth of oneness for you. For instance, seeing a beautiful sunset or walking hand in hand with your beloved might cause you to realize that you are one with God.

My God, my God,
why have You forsaken me?

Psalm 22 begins with these words: "My God, my God, why hast thou forsaken me?" It was this verse of Scripture that Jesus quoted when He spoke from the Cross. In doing so He uttered a prevalent human belief— that Spirit can turn from its creation. This is not true.

Pause now and read Psalm 22. In it you will find the crucifixion experience. There is reference to bargaining for Jesus' garments, words of mockery, and the piercing of hands and feet. Note in particular verses 27, 30, and 31.

I believe Jesus quoted Psalm 22 from the Cross not because He felt forsaken, but because we feel forsaken. He was drawing our attention to the psalm, for within it there was a message of hope and a clear indication that Jesus was not forsaken. The Cross experience is outlined, but so is the fact that "men shall tell of the Lord to the coming generation, and proclaim his deliverance to a people yet unborn" (Ps. 22:30-31). We are the people "yet unborn." Let us know that we, like Jesus, are not forsaken. Our circumstances may be dire as were His as He hung upon the Cross, but Spirit is with us just as it was with Jesus.

Consider the idea that an ancient culture of spiritually minded people once taught the children that the great Spirit was always with them. As the little ones began to learn this idea, they were instructed to turn quickly and look over their left shoulder in an attempt to see the great God watching over them. No child ever saw the Spirit the wise ones spoke of, but there was a growing awareness of the great God.

Be like the children of these ancient people, and look often over your left shoulder today. It is doubtful that you will see anything, but there will be a growing awareness of the presence and power of God.

I will never leave you.

Listen, listen, listen to my heart song.
Listen, listen, listen to my heart song.
I will never leave you; I will never forsake you.
I will never leave you; I will never forsake you.

These word are often sung at spiritual retreats. Over and over again these words are sung by the participants as an echo of what they deeply believe God is "saying" to them. Then they sing the words as an expression of their love for one another. This is an unforgettable experience.

God is omnipresent—everywhere equally present. Spirit cannot forsake you or leave you. Where does an omnipresent God go? There is no place to hide. The mountains and forest declare the grandeur of God, the seas God's mystery, and space the limitlessness of the unseen Presence.

Children of modern times learn the saying, "There is no spot where God is not." If this is true, why do you feel alone and forsaken at times? Remember a time when you felt alone. Allow yourself to re-experience the feelings if they emerge again. Then ask, "Why did I feel this way when God was with me?" Write any thoughts or impressions in the space below:

"I shall dwell in the house

of the Lord for ever."

"Surely goodness and mercy shall follow me all the days of my life; and I shall dwell in the house of the Lord for ever" (Ps. 23:6). These are familiar words, for they conclude the Twenty-third Psalm. They also point to our destiny, for we will dwell in God's house forever. Some people believe that this house is heaven and that it is available to us after a good life upon planet Earth. Other people who know the symbolism of the Bible insist that God's "house" is God's presence or, more accurately, an awareness of God's presence.

As Paul pointed out, all of us live and move and have our being in God, but we may not be aware of this presence. It is our destiny to consciously know this truth and to live life accordingly.

Beautiful churches, temples, mosques, and synagogues have been built through the ages. We enter these places and are in awe of the architecture and artistry of these man-made structures. However, though the walls, floors, and ceilings may be beautiful, their function is to set forth the presence of God. The church is not the visible structure, but the unseen "space" between the walls. It is in this space that we live and move and have our being. That which appears empty and void is the house of the Lord.

Today become consciously aware of the "space" in which you dwell. Every structure defines space. A wise architect like Frank Lloyd Wright designed structures that remind us that the space in which we live and work contains the presence of God. Walk into each room of your house, stand in the middle of the room, and become receptive to the space. Remind yourself that this space is the house of the Lord; it is God's presence.

God is closer than hands and feet.

Up to this point of *Week 18*, we have considered the idea that God is close—around us and enfolding us. This is only a portion of the truth. Others have had the insight that God is closer than hands and feet. The omnipresence of Spirit transcends the idea of closeness.

When we consider the idea that Spirit is closer than hands and feet, there is a natural tendency to think that God is within us. This enlivening thought and idea, if it is true, explains why we can never be forsaken or forgotten. Wherever we are, God is.

When the sky grows dark this evening, light a candle and place it in the center of the room. Sit back from the candle and see the flame as a point of light. Next imagine that this light is the image of God and that it is centered in the midst of you. At first it may be only a point of light, but Spirit declares, "Let your light shine." Return to the idea of the indwelling light and express your willingness to let it shine. Record in the space below any experiences or thoughts that come to you:

Today I awaken to my oneness with God.

Today is a Remembrance Day. Consider a time in your life when you felt close to God. These times are usually marked by great peace in the midst of difficulty, a feeling of being loved when no one is with you, or a wondrous joy when nothing has happened in your outer life. Perhaps some keen insight has come to you. Maybe the insight is uplifting, but it may be something that you don't particularly like, yet which still rings true.

Record the happening:

When you stop to consider closeness with God, there is usually the realization of a time when you knew God was with you. Sometimes you try to explain away such happenings or you simply forget. The consciousness of the moment drifts away from you, and life "returns to normal." It is possible that you have not experienced oneness with your Creator and have not yet had such an experience. You will, for it is your destiny. In the weeks to come, practical help will be given to prepare you for what lies ahead.

I am closer than you think.

When Spirit begins to reveal itself to us, usually one of the first truths we discover or "hear" is God declaring, "I will never leave you; I am with you always." Later in the relationship, God reveals a greater truth: "I am closer than you think."

It is like two people in love revealing more and more of themselves to each other. We cannot bear the truth of God or of our own being all at once. Day by day, insight by insight, the relationship grows.

God is more than within us. The closeness is greater than water in a cup or even the breath in the body. We are made in the image of God. Some people have said that God is in us in the same way that the ocean is in the wave. It is a beautiful analogy, but all human concepts fall short when describing our oneness with God. A whole section of this book is dedicated to discovering what it means to be made in God's image.

No matter what your current understanding of your oneness with God, open yourself today to a more intimate closeness. Spend fifteen minutes in stillness today, sensing Spirit's words, "I am closer than you think."

"I and the Father are one."

Jesus said, "I and the Father are one" (Jn. 10:30). When He spoke these words, they were so foreign to the people that they picked up stones to kill Him. But for many, this statement is the beginning of a spiritual journey. Oneness with God is something many never consider. To them, God is always far away. Here is a simple poem that declares our oneness with God:

Oneness

When I hear the howl of the wind
and that "still small voice"
and know they are uttered
by the same power,
the Father and I are one.
When the energy of a storm
rages within me
as zeal and zest for life
I have the power
to become what I am.
When I watch my son become a man
and a seed become a tree
and know they meet
at the crossroad called life,
the Father and I are one.
When I observe the order
of the heaven,
and the irresistible force of love
moves through my life

the harmony of the universe is mine.
When I feel a gentle breeze
against my face,
and the loving squeeze of my love's hand,
and know they stem from the same heart,
the Father and I are one.
When Christ, my "hope of glory,"
can be seen within me
and in my life,
I am what I am.
When the sunrise and sunset
each marks a new beginning
for my eternal life,
the Father and I are one.

Logically, we understand that we and the Father are one, but this is not enough. Our souls long for the experience of oneness. Only experience feeds us and fills us to overflowing. We can compare ourselves to a man who has not eaten for days. Don't tell him about a sumptuous meal. Don't describe the taste. Let him eat!

Some of the following weeks' activities are designed to help you do your part in preparing for the experience of the presence. For today, consider your oneness with God and write a poem on the following page that expresses the way you feel.

Week 18
Day 126
continued

Week Nineteen
"Be Still, and Know"

It is good to have the world declare to us our oneness with Spirit, but it is better to have God revealed to us. Long ago the Psalmist heard these words, "Be still, and know that I am God" (Ps. 46:10). Any encounter with Spirit is a life-transforming experience. It must have been so for the Psalmist, and it is for us.

Our responsibility is to be still. These are simple words, but for an active individual in a fast-paced age, being still is a challenge. As we enter into the "activity" of stillness, let us do so with the idea that when we are still, we can sense what is perpetually occurring within us.

Begin being still by finding a quiet place and allowing yourself to sense the rise and fall of your chest. This happens perpetually, but you are usually not aware of it. By being still, you are beginning to be aware of inner processes which happen all the time.

Next allow yourself to sense your heartbeat. At first you might place your hand over your heart or your finger on a pulse point. Eventually, take your hand away and feel the heart beating in your body.

Now you are prepared to sense the deeper, more serene activity of Spirit in your soul. Rest quietly for a few moments, and let your soul become sensitive to whatever it is that is occurring within you. Do not record any thoughts, feelings, or images. At this point your purpose is not to gain results, but to be true to the process of being still.

By being still,
I know what I have not known before.

"Kung Fu" was a television program about a Chinese priest named Caine who traveled the American West, touching people's lives and bringing to them a sense of the Presence. During the program, there were flashbacks to Caine's training in the monastery. In one episode, Caine as a novice was asked by his blind teacher if he knew of the grasshopper at his feet. Caine asked how the teacher could hear such things. The wise master answered with a question, asking how it was that Caine did not.

Meister Eckhart said, "Nothing in all creation is so like God as stillness." A promise is given, "Be still, and know that I am God" (Ps. 46:10). Stillness is an extended hand offering us all the wonders of the universe. To some it is strange that stillness begets God's gifts, but it is so.

Attempt to become still at least twice during this day. Use whatever skills you have previously learned, and then rate yourself and the stillness you have achieved on a scale of 1 to 10, with 10 representing a restful quiet and 1 a state of unrest. Please do not look ahead to future days and their activities. Indicate below your degree of stillness. Let there be no condemnation regardless of the stillness you experienced.

1   2   3   4   5   6   7   8   9   10

This is normal. Everyone who walks the path of stillness encounters the wandering mind. It is like traveling across the country; it would be naive to think that we could move from where we are to our destination without having a few distractions or stops upon the way.

Do you remember when Jesus was in the Garden of Gethsemane and went aside to pray? He brought several of His disciples with Him—Peter, James, and John—but they fell asleep. Sleep is another traveler on the path of stillness. Let us not believe we will avoid meeting this one. We will meet him; we will fall asleep when we are trying to pray.

The wandering mind and sleep are companions in the early stages of our spiritual lives. It is for this reason that the many religions of the world have provided us with numerous practices which allow us to remain awake and centered in God rather than following the wayward ways of the meandering mind. Some cultures focus upon sounds and words to quiet the mind. Others have their devotees keep their eyes open and look at candles, pictures of saints, or objects, or have them think about significant spiritual happenings. Some people simply observe their breath.

There are undoubtedly hundreds of prayer and meditation techniques. We will utilize a few, but do not place more emphasis upon them than is necessary. Their purpose is to help us concentrate the mind and to lift it up so that we are better able to experience God's presence. We will discuss this lifting process in more detail in coming weeks.

Twice during this day, preferably in the morning and in the evening, practice the following exercise. Imagine yourself as the Psalmist in Psalm 46. You are in prayer. See yourself in the traditional dress of biblical times. You might imagine some difficulty that this person is having. Maybe the details of the problem are explained to God. And then the words, "Be still, and know that I am God," rise from within. Let this be your experience!

"You shall have no other gods before me."

The degree of success of yesterday's exercise is not important. Perhaps there was progress or maybe the mind was as unruly as it was the day before. It is all either *seeming* success or *seeming* defeat. The mind is like a butterfly fluttering from thing to thing; like a river, for it meanders in valleys. Butterflies and rivers are accepted by us, and the mind that meanders and flutters must also be accepted. This is the heart of today's activity.

The commandment is "You shall have no other gods before me" (Ex. 20:3). When we are trying to focus upon God or spiritual things and the mind wanders to our concerns and worries or other earthly issues, this does not call for condemnation. It calls for acceptance.

Try to be still in any way that seems workable for you. Once again, it is suggested that ten to fifteen minutes be taken in the morning and in the evening. The added ingredient today is acceptance. Let there be no condemnation. In the stillness that is God's presence, there is no condemnation.

I observe unconditionally.

Today more guidance is given which will assist you in becoming still. The breath will be a center of your attention, for it is like Spirit—unseen, and yet it sustains our physical bodies.

This activity requires two fifteen-minute periods. In the first, focus upon your breathing. Inhale through your nose and exhale through your mouth. Give the gift of your attention to the rise and fall of your chest for a time, and then center your attention just in front of your face where the unseen breath is entering and leaving your body. This simple centering exercise is to be done for the entire first fifteen-minute period. You will discover as you do this that you become relaxed. This is significant, for there is no tension in God.

The second fifteen-minute period is to have an added ingredient— unconditional observation. When you discover your mind wandering, observe it for a time. In what "direction" is it drifting? Family, work, worry, the past, the future? Observe this movement of the mind as you would a butterfly moving from flower to flower. Consider that the meandering mind simply is. It is not bad or good; it is. Then return to your breath again. With this activity, acceptance is becoming more a part of you.

You will find as you grow spiritually that acceptance is paramount. The practice of prayer and meditation always activates the cleansing power of Spirit. Images from the past and even hurtful emotions from as far back as childhood emerge. They are not to be resisted. Through acceptance, they are healed.

I and the light are one.

Today we will be exposed to a technique which has been used through the ages to center and lift the mind.

Put aside twenty minutes this evening after the sun has set. In a darkened room, light a candle, sit about a foot from the flame, and observe it. Observe and accept the mind when it wanders, and then return to the flame. Observe every detail of the flame. Occasionally, take note of the shadows that are cast by the light. Ask this question: How are this candle, its wick, and the light related to my life?

Record any insight in the space below:

I sing a new song.

Visual helps, images, and objects can be the focus of the mind and help still the soul. Humankind discovered long ago that sound also can assist us in being still. Single words are intoned in some cultures. Seemingly meaningless sounds are often uttered for extended periods of time. Some people speak statements of truth, and still others sing the same words. Sound has a special quality in that it is of the moment. No one has ever heard a sound in the past or in the future.

Charles Fillmore, co-founder of the Unity movement, loved the old saying, "He who sings prays twice." Mr. Fillmore was aware of the power of singing. The feeling nature can be engaged, and the meaning of the words seems to root itself more deeply in us.

Today's exercise is to be done in the privacy of your home. Form a statement or affirmation consisting of seven syllables. This statement must be meaningful to you. For instance: *I am filled with God's grandeur*, or: *I sing a new song of love*. Now sing your seven syllable phrase to any tune which seems right to you. Sing it over and over again until it fills your mind. Then cease singing and rest. When the mind wanders, sing again, and be still once more. Continue this process for twenty minutes.

If you repeat this experience daily, eventually you will discover that less and less time is spent singing and more and more time simply being still.

A simple truth

Today we combine several centering ideas. We will use the seven-syllable affirmation used by Jesus, "I and the Father are one" (Jn. 10:30). No audible sounds will be uttered, for we are going to *think* this statement in concert with our breath.

As you inhale through your nose, think the words: "I and the Father," and when you exhale finish the affirmation of truth: "are one." Do this several times and then rest. Watch the mind and its degree of stillness. Does it wander afar or does it remain near to the truth of being, our oneness with God?

Return to the simple truth of oneness again, and let your breathing actually "utter" the words. If this is done enough, the time will come when any thought of your breath will return your mind to the words: "I and the Father are one."

There is one other ingredient you can add to this exercise. As the breath and thought are joined, center your attention at the top of your head. Think of each breath entering and leaving through the crown of your head. Notice that three things are unified in this practice. There is breathing, a simple truth, and concentration on a specific portion of the body.

Be gentle with yourself in this exercise. Be patient, and you will find that you are being still!

Note: Read *Day 134*'s lesson before rising tomorrow.

Week Twenty
Talking to God

This is destined to be a week of companionship. We may be alone during this week, but we will soon find a new definition of the word *alone*. Alone means being with God.

At times we cry out for companionship and in doing so fail to acknowledge the truth that God is with us. If God were a person and we treated God so, God would be the most rejected of all people in the universe.

During this week, let us talk to Spirit as if it were at our side. This practice of the presence has been done before, and those who have persisted have found a constant consciousness of God that nearly overwhelms them.

In the 1500s there lived a Carmelite monk named Brother Lawrence. He spent most of his life in the infirmary kitchen of the monastery. However, this simple monk spent his time wisely as he talked to God and ultimately felt a closeness to the Father that was evident to those around him. In fact, his superiors often came to visit him to learn of his relationship with God and how they might have the same experience.

Move to the first day of this week as you begin to practice the presence. Remember, being alone means being with God.

*This is the day that the Lord has made,
I rejoice and am glad in it.*

There are many things that we do in the course of a day. The practice of the presence of God may seem like simply talking to God, but it is more than it appears. Contemplation is wed to the activities of daily life. This week is unique in this book. Each day's lesson and activity are to be treated as cumulative. The previous day's activity is to be repeated every following day. All seven activities will be performed on the last day of *Week 20.*

The purpose of the practice of the presence of God is to hold in mind continuously a thought of Spirit and spiritual things. God must not be seen as separate from daily life, but unified with it.

When you first awaken today, do not rise from your bed, but instead remain still and say to God: "This is your day. I will rejoice and be glad in it. What shall we do together today?"

Before you begin to move your arms and legs and continue your day as you normally would, consider that the strength and energy enabling you to get out of bed is the strength and energy of God. Then slowly, very slowly rise from your bed with the conscious awareness that God is your strength. Perhaps you will be able to sense the power, strength, and energy that God is.

Begin today as you did yesterday. Remember that the day is God's and rejoice and be glad in it. Be sensitive and open to experiencing the power God is in your simplest movement.

One of the typical things you do each morning is to bathe or cleanse yourself. In the practice of the presence of God, a parallel is drawn between washing and an activity of Spirit. As you are showering or bathing, let your mind return to the ancient ritual of baptism. See yourself standing beside the Jordan River watching people being baptized. Allow the act of bathing to bring to your mind the need for spiritual cleansing. See yourself immersed in the River Jordan, cleansed on the outside and purified on the inside.

"I have food to eat of which you do not know."

Return to the two previous days' activities and perform them again. Now another part of daily life is wed to the contemplation of spiritual things— eating.

As you drink water, remember Jesus' words to the Samaritan woman, "Every one who drinks of this water will thirst again, but whoever drinks of the water that I shall give him will never thirst" (Jn. 4:13-14). As you eat, recall the words, "I have food to eat of which you do not know" (Jn. 4:32). During another meal you might join the Hebrews wandering in the wilderness and help them gather the manna or daily bread that sustained them during the years prior to their entry into the Promised Land.

There are so many spiritual illustrations to remember while we nourish our bodies. There are the feeding of the five thousand, the ravens which fed the prophet, and the Last Supper. As you eat, be nourished by more than food. Truth is your daily bread.

With God nothing is impossible.

As the day begins, continue with the previous days' practice of the Presence. During the course of the day, there will be some task that must be performed. Maybe it is easy, and you have performed it many times. If this is the case, you are probably confident of your ability to do this task. Or perhaps something new challenges you, and you wonder how it can be achieved.

No matter what the task at hand, it can better be achieved when you take the stance: *I of myself can do nothing. With God nothing is impossible.* One reason we sometimes fail in doing a job, or perform it inadequately, is that we try too hard. We assume we must do it, and yet we do not believe we have the resources. There are even times when the job before us seems impossible. During these times John Flavle's statement, "Man's extremity is God's opportunity," rings true.

If you have an impossible task before you today, stand still and remember that nothing is impossible with God. Once you begin to act, the energy, wisdom, and resources necessary for the completion of the project will become evident.

On the other hand, it is likely that there is no impossible task before you today. Instead you have the opportunity to practice the Presence in a way that allows you to experience the ease with which a thing can be accomplished when Spirit is your partner and is allowed to express itself through you. Simply remember that you of yourself can do nothing. With God nothing is impossible. Then begin. Act with boldness, daring, and the expectation that all is well.

Write the results of your experiment:

Week 20
Day 137
continued

I behold the Christ in you.

Continue as with previous days.

Unless we live isolated lives, we come in contact with other people on a daily basis. These may be family members, neighbors, co-workers, strangers, those we like very much, or those we wish we could avoid. When we practice the Presence, we do not judge by appearances or by what a person says or does. Our purpose is to behold the Christ in that individual.

Please return to *Week 16, Day 109*, reread the story of Mother Teresa, and then return and do today's exercise.

You have a formidable task before you today. It is to see each person you meet as the Christ in disguise. Some people will have better disguises than others. It is not necessary that you say anything to anyone. Simply let the words *I behold the Christ in you* flow through your mind. The challenge is to do this at least once with every person you meet.

All throughout the day
I enjoy monastic moments.

To the previous day's practices we now add monastic moments. These are refreshing pauses and remembrances during the day.

With great regularity, pause during the day, and for twenty to thirty seconds remember that you and the Father are one. These monastic moments, added to the other things you are doing, will add a sense of the Presence to your waking hours.

How many monastic moments did you enjoy during the day?

In my dreams,

Spirit illumines me.

Week 20's activities offer but a few suggestions for practicing the presence of God. Remember, contemplation and a remembrance of spiritual things must be wed to daily activity.

Consider other things that you might do to enhance, deepen, and enrich your oneness with God. During the day, do this thing, for it is your own. As you began your day with God, so you must now end the day with God. Lie down to sleep, and let these words be the last that flow through your mind: *In my dreams, Spirit illumines me.*

Week Twenty-One
God's Will

God's will is a mystery to us. Is it God's will that a certain man marry a certain woman or that a family move to a particular city? Is it God's will that we die or that we be healed? Does God will earthquakes, famine, flood, disease, or plane crashes? Notice that these questions relate to our earthly experience. The truth is, God's kingdom is not of the earth and neither is God's will.

God's will is not of the earth.

Our concerns are worldly, and naturally we have wondered if what we want is also what God wants for us. To enlist the aid of the Almighty would be immensely helpful. Aligning our will with the divine will would assure us of the fulfillment of our desires. Please note that in most cases our desires are earthly, for we have specific needs which we feel must be met. We may not have entertained the possibility that God's kingdom is not of the earth and that neither is God's will.

Make a list of the things that you have considered to be God's will or wished were God's will. Here are a few possibilities: a healed body, a new job, a vacation trip overseas.

Are these things earthly in nature? If you answer yes, it is likely that what you hope is God's will is not God's will at all.

God's will is the same for everyone.

The will of God is not specific to one human being. Spirit has no favorites. If two men want to marry the same woman, could it be God's will that one man marry the woman and another not marry her? God's will is the same for every human being. It is not about marriage and places to live and work, for everyone cannot have the same earthly experience.

Make a list of things specific to you that you have hoped were aligned to the will of God:

Are you willing to consider that these things could be experienced by everyone on earth simultaneously? If you answer no, it is likely that what you hope is God's will is not God's will at all.

God's will fulfills my every human need.

It is inconceivable to believe God's will would leave us in a state of lack and deprivation. The promise, "Thy will be done, On earth as it is in heaven" (Mt. 6:10), must be fulfilled. God's will, although not of the earth, must manifest itself upon the earth and fulfill every human need, as well as desires which we are just beginning to sense. That which seems so complex is actually very simple.

God's will is powerfully simple, and in the quietness of our souls Spirit speaks its will: "Know me." This is the same for everyone. It is not of the world. It is from above. If we respond to divine will and let our purpose be to know God, it is reasonable to assume that all wholesome, earthly desires will be fulfilled. Perhaps they would be fulfilled without making them the object of our lives.

In the space below, write the two words that describe God's will for you and every human being. Four lines have been provided, but this space is not required. Write in the center of the top line the words *Know God*. Can you see how simple God's will is? how all-encompassing?

_____

_____

_____

_____

God's will is not death,
but that I know God as life.

The mystery is no more. We can now be aligned to the one will. There need be no doubt as to whether it is God's will that we live or die. God's will is not of the earth. The life that God is transcends earthly experience. God's will is simple: Know Me as life.

When we come to know Spirit in this way, there is no death. Life is and shall ever be. The body may be shed, but the pure and perfect life of God remains. This life is not ours, for we have no being without the life of God.

Utilize some of the prayer techniques you have used in recent weeks and consider today's statement: God's will is not death, but that I know God as life. Can you see how today's idea solves the question of whether life or death is God's will?

God's will is not that I be in a certain place, but that I know that wherever I am, God is.

The insights of truth must be applied to daily life. This week's work outlines a foundation principle which we can return to when facing any human challenge or difficulty. Let there be no wondering about divine will. God's will is "Know Me."

For instance, assume you are considering moving to another city or even another country. In the past, you would ask whether it is God's will that you move to another location. However, when God's will is "Know Me," you must approach this matter differently. Spirit is everywhere equally present, and therefore it does not matter to God where you are. You are always in the Presence. The question is: Will you know this truth and experience it?

This understanding of will demands that we change our approach to living. Life is simplified, and we realize as never before the need for the inner journey, which is the theme of this second 13-week segment of *A Daily Guide to Spiritual Living.* If life's problems are to be solved, we must put aside the need to find a solution and be willing to know God.

Utilize some of the prayer techniques you have used in recent weeks and consider today's statement: God's will is not that I be in a certain place, but that I know that wherever I am, God is. Can you see how today's idea solves the question of whether you will live on the West Coast or the East Coast or north or south?

Note: This approach to life does not disallow us having a sense of guidance about living in one place or another. The guidance will be the fruit of knowing that God is wherever we are. If this seems confusing, let it go for now and know that we will expand on this idea in future weeks. In the meantime, let your will and God's be one.

God's will is not earthly riches or poverty, but that I know God as my source.

Prosperity and security are key issues for human beings. We want to be able to provide for ourselves and our families. Actually, we are seeking security. We believe this is achieved by having enough money to secure our future days. We wonder if it is God's will that we drive a certain car or are employed by a particular company with the salary and benefits that will enable us to feel secure. We now know such things are not God's will. However, that does not mean we are to live insecure lives or lack for any good thing.

Spirit's will is that we know God as our source. The Bible declares in various ways that we trust in God. Let us not think for a moment that the Almighty is going to pull some strings for us, and we are going to get that raise. God does not work in this manner. The universe is devised in another way. In fact, the design is incredibly simple. Our awareness or thoughts tend to manifest themselves first as feelings of security and then later as prospering ideas, job opportunities, and increased salary and benefits. Our function is so simple; know God. When we are one with this will, all is well.

No longer do you need to question the Lord of your being and wonder if a job is to be yours or how your needs will be met. Know God, act upon the guidance that comes from this consciousness of Spirit, and be sensitive to the ideas and opportunities that present themselves to you.

In the space that follows, outline the steps you are going to take to open yourself to an awareness that God is your source. You may wish to refer to the past weeks' ideas as you determine what is best for you.

Week 21
Day 146
continued

204

God's will is not a human relationship,
but that I know God as love.

Once again the wisdom of God is evident, for when we know God as love, loving relationships abound. A father and his youngest son have a running dialogue about love. The father maintains that the son's stuffed polar bear named John is filled only with stuffing. The son believes, or so he says, that the stuffed animal contains love. They kid about this, but the father's stance is that his son is filled with love, and when he hugs and loves John, the stuffed polar bear, his son feels the love that flows from within himself.

The search for a relationship is actually a search for love. We attempt to find love in the arms of another, but we may be, as the song says, "looking for love in all the wrong places." God's will is not that we are wed to a certain person. God's will transcends human relationships. God's will is the center out of which all wholesome relationships arise. God's will is that we know God as love. Once we discover love within ourselves, we will not look for others to fill the void we feel inside, and we will begin to express the love that we are. Will there be loving relationships? Absolutely! They are destined to be part of our lives, but only when we are attuned to divine will.

Outline the steps you are going to take to open yourself to an awareness that God's love is within you. You may wish to refer to a past week's ideas as you determine what is best for you.

Week 21
Day 147
continued

Week Twenty-Two
Not My Will, but Yours Be Done

Last week we became familiar with God's will, Know Me, and reacquainted ourselves with the need to purify our desire. Prior to last week, we struggled to determine divine will and hoped it was one with ours. When we were unsure of God's will, we tried to mold it to our own.

Today you begin a process that results in only one will, God's will, being active in your life. Your purpose will be simplified, and all activities will eventually flow forth from this purpose. There will be no more questions about whether some happening is God's will. The events of the world will be accepted without resistance and the "business" of knowing God will finally become the driving force of life.

Read the account in The Gospel According to Luke (Lk. 22:39-44) in which Jesus declares, "Not my will, but thine, be done." Be prepared to speak these words whenever you are tempted to let your purpose or reason for acting, speaking, or being be less than Know Me.

Week 22
Day 148

I acknowledge
that I have a will of my own.

We know that God's will is Know Me. But it does not take long to realize that you also have a will of your own.

This does not mean that your will is always destructive. We live in a three-dimensional world, and there are things which we must do that are a natural part of life on earth. There are places to go and items to buy, things to do, and people to see. These actions are not the fulfillment of God's will, but may still be very necessary for human existence. At times we may simply want to go to a movie or read a spy novel. These are expressions of our will.

The will to live is considered by survival experts to be the strongest and most necessary ingredient when one is alone in the wild or enduring great hardships. The strength of this will has helped many a person survive the trauma of tragedy.

Today's lesson requests only one thing of you—the acknowledgment that you have a will of your own. In the space below, list several expressions of your will. At this time, do not look for examples that are willful, but for those which relate to life on earth. Examples might be wanting to win a tennis match or finish writing a novel. Remember that God is not concerned about the outcome of any tennis match or the finishing of a novel. Wanting to play good tennis or finish a novel are examples of our will.

My will can be opposed to God's will.

When Jesus was born and the word went forth that a new king was in the land, King Herod did not bow down and pay homage to the new arrival. King Herod, symbolizing the human will, sought to preserve his way of life by opposing the newborn.

Spirit's will, Know Me, will be opposed by our human will. Rather than being willing, willfulness will be the rule of our lives at times. Today let us become aware of a few characteristics of the human will.

First, it wants its way and knows exactly what that way is. Specific outcomes are foreseen, and great effort is expended to "make it happen." When divine will is active, our efforts are to know God, to experience the Presence. We are then willing to allow this revelation to change us, mold us, and transform us in whatever way is best. The only specific desire we have is an awareness of God.

Second, the human will is willing to have its way at someone else's expense. Divine will knows that when we know God, all are blessed.

Today become aware of your will and its tendencies. Describe in detail three examples of your will in opposition to God's will. Let one of the examples be the most recent you can remember. The other two may be from the past.

1.

Week 22
Day 149
continued

2.

3.

I cannot serve two wills.

Willingness and willfulness are not companions. They cannot rule the same kingdom. There will be either one or the other. God's will, Know Me, is eternal and can never perish. Our will may persist, but its days are numbered.

Today is a day of choice. "Choose this day whom you will serve . . . but as for me and my house, we will serve the Lord" (Josh. 24:15). Today is more than a choice to fulfill God's will. It is a choice to declare in thought, word, and deed, "Not my will, but thine, be done" (Lk. 22:42). Today's choice is to acknowledge the conflict we feel inside when we attempt to do our will instead of Spirit's.

We cannot go on forever following our will. An alcoholic must eventually choose to let God's will be done. Slowly but surely, we choose to let life's challenges be answered by becoming aware of Spirit.

Let today be filled with monastic moments. Pause for many ten-second intervals and say to yourself, "I cannot serve two wills." Then declare: *As for me, I choose* _____. Insert either *my human will* or *God's will.*

There is only one will.

There is only one will that endures, the will of God. Our will is like the buildings we build. Many are majestic and endure for eons, but eventually, even they crumble. The seven wonders of the world are nearly history. The pyramids of Egypt are all that remain, and they are not what they once were. Our will and its acts are temporal. Only God's will remains. It is just as pure and thought-provoking and filled with possibilities as it ever was.

The will of God alone endures. When our will is fulfilled, we rejoice, but the universe is silent, and eventually our joy is no longer even a distant echo. When God's will is done, the universe rejoices as do we, and the sound of our joy never ends.

Be sensitive to the activity of your will. When it asserts itself, reinforce yesterday's activity by declaring: *There is only one enduring will, the will of God.* Then do that will!

Without God,
may my will never be fulfilled.

When our will opposes God's will, may it never be fulfilled. Our will does not result in harmony. It gives birth to chaos. Of course, at first we are convinced that all is well, but the passage of time reveals another "truth."

Give three examples of instances when your will was fulfilled and upset followed:

1.

2.

3.

May God's will always be fulfilled.

If God's will is to be fulfilled, we must open ourselves to experience the Presence. Only when we know God is the will of God satisfied. Spirit is gentle with us and affirms that the choice is ours, but something is demanded of us. No longer can we expect harmony by trying to create it. Our purpose and work are to know God. This is why, on an earlier day, it was stated that our first step is to stand still.

When you are challenged by a difficulty, stop your efforts to solve the problem and remember this day and its affirmation: *May God's will always be fulfilled.* Put aside what you think is the perfect answer. There is only one answer to the challenge. God must be known.

As Jesus drew near to His crucifixion, He went with three of His disciples to the Mount of Olives and prayed. He wanted God's will rather than His own to be fulfilled. This is often interpreted as Jesus' request to know whether He was to be crucified or not. This is a reasonable interpretation of the statement, "Not my will, but thine be done" (Lk. 22:42). But there is another possibility. Perhaps Jesus' statement implies that He knew He was destined for the Cross, but that the only way to face such an experience was through oneness with God. Only by knowing God, by experiencing the Presence, could a resurrection be the fruit of a crucifixion.

Dear friend, God must be known. May God's will be fulfilled in your life.

God's will is the law of my life.

There are certain principles that are the foundation of a person's life. Some people believe life is a struggle, and their belief is confirmed. Others feel humankind is basically sinful, and the worst is expected. Amazingly, these people see very little of the good that occurs on earth or that could occur in their lives. These basic primal beliefs become the law of life for these people.

There is a law of life for us, and it is God's will. Will denotes action and accomplishment, but the beginning of a sacred work is stillness. First, there is God's will; then there is God's work being done. We yearn to know God, and eventually the Almighty becomes a friend. Then we are given a God mission that fulfills our purpose and fills us with creativity.

God's will is the law of your life. In the beginning is God's will. If you can remember these ideas and let them be the beginning of your acts, your life will change. Rather than oppose the natural tendency of the universe, you will be an important part of it. God's will, as you now know, is not of the earth. It is not interested in ordinary happenings. It is the cause of extraordinary occurrences.

Let today be a perfect expression and outworking of this law of life. Let the day begin with your allegiance to God's will. Often during the day, say and then enact the idea: *In the beginning is God's will.* Knowing God will be the heart of this day. You will never forget it. In the evening, list a few activities which you began as you sought to know God.

Week Twenty-Three
Knowing What to Ask For

A promise is given: "Ask, and it will be given you; seek, and you will find; knock, and it will be opened to you" (Mt. 7:7). Another promise is given: "It is your Father's good pleasure to give you the kingdom" (Lk. 12:32). If these promises are true, why are we unfulfilled? Something is being offered to us, and we do not know how to receive it.

The problem is that we do not know what we are being offered. It is as though we think we need a new car, and therefore we ask for it, but a boat is being offered. We do not think we need a boat, but it has been raining for thirty-nine days and thirty-nine nights.

The truth is, the promises are true. God is offering us something, but because we don't know what it is, we cannot receive it. When we know what is being offered, we will know what to ask for, and we will be fulfilled.

Before you do today's lesson, acknowledge the following idea: *I do not know what to ask for, but I am willing to learn.*

I know what to ask for.

Finally, we know our heart's desire. For too long we have come to the fountain of All-Good with a thimble instead of the fullness of our soul. We have asked for so little, thinking we have asked for everything. We have asked for healing, a new job, peace of mind, a loving relationship, and a creative mind. All these requests seem reasonable. Why are they not fulfilled?

List a few reasonable "things" you have asked for in your life, but have not received:

The universe is more simply structured than we have imagined. We are to go directly to the Creator for what we want. This does not mean we go to God asking for healings and new jobs. We go to "headquarters," as Charles Fillmore stated, asking to know God. This consciousness of God will then appear in our lives as a restored body, a new employment opportunity, or a creative idea.

Rejoice today, for you know what to ask for—an awareness or consciousness of God. This consciousness is the fulfillment of every desire and can manifest itself in your life in ways that meet and exceed human expectations. Today is a grand new beginning. God's will and your desire are unified. Life will be simpler from this day forth.

I want to know God.

There is a practical side to this new way of life. In fact, for a time the challenges of daily life will quicken in us the desire to know God. After a while, knowing God will be our way of life, not our answer to specific human problems.

In order to complete today's activity, you might want to return to the place of wisdom of *Week 11, Day 74.*

Please complete the following sentences:

1. When I have a decision to make, I want to know God as _____.

2. When I have a healing need, I want to know God as _____.

3. When I have a need for money, I want to know God as _____.

4. When I feel alone, I want to know God as _____.

Answers:
1. Wisdom
2. Life
3. Source
4. Love

I ask, believing.

The following verse of Scripture is the foundation of humankind's approach to asking. "Whatever you ask in prayer, believe that you have received it, and it will be yours" (Mk. 11:24). In the human mind, the *it* to be received is of the earth—cars, healings, jobs, loving relationships, and so forth. Because of this misunderstanding, affirmative prayers are uttered. "I give thanks that my body is restored to perfect health." "I am now being attracted to the perfect job, which will bring me fulfillment and financial plenty." "My life is now filled with the love of a person with whom I can share my life." There are laws of mental science that allow for the fulfillment of these human desires, but remember, this is a guide to spiritual living. There is a greater joy awaiting us.

The *it* is not of the earth. The *it* being offered to us, which we can receive, is Spirit. God is offered to us—an awareness of the Presence. Who would ask for a car, a healing, a job, when the Creator is offered to us? Below, write affirmative statements which express the belief that we have received an awareness of God as wisdom, life, source, and love.

1.

2.

3.

4.

Examples:
1. I am one with the wisdom of God. I let the light shine.
2. I am divine life being lived.
3. I am safe and secure, for I am a fountainhead of All-Good.
4. There is but one love in my life and in all the universe—divine Love.

My desire is pure.

How confusing life is when many desires fill the mind and heart. We are pulled first in one direction and then in another. Today our desire is singular and pure.

You return home one day, and a present is on your doorstep. It is a gift from a dear friend, and you are delighted. But a sadness comes over you, for you have missed your friend. The gift represents some tangible demonstration, such as being healed of a disease or finding the person of your dreams. There is happiness, yet the highest desire of the soul for God is not yet realized, so there is also sadness. On another day, you return home, enter your house, and smell a sweet fragrance in the air. It is the perfume of your dear friend. A sadness comes upon you again, for you have just missed your friend. It is nice to know that this special one was here, but it would be better if you had had the opportunity to commune with each other.

These modern-day parables illustrate our most heartfelt desire. The friend in the stories is God. You give thanks for the gift that is a tangible blessing, but you will always sense a void until you can commune with God, your friend. The fragrance represents a feeling of peace or love or some insight or truth that thrills you. You are delighted, but "gifts" and "fragrances" are no substitute for God.

Many of the games played by our lesser self, our ego, cease when our desire is pure. The lesser self is disarmed when we desire only God, for nearly all its ploys and antics require a relationship with something other than Spirit.

Today, please devise an activity that will assist you in purifying your desire. Write the exercise in the space that follows:

Week 23
Day 158
continued

I ask through waiting.

During an earlier lesson, we said that it would be necessary to revisit the idea of waiting. Ultimately, each person will discover that waiting is one of the greatest skills that can be learned on the inner journey.

Our desire is pure. We ask for and desire the consciousness of God. The question now is how do we prepare ourselves to receive? Preparing to receive is our work, but know that God is not achieved. We can achieve many things in life, but God consciousness is not won in the same way that we win a tennis match. Union with Spirit is not facilitated in the way a merger takes place between two companies. We have our work to do, but humility is the key.

Remember the image of being in a garden and seeing a beautiful dove resting nearby? We are struck with the beauty of this creature and want to caress and love it, so we move toward the winged one only to find that as we draw near, it flies away. After a few tries, we humbly realize that through our efforts we will not touch the dove. So we close our eyes and wait with our desire extended like an outstretched hand. After a time, the dove descends upon us and rests on our shoulder. This is God's way.

To wait with a heart yearning only for God is today's work.

When you can, enter into your sanctuary or quiet place where you consistently commit yourself to a spiritual work. Take a few deep breaths, and let the following words and ideas carry you to the garden and the dove.

My desire is pure.
My outstretched hand is my yearning heart.
And so I wait . . .

There is only one desire of my mind and heart.
Like a treasure hidden, I have discovered it—
My desire to know God.
And so I wait . . .

Only my God can fulfill me.
Only when we are one is my life fulfilled.
And so I wait . . .

Note: When your mind drifts during your period of waiting, come back to one of the above statements, say it to yourself, then wait again . . . and again.
Remember: Waiting with a heart yearning for God is today's work.

I ask through my actions.

We are learning to ask through waiting, but life is not always stillness. Prayers cause us to move our feet, for "faith apart from works is dead" (Jas. 2:26).

It is a spiritual truth that what we seek is within us. Therefore, we experience through expression. Memorize this statement, for it will become a great friend on the journey. *We experience through expression.*

When we understand this principle, we are called to action. If we are to experience love, then we must express love. We feel peace when we express it. Security comes through giving. This powerful principle is a foundation for a life of God-ordained actions. The challenge is to determine how we express love, peace, and the other aspects of Spirit.

This is your challenge today. Love is within you and is not experienced unless you express it genuinely. By expressing love, your actions are asking to know God as love. You will be a blessing to others, but you will also find yourself blessed. This is the way Spirit has devised the universe. You are blessed by being a blessing.

In the space below, record your expression of love. Notice that with the expression there was the experience of love. To waiting you can now add action as a way of asking to experience the presence of God.

*From one desire,
all desires are met.*

God's way is so simple, and our ways are so complicated. The following is a description of the human condition. It is time to go to the grocery store, for the cupboard is bare. There are many items that need to be purchased. We drive to the grocery where milk is sold and then on to another store where butter is for sale. Each food item is sold at a different location, bread on one side of town and vegetables on another. It will take days, literally, to do our grocery shopping. What is the solution to this problem?

What is your suggestion?

One suggestion is that the food stuffs be consolidated into one location where you can go to purchase what you need. When it comes to food, we understand the necessity of a neighborhood store, but when it comes to more enduring qualities of life, we roam from place to place. We go to people for love, books and wise ones for wisdom, jobs for security, and so on. What an inefficient and tiresome way of life.

All we need to do is go to God for God, not for the specific items we feel we need. From this awareness, all else is provided.

Today rejoice in the simple truth that God is your heart's desire. Memorize these two statements, for they are true companions for the journey: *From one desire, all desires are met. Go to God for God.*

Week Twenty-Four
The Mystery of Power

Let us not be deceived by earthly forms of power: the wind, water and steam, the warming rays of the sun, and the energy of the atom. Nor should we think that power rests in the hands of the rulers of countries. Remember, Jesus' promise was that the meek shall inherit the earth.

Who are the meek? What do they know that enables them to inherit the earth? They realize that true power is not of the earth; true power comes from knowing God. *True power is a consciousness of Spirit.*

The human approach to life is to achieve one's goals through work. Much effort is expended, and some of it leads to exhaustion. The meek know that being is prelude to doing and accomplishment. The meek prefer to inherit the earth. To inherit is to "acquire" a thing, not because of what we do, but because of what we are. The meek do not pursue the earth; they pursue God, and then this consciousness of Spirit manifests itself. Imagine the fruits of a consciousness which is Spirit.

There is no personal power.

When we judge by appearances, there seem to be numerous powers on earth. People are powerful. Money motivates people. The forces of nature leave us awestruck. Yet, none of these is power. They can cause changes in outer conditions, but they cannot change the core of things or the truth of who we are. Only that which created us the way we are is power.

This is an important lesson to learn. We are spirit, and nothing of the earth has dominion over us. Do not be surprised by this realization, for during the next three months, we will allow this idea to unfold from within us. For now, realize that the only power there is is God. Therefore, there is no personal power.

List ten "things" that you have considered to be power:

1. _____

2. _____

3. _____

4. _____

5. _____

6. _____

7. _____

8. _____

9. _____

10. _____

Life is consciousness of God.

For many years we have believed life is consciousness. This statement indicates the relationship between our dominant thought patterns, attitudes, and beliefs and what occurs in life. We cannot think in a negative or downward fashion and expect to have positive experiences. Perhaps it is true to say that experience is consciousness. The seeds we sow, we reap.

However, let us redefine life. Life, *as it is meant to be*, is a special state of consciousness—a consciousness of God. Our time on the earth is filled with many experiences, but how often do these happenings rise out of a consciousness of God? Life—dynamic, wonder-filled, overflowing good— is mothered by an awareness of God. All else is experience.

Through our five senses we can build an awareness of our world, but through stillness, prayer, and meditation, we become aware of the kingdom of God within us. We may raise a family and remain on the job for thirty years, but we merely exist until we are aware of our God. Then we are born and come alive.

While we exist, we believe in personal power. When we come alive, God is the only power in our lives. It does not make things happen; it reveals the way things are.

Please list the areas of personal power you have held in the past. (For example, perhaps you felt you were responsible for the life of your child or you wielded power on the job.)

I go the extra mile.

For humankind, power and might may seem to be one. We think of power when we hear the thunder of the water as it flows over the spillway of the dam. This is not power. The power is at the base of the dam where the water is still. Here great pressures are exerted in quietness.

Consider the story of a man who lived in biblical times. He stood on the roadside watching Roman soldiers marching through his village. Suddenly one of the soldiers stopped and called to him. The man's breathing quickened as he hurried to see what the soldier wanted. It was as he feared. The soldier commanded him to carry his pack for one mile. This was a law that had been decreed in the land. Any Roman could have an inhabitant of Palestine carry his burden for one mile.

Begrudgingly, the man took the pack and began his trek down the dusty road. The sun was hot, but the man's face was flushed red not because of the heat, but because of his anger. The soldier smirked as he saw the anger, for he realized that another Israelite had felt the might of Rome.

After traveling about half a mile, the Jew remembered hearing a rabbi named Jesus say, "If any one forces you to go one mile, go with him two miles" (Mt. 5:41). Now the man understood what Jesus was saying. During the first mile, the Roman soldier would be in control. The second mile, the man carrying the burden would reclaim his dignity, for the second mile was his choice. After one mile the soldier looked around to find another Jew to carry his pack. The man who had walked with him for a mile said, "May I carry your burden for one more mile?" The Roman was shocked and now knew that these were not a conquered people.

Look for opportunities to go the extra mile. Do what you are told to do, but also do a little more than you are asked. As you do, you will have a better understanding of the power of God within you. On the next page describe the extra mile you walked:

Humility calls into expression
the power God is.

Many of us would like to be powerful. We want to wield power, we say, not for ourselves, but for the common good. We can even build up a sense of esteem and begin to believe that we are powerful beings. The difficulty is that this "structure" has no firm foundation and will eventually collapse.

We do not call forth the power God is through force of will and human effort. The most powerful people who have ever walked the earth have had a marvelous sense of esteem about themselves, but this positive regard was balanced with the realization: *I of myself can do nothing.* There is humility and thus no sense of personal power. Where there is no "power" to oppose the power of God, the wonders and mysteries of Spirit are made known. We call them miracles. When we are powerless, we awaken to the Presence, and the power of Spirit is released from within us. This power is always for the common good.

In order to gently enter into the powerlessness which calls for the power of God, list ten things you are powerless over:

1. _____
2. _____
3. _____
4. _____
5. _____
6. _____
7. _____
8. _____
9. _____
10. _____

Thankfulness is a call to power.

Acts 16:25-26 tells of a time when Paul was in prison. It was midnight, and he and Silas were singing and praising God. Suddenly, there was an earthquake, and the doors of the prison were opened and the prisoners' fetters broken. They were free.

Naturally, they were free. Their souls were free. Their prayers, praises, and songs had lifted them up into a state of liberty. The world around them had to reflect the inner world. Charles Fillmore declared about this event in Paul's life, "Spiritual forces act through exalted thoughts."

Wherever there are exalted thoughts, the power of God is released. Notice that in this story there is nothing in the outer for which to be thankful. The men are in prison, but they make a choice to praise, pray, and give thanks. The power of God is released from within us in this way. Notice, also, that there is no attempt to wield the power or direct it in a particular way. Paul and Silas' purpose is exalted thoughts.

Put this principle to the test today. In a way to be determined by you, let your soul be filled with thankfulness. Give thanks for all aspects of your life. Give thanks for the goodness of your life as well as the challenges. Give thanks, and wait three days. Within three days, the power of God will be released from within you. Record the happening in the space below, but during your period of waiting, do not try to determine the expression of this power. Remember, there is no such thing as personal power.

Not by power, nor by might, but by Spirit.

True power is a consciousness of Spirit. When we become aware of our God, a window or door is opened which allows the expression of Spirit.

Our work is not to direct or wield the power. We are not to expend great effort and try to accomplish things by might. This only leads to exhaustion. Our purpose is to know God. Then the door is opened, and God's work is done. The work is effortless and enduring. We are amazed at how much is accomplished with so little effort. In fact, extraordinary things occur when the door is opened wide. During our time, the extraordinary happening is called a peak experience. Rest assured that in some way the power of God has been released.

If you have not had a peak experience in your life which you can express in a few sentences, research this subject and describe a peak experience someone else has had. A great example of such an occurrence happened in 1968 when Bob Beaman's long jump broke the world's record by over twelve inches, and he never came close to jumping so far again. Peak experiences are all around us and in every area of life. Describe your peak experience or a peak experience you discovered:

By grace . . .

We must remember these two words. They can prevent us from trying too hard. Fruitless effort is our specialty. It does no work. It is like pushing against a great building. We may expend much energy and be exhausted at the end of the day, but nothing is accomplished.

Remember that our work is basically to know and experience God. There is much for us to do in preparation for this "happening," but do not think God is achieved in the same way that we climb a mountain. Many a "climber" is shocked and delighted when he comes to know the Creator at a time he least expects it. He has tried and tried and tried. Exasperated, he quits and suddenly becomes aware of Spirit. Is it any wonder that we say, "By grace . . ."?

For many people, God is like a mountain to be climbed through human effort. On this divine mountain there is a high meadow. It is a beautiful place, but while here we are aware that the summit is still before us. It is shrouded in a mist. We want to go higher, but we cannot. We do not know the way. We must wait until a guide comes to show us the path to the peak. Watch for this guide. Her name is Grace. Every "mountain climber" knows the summit is reached by Grace.

Once during this day, set aside at least twenty minutes for the following experience. Picture in your mind a high mountain meadow where the mountain rises again. There are clouds and therefore no path is visible, but with patience and waiting, the summit can be realized . . . by Grace. Wait for her, and allow her to take you higher.

Week Twenty-Five
God Is Enough

A fundamental truth is that there is one Presence and one Power in the universe. We seek many things; however, nothing but a consciousness of God will satisfy us. An awareness of Spirit will manifest itself in ways that meet every human need. There is contentment and fulfillment *in* God, not *from* God.

There may have been periods in your life when you felt great unrest, when nothing seemed to satisfy you. There may have been no great void in your outer life. In fact, there may have been much to rejoice over. Your world may have been full, but your soul empty. Perhaps you kept looking to the world to find something which would "fill you up."

Now comes the truth: *God is enough.* Let this simple affirmation become more than words to you now. Let the phrase become your friend. Whenever you feel a sense of lack and begin to look outside yourself for what you think you need, let your "friend" ground you again and bring you home.

Only God can fulfill me.

The search for happiness and fulfillment can continue indefinitely. In fact, the quest will continue as long as we look to the world for what only God can provide. Today is a new beginning, for we consciously acknowledge: *Only God can fulfill me.* Perhaps this is the first day in our lives that we declare: *God is enough.*

We are so conditioned to believe that our five senses bring us joy. We see a beautiful sunset or are touched by a meaningful movie. We taste good food. We feel the gentleness of the wind and the warmth of the sun. We smell the fragrances of the flowers and high mountain pines. We hear the bird's song and the sound of beautiful music. We welcome kind words. Much of the joy and happiness we experience in life comes from the world and through our five senses. A part of us is fed by these messages, but another part finds joy and fulfillment in God.

It is obvious that only the spiritual aspect of us can say: *Only God can fulfill me.* This is a natural step in our inner journey. Everyone must walk this path. Long ago we sensed this truth, but we ignored it, and pursued the obvious—happiness in the world.

Now a new day begins.

List a few "things" which once brought you happiness, but today bring you little satisfaction:

Are you willing to consider the idea that the search for contentment will go on until you become conscious of your God? If the answer to this question is yes, write in the space below: *Only a consciousness of God can fulfill me.*

These are simple words, but they offer you a new life.

Spirit is my everything.

The things we truly value go unnoticed by the five senses. Who has seen love or touched peace? Does joy cast a fragrance in the air? Can we really taste freedom? Does wisdom or life have a voice? The senses are our servants and allow us to become conscious of the world, but with what sense will we awaken to the Almighty and come to know who and what we truly are?

It is through the eyes of love that we see the truth about another person. If our hearing is acute, we hear not so much the birds' song as we perceive the still small voice. It is Spirit that is like a fragrance, for when we are still we know of the Presence, but when the winds of human turmoil blow, the "fragrance" seems to drift away. We can reach out to people, but it often seems that Spirit reaches inside of us and touches us in ways that defy our understanding. Many tastes seem to meet our appetites, but after having drunk the tasteless living water, we will never thirst again.

There is only one Presence and one Power in the universe, for it is written, "In the beginning God . . ." (Gen. 1:1) All that is sensed and all that is known, whether through the five senses or other faculties of the soul, is God. From this, we conclude: *Spirit is my everything.*

Sense what is physically around you today, and remember, Spirit is your everything. What have you sensed that reminds you of the allness of Spirit?

Sense what is within you today. Be aware of "things" that you value which cannot be noted by the senses. Is it evident to you that Spirit is your everything? If the answer is yes, why?

The love God is is enough.

How long have we searched for love? From how many people have we sought love? At times we seem to find it, but then the excitement and passion of the moment die away and love seems no more. We postulate, "I found love in the arms of a person once; I can find it again." And so the search continues!

Thank God for the inner journey. The love we seek is within us. It is the love God is, and it is enough.

Make a list of the people from whom you have sought love:

A covenant is now presented to you. If you believe the love God is is enough, sign the covenant and practice it for a period of forty days.

I believe that the love God is is enough. Because of this truth, I do not seek the love of other people. For a period of forty days, I journey inward to find the love God is within me. During this time, I will start no new romantic relationships or do things previously practiced only to solicit "love" from others. My forty-day quest is to experience the love God is. I expect a powerful, loving relationship with the Presence and a conviction born of experience that affirms: The love God is is enough.

_____

Signature

The life God is is enough.

Can there be any other life than the life God is? Aren't the life expressions of plants and animals divine life made manifest? Can we have life separate from God? Can death destroy the life God is? Is death a barrier to God-life?

On an earlier day, we said that life is consciousness of God. This is why Jesus spoke of being born again. We are not truly alive unless we are conscious of Spirit. We may attempt to have and enjoy a life separate from God, but that life contains the seed of death; that is, it cannot go on.

Let us seek life in God. This search has not always been uppermost in our minds. We believed we could find life in many places and in doing many things. Some people attempt to find life through the love of other people. We say, "I am alive when I am loved." The wise ones say, "I am alive when I express the love God is." Some people attempt to come alive through learning and accumulating knowledge. They say, "I am alive when I am learning." The wise ones say, "I am alive when truth is not simply stored in me, but when it is applied for God's glory."

On what does your life depend?

Is there something you must be doing?

Do you have to have something or be with a particular person to be alive? If yes, what or whom.

Remember, life depends not upon a person or thing, but upon your awareness of Spirit. Memorize the following statement if you have not done so already: *Life is consciousness of God.*

The wisdom God is is enough.

The path of direct knowledge is within us, and it leads to the secret place of the Most High. Facts can be found in the world; Truth cannot, for it must be spiritually discerned or revealed by God. People can be storehouses of facts, and they are often willing to share this knowledge with others. The knowledge is then duplicated and stored in another "location," but lives do not change. This wisdom is *not* enough.

The wisdom God is is enough. This truth or light is within you now. Creativity, clear thinking, wise decisions, intuition, and reason for being come from this source. Other people cannot light your path. You have a light within you that illumines. It must be released. There is only one reason to seek the counsel of another person: to receive insights which help you let the light already within you shine.

May Rowland was the director of Silent Unity, a worldwide prayer ministry that continues to assist people from around the world. A worker was given added responsibilities, and decisions had to be made by this person. Time and time again, the individual would come to May and ask her what she should do. Finally, Ms. Rowland told the woman that she had the mind of the Christ, and she would know what to do. These simple words gave the worker the opportunity to let her light shine.

Times of puzzlement are opportunities for us to experience the wisdom God is. This wisdom is enough. Whenever we are confused, we can discover the all-sufficiency of divine Wisdom.

Today a potentially puzzling statement is given to you. Do not ask anyone for the answer to this puzzle. Even if it takes years, seek the answer only from the spirit of Truth within you. Then you will know that the wisdom God is is enough.

"Light and darkness are as one to God."

The peace God is is enough.

For most of us peace is directly related to what happens in our world. We envision what we think is best, and we try to make it happen. Through the years we have even taken the stance that if we have inner peace, we will have peace in the world. This is certainly true, but let us not seek inner peace just so the world will be free of war. Let us know peace because it is our natural state.

True peace, the peace God is, passes understanding. Even in the most difficult human challenge, the peace transcending logic is present. It is the quiet and stillness experienced by a person after a loved one has passed. In the outer world, there is nothing to be peaceful about, but the relative who remains is nevertheless at rest and calm.

Let us not look for peace to be established. Peace is here. We must make no demands that certain things happen.

In the past, what did you believe must happen before you could have peace?

Today, invite the peace that passes understanding into your life. You do this by letting things happen rather than making them happen or demanding that certain things occur. During this day, your peace will not depend upon anyone or anything. You are free of the world, free to experience the peace that passes understanding. Remember, there is no peace in the world. The peace is in you.

There was a woman who had a favorite word—*perfect*. She experienced much peace, for she sincerely believed that what happened in her life was

perfect. It is interesting that as the years went by more and more of what happened in her life was that which all of us would desire and enjoy. She had found peace in herself, and therefore she was able to say to the world— *perfect*.

What do you believe must happen before you can have peace?

The prodigal has returned!

We have been in a far country looking for contentment, love, wisdom, life, and peace; we have found it in God. Why must we travel around the earth only to discover that the treasure is in our own backyard? The answer is simple: because we have not looked within ourselves. The world holds promise, but not the meaning and purpose for which we yearn.

The prodigal has returned to its Creator. God is enough. Spirit is our everything. A consciousness of Spirit manifests itself as the fulfillment of every earthly urge.

In the weeks to come, you will probably experience the temptation to venture into the world again to find love, wisdom, peace, or plenty. During these times, please remember how welcome you are at home. A consciousness of Spirit is the house you are destined to live in forever.

When the temptation comes, return to this week and move through the exercises again. When you come to that day, slowly say these words out loud: *Only God can quench my thirst. Only Truth can set me free.*

Week Twenty-Six
Summary

Inner change calls for an inner journey. What we seek is at hand, for it is within us. As we begin the inner journey, the first thing we face is ourselves, and forgiveness of the painful past must occur. Next we cease saying no to God and begin to say yes. In fact, our quest becomes a relationship with Spirit. It is like finding a friend and realizing oneness has always existed. It is accurate to say, "I and the Father are one."

This oneness is aligned with divine will. In the quietness of the soul, the still small voice of God whispers, "Know Me." Soon we discover that God is enough.

Return to any day or combination of days that you have not understood or which you think need more work or review. Repeat the lesson(s) as *Week 26*'s work.

Resist the temptation to skip the review and continue with the next section, *"Know Thyself."* The continuation of the spiritual journey can wait for one more week.

In the spaces on the next page, write the lessons you chose to review:

Week 26
Days 176-182
continued

Day 176   *Week* _____

             Day _____

Day 177   *Week* _____

             Day _____

Day 178   *Week* _____

             Day _____

Day 179   *Week* _____

             Day _____

Day 180   *Week* _____

             Day _____

Day 181   *Week* _____

             Day _____

Day 182   *Week* _____

             Day _____

Section Three
Know Thyself

What Am I?

While on the inner journey, we come face to face with the sacred human. As we continue on our way, there comes a time when we have to respond to the ancient call, "Know thyself."

Perhaps Plutarch, the Greek moralist who asked us to know ourselves, discovered what he was and found himself to be something common to all humankind, yet grand and beautiful beyond words. No one can reveal the truth of being to another person; however, the gift given by the person who knows what and who he or she is is an invitation for everyone to make the same discovery.

The inner journey continues as you come to know yourself and learn your true identity. Your beginning is the insights of the past and the confusion they create. The Scripture declares that we are made in Spirit's image and likeness, but no one has seen this image. Perhaps who we are cannot be seen with the human eye, but can be known with the mind. It is as Paul said, "We have the mind of Christ" (1 Cor. 2:16). And if this is true, then we have the capacity to know ourselves and discover who we are.

May the next three months of activities and exercises allow you to discover who and what you are. Begin by giving twelve answers from the human viewpoint to the following statement:

I am

I am

Week 27
continued

I am

I am

I am

I am

I am

I am

I am

I am

I am

I am

I am made in God's image.

You are made in God's image. What God is, you must be. You are like the orphan searching to find its mother because knowing the mother will help the child know itself.

You are made in God's image, but you must be cautious of the law of reversibility. Through this false principle, we make God in our image and likeness. We look at our bodies and assume the Creator has arms and legs. We feel anger and believe the God that is love can lash out at its creation. What human qualities have we assigned to the Almighty?

1. _____

2. _____

3. _____

4. _____

5. _____

6. _____

7. _____

8. _____

9. _____

10. _____

11. _____

12. _____

Week 27
Day 183
continued

List some spiritual qualities of God (for example, love, strength, eternal, changeless):

1. _____

2. _____

3. _____

4. _____

5. _____

6. _____

7. _____

8. _____

9. _____

10. _____

11. _____

12. _____

These qualities are your true nature!

You can do the things that I do.

Today we accept the truth that our destiny is to do the things that Jesus did. A full acceptance of this truth requires that we come to understand who Jesus is.

There was once a young man who had reached the stage in his own spiritual development where an answer to the question "Who is Jesus?" had become crucial. In the process of his search for the answer, he uttered the words, "I wish Jesus would come to me and tell me who He is." Immediately, he began to feel a presence and knew an answer was coming.

A verse of Scripture filled his mind, "Truly, truly, I say to you, he who believes in me will also do the works that I do; and greater works than these will he do" (Jn. 14:12). Then an image filled his mind. Jesus was standing on a mountaintop of consciousness and in essence saying, "You will stand in the awareness in which I currently stand." Then Jesus looked ahead for Himself and then back at humankind. In this image, He declared the truth of the Scripture that there were greater things we would do.

The message was clear. To the young man Jesus was saying that all humankind will someday stand in consciousness where He is, but that there is more growth before Him and before us. These are the "greater works."

Some people think the greater works are technology. As great as they are, scientific discoveries and their application to daily life do not compare with the unfoldment of spiritual consciousness. The issue is a consciousness of God, not technology and labor-saving devices.

Jesus is the expression of what humankind is destined to be. Could it be that Jesus is the prototype for all humanity, our Way-Shower for the spiritual path?

Pause often throughout this day to hear the words, "You can do the things that Jesus did and greater works than these shall you do." If this idea

 *Week 27*
Day 184
continued

is unsettling to you, spend a few moments writing out your understanding
of why in the space that follows:

Most religiously oriented people have a favorite verse of Scripture that is
meaningful to them. Charles Fillmore, co-founder of Unity, found the
following verse transformative: "The mystery hidden for ages and generations . . . which is Christ in you, the hope of glory" (Col. 1:26-27). Most
scholars believe that at the writing of Colossians, approximately thirty years
had passed since Jesus' death and resurrection. Because of the reference to
a mystery hidden for "ages and generations," it is unlikely that the apostle
Paul was thinking just about the earthly Jesus.

In truth, when Paul used the word *Christ* he was referring to the image of
God in Jesus, or our divine potential. In certain spiritual ways of life, a
distinction is made between Jesus and the Christ. It is said that Jesus walked
on the water, but the Christ made the feat possible. Christ is our spiritual
nature, and it rests in us in "silent repose."

The Christ came alive in Paul, and he wrote, "It is no longer I who live,
but Christ who lives in me" (Gal. 2:20). Each of us is destined to be born
again or to awaken spiritually. The image is our hope of glory, love, peace,
and joy. The Christ is who we really are. This does not diminish Jesus. It is
His message, for He said that we would do the things that He did and even
greater things.

There are numerous examples of individuals expressing their divinity or
having the Christ come alive in them. Please list below four people that you
believe have allowed their Christ selves to live in them:

1. _____
2. _____
3. _____
4. _____

I am a child of God.

_____

If we want to know our identity, it is best to ask our Creator directly, "What am I? Who am I?" Many people have asked these questions. The answers have been varied. Jesus heard the powerful words, "This is my beloved Son, with whom I am well pleased" (Mt. 3:17). Charles Fillmore wrote: "Spiritually you are My idea of Myself as I see Myself in the ideal." Others have heard the simple truth, "You are My beloved"; still others, "You are My child." It is helpful to know what other people have experienced when they attempted to discover their identity, but there is no substitute for your own experience.

Utilize some of the prayer and meditation techniques from previous days and gently ask, "What am I? Who am I?" and then listen. Do this for the remainder of this thirteen-week segment of *A Daily Guide to Spiritual Living*. Record your insights below:

. . . and if a child then an heir.

We are children of God, offspring of the Almighty (see Galations 4:7). To what are we heirs? On earth, parents work hard to achieve much and usually will their earthly possessions to their children. One day the parents die and their earthly belongings become the property of the children. That which has created us will never die, so what is our inheritance?

Spiritual illumination reveals that Spirit has only one "thing" to give to its creation, and it is the gift of a consciousness of itself. Obviously, this "Parent" does not die in order for us to receive, but instead we die to our earthly way, so we might come alive and receive what is perpetually offered to us. Inheritances are offered, but they must be received.

If Spirit is offering a consciousness of itself to you, what must you do to receive your inheritance?

How will you know that you have received your inheritance?

I have the mind of Christ.

Paul knew who he was, and he knew our nature as well, for he wrote, "But we have the mind of Christ" (1 Cor. 2:16). A casual look at the world leaves us with the deep impression that this is an intelligent universe. There is wisdom in the growth of living things, the migration of the birds and whales, and the thoughts that move within our minds. And wherever there is intelligence, there is a mind. In the instance of Paul's quote, the mind is divine. It is a supermind pervading the universe, and it is filled with ideas. This same mind, Paul concluded, has been given to us. Through this mind, we may know the secret of life and the mysteries of the universe.

List twelve examples which tell you that this is an intelligent universe:

1. _____
2. _____
3. _____
4. _____
5. _____
6. _____
7. _____
8. _____
9. _____
10. _____
11. _____
12. _____

In the space below, give an example that illustrates that you have the mind of the Christ. For example, perhaps you knew something was going to happen before it happened, or some solution to a problem suddenly popped into your mind without you giving it any thought.

The one becomes the many.

Individuality is one of the most powerful and far-reaching principles at work in our lives and in the universe, but it is also part of our mundane daily existence. For instance, a mother is preparing the family's favorite dessert. A recipe lists the ingredients needed and how they are to be blended together and cooked in order to provide the family with a German chocolate cake. The recipe is helpful because it is a blueprint for the cake, but no one eats a recipe. *It must be individualized.* In this way, there is a movement from the abstract, unseen world to the concrete, observable world. A baseball game, whether T-ball played by youngsters or baseball played by all-stars, is an individualization of the rules of the game. It is only on the playing field that the umpire can shout, "Play ball!"

God is the Great Principle of the universe, but principle does not "live" until it is individualized. This individualization is not the man, woman, or child that can be seen with the human eye, but the spiritual being realized by the Christ mind.

Survival experts say the will to live is the most important factor when a person is alone in the wilderness. This will to live is more than the desire to draw another breath. It is the force of God seeking to be individualized through us.

Give an example of individuality:

Is it so strange to consider that Spirit desires to express or individualize itself?

Give two names that describe God individualized:

1. _____

2. _____

Possible answers:
1. Christ
2. Image of God

Week Twenty-Eight

Revelation

Someone once asked how we can know many of the spiritual truths and principles that govern our lives and still not live life according to our full potential. The answer is that we intellectually know the truth, but that truth is not lived until there is revelation. When the periphery of the mind is filled with truth, our vocabulary changes, but we still do not "walk the talk." When the truth is revealed to us, we are stirred, and our lives change forever.

When we know something intellectually, we reach down with cupped hands and drink from the river of truth. When there is revelation, the river surfaces from within us as living truth. When we know truth intellectually, we sometimes speak the truth we "know" to convince ourselves and others that what we say is true. When there is revelation, we do not speak; we listen. In learning truth, we often say or think the truth again and again in order to memorize it. When there is revelation, the truth is spoken once by the indwelling Christ, and we never forget.

Acknowledge a spiritual truth or principle which you know intellectually, but are not yet able to express:

Spiritual things must be spiritually discerned.

Moses spent years in solitude, and his aloneness allowed him to see the burning bush. Horeb (which means solitude), the mountain of God, is where the bush was located. Most likely, Moses had tended his flock upon this mountain before, and perhaps he had even seen the bush many times, but it was not on fire on other days. Or was it? Many believe that every living thing is ablaze with the presence of God, but that we do not have the vision to see. Through solitude, the radiant truth about the bush was revealed to Moses.

It is one thing to see the beauty of a hardwood forest on an autumn day, but imagine when we can see as Moses did. This sight comes through revelation.

Take time today to sit and observe a bush, tree, or plant. Do not try to see the brilliance of God's presence, and do not judge by appearances. There is more to perceive than the eyes can see. Observe every detail of the living thing. Note the smallest part of it, and then see it in its entirety. Remember, the ability to see the burning bush rests in revelation, not your efforts.

After this exercise, affirm and then memorize the following statement: *Through grace and revelation, I live in a new world.*

The living truth comes from within me.

Some people think knowing the truth means that we must say the truth again and again until it is absorbed by our subconscious mind. Then it will impact our lives, and we will live as we are destined to live. Why then does the Bible say, "I will put my law within them, and I will write it upon their hearts" (Jer. 31:33)?

There is no revelation when we insist upon affirming truth with the purpose of impressing our subconscious mind. Revelation, and thus transformation, comes when the truth or law written on our hearts is allowed to rise from within us.

A young boy at his grandfather's well pumped and pumped, yet not a single drop of water filled his bucket. Then his wise grandfather came, poured a little water down the well, and instructed him to pump again. He said it was necessary to prime the pump when it had not been used for a while.

Truth is within us, and therefore need not be added to us. However, it is helpful to speak the truth in the same way that it is helpful to prime a pump.

Select one of the following statements, or make up one of your own, and prime the pump today. Keep this truth moving within the mind, but also remember to pause and allow the truth to come from within you.

I am God's beloved child.

I am rich. I have no needs.

I am divine life being lived.

I find no peace in the world.

Indicate which statement you used and today's date:

I am willing to think in a new way.

We are not a storehouse for Truth, but an opening through which Truth may be expressed in the universe. Some expressions of Truth are amazingly different from our previous opinions. Truth can be shocking. Often as Truth is revealed to us, we will say, "I did not know. I had no idea."

A young minister once served a ministry which met on Sunday mornings near a beautiful rose garden. Before the service, he would stroll through the garden and open himself to the absurd thoughts of Spirit. Often he was stirred by what he "heard."

One day he asked why a flower as beautiful as a rose had to have thorns. It did not make sense, he thought. "Because beauty is not to be touched or tampered with," he was told. "It is to be observed and allowed to lift our souls."

On another occasion the young minister was sitting and watching great oak trees sway with the wind. He thought the wind was moving the high branches of the trees. "Have you considered," he was asked, "that maybe these great trees move and create the wind?" Absurd, yes; but unless one is willing to consider such thoughts, revelation cannot be part of us, for truth is stranger than fiction. Much Truth that can be revealed to us will seem absurd at first, but eventually it will be as cherished and comfortable as a good friend.

In the instance of the trees moving and creating the wind, the young minister paused and considered the prompting of the inner voice. Slowly a smile crossed his face, and he said, "Of course." This did not mean that he had come to believe trees move and create the wind, but that he now realized how important it is to think in a new way.

This day is declared to be an Absurd Day in which your mind is willing to entertain the revelation of Truth. Undoubtedly during today you will catch a glimpse of Spirit's sense of humor. Enjoy, and record any absurd thoughts in the space below.

I enjoy the mystery,
but invite the revelation.

Revelation does not come through struggle. It comes when we are content. For years a young Truth student felt that a greater good was awaiting him. He longed to know the nature of this mission and what was before him. Numerous times he asked, "What lies ahead? What am I to do?" The question "what" created incredible amounts of tension and inner turmoil. While his moments were filled with beauty, he was not enjoying them because he wanted to know the future and the God mission that was just around the bend.

After years of inner struggle, he received the help he was seeking. "Be content with the mystery," his guidance revealed. It took a while, but eventually he ceased asking "what." He became content with the mystery. Strange, but as soon as he was content with the mystery, the revelation began, and the God mission was revealed.

Outline the most mysterious part of your life. Perhaps you are concerned about your job, your retirement, your health, or a relationship. Describe below the "unknown quantity" of your life:

Now, cease asking or thinking about what is going to happen. Instead, begin to work prayerfully with the idea: *I am content with the mystery.* Today's activity could take days, if not weeks, before you begin to enjoy the mystery. On that day, the invitation to revelation has been given!

No one is the source of my wisdom.

We come complete with instructions, for we have the mind of the Christ. Insights assisting us in daily living can come from within us, but this cannot happen until we cut our ties with the "wisdom of the world." No one can be the source of our wisdom and our help for daily living. The wisdom is within us and must be relied upon. As long as we turn to others to tell us what to do, we will not perceive the indwelling light.

The truly great thinkers of our world have not tried to live by the light of others, but have come to believe that they could *know*.

Who have you looked to in the past as a source of wisdom and guidance?

_____

Perhaps this person was helpful, but now is the time to be weaned from the wisdom of the "wise ones." The individuals we turn to should now assist us in finding wisdom within ourselves.

Please identify who you can turn to, not to tell you what to do but to assist you in finding the wellspring of light within you:

_____

From this day forth, your approach to life is to let the Christ mind guide you. Seek other people only to help you experience union with the light.

Write a covenant that declares your intention to live this way:

_____

Signature and date

"Unanswerable" questions invite revelation.

Confusion can be the mother of wisdom, new insights, and revelation. When a question is asked and we have no immediate answer, but believe there is an answer, we invite revelation into our lives. We have come to the limit of our comprehension, and therefore stand on the edge of the kingdom of God from which all revelation comes.

Today three questions are asked. It is hoped that at least one of them will bring you to the edge of your intellectual knowledge, and therefore the question will become an invitation to revelation.

Question one: Why are sickness and health as one to God?

Question two: What is the sound of one hand clapping?

Question three: Please read Luke 14:26. What is the meaning of this verse? Jesus' message is one of love. How can He say we must hate our own mothers and fathers?

Your answer to your chosen question:

Revelation is Spirit's work.

It appears that revelation is our work, but that is not true. Revelation is Spirit's work. There is nothing we can do to force the wisdom to come from within.

Our allies are "waiting" and "letting." God let there be light, and so must we. We let go having to know, and we wait. Then suddenly, the answer comes; we know. The spiritual dawn does not creep upon us. The mind is not filled with gray and then the colors of the day. There is night, and then there is day. Suddenly, without warning, there is light.

Half of each day of your life is spent in letting, though you may not realize it. The exhalation of your breath is letting. A supreme example of this is the human sigh, the sign that a human being has released his grip on life, if only for a moment. As you spend your time in daily prayer and meditation, give special attention to the exhalation of your breath. Let go and sigh . . . and then wait, for as you know, waiting is the heart of our way of life.

Remember, Spirit "hears" every human sigh and knows that when a human being lets go, God's work can be done!

A deeply distraught young man was driving down the highway and crying. The tears and emotion began to cloud his vision, so he pulled to the side of the road, placed his head on the wheel, and sobbed. In the midst of the emotions, he heard a voice say, "Stop struggling." His turmoil turned to peace.

When we let go and the revelation comes, the insight we receive transcends the messenger. This is as it should be, for the king's messenger is welcomed not because of himself, but because he carries the decree of the king. The words "stop struggling" were the messenger, but the decree was peace. This is the way it is when there is revelation. We are stirred, and our

lives are changed by seemingly simple means. But we must not be deceived. Instead, let this be a sign that tells us our experience is genuine.

There is also another characteristic of revelation—our transformation. The people were amazed that Jesus spoke as one having authority. Authority comes from revelation. Jesus spoke not of what He had learned from man, but of what He had learned through revelation.

Do not try to speak with authority. You will only raise your voice. Instead, let revelation lift you so you are more aware of what it is to be made in God's image and likeness. Children work mathematical problems but cannot apply the principles to the economic realities of life. Then suddenly they understand, and they possess another practical tool for daily living. There is nothing more practical than the experience of who and what you are.

List four people you have heard speak with authority:

1. _____

2. _____

3. _____

4. _____

What response do these people quicken in you?

Week Twenty-Nine

Herod

We are spiritual beings, and revelation illumines us to our true identity and the truth about the world. Revelation awakens us, and we become spiritually alive. It is like a birth. But there is a part of us which we have created that resists the birth. It is Herod, the one who tried to destroy Jesus. The Herod we shall face is not the literal Roman puppet who ruled Palestine two thousand years ago, but our human will which opposes the things of Spirit.

Spirit has given birth to its creation, the image of God. This indwelling Christ is our true identity. It is who we really are. But there is also Herod— our creation. Herod is who we think we are. It resists the spiritual birth and rebels when it learns that another king is in the land. It tries everything it can to remain in control. However, once we reach this point in our spiritual unfoldment Herod will die, just as he did in the Christmas story. He does not need to be resisted, but it is helpful to know some of his ways. When we know and understand our human tendencies, it becomes more difficult to be deceived by our human will.

Who's on the phone?

Two friends once discussed the difficulty of determining whether the thoughts moving within their minds were "uttered" by Herod or the Christ. The phrase they used was, "Who's on the phone?"

Who's on the phone? Is it our God self or our lesser self? Actually, in the early stages of our spiritual growth the question is not difficult to answer. Our lesser self is not deceptive. The thoughts moving through the mind are negative and limiting. For instance, we consider going back to school for more education, so we can get a better, more creative job. Who's on the phone when these words fill our mind? "You never were very good in school. And besides, why start over again?" Or perhaps we might hear, "You will never get out of the rut you're in. You don't deserve a better job."

Our God self does not speak in this fashion. Only our lesser self would have such a dim view of us and the world. However, as we progress in our spiritual growth, Herod will become more subtle and deceptive. We will consider this idea later in the week.

In the meantime, what is the prominent negative thought or statement that Herod has said about you?

What feeling does this statement generate in you? Describe this feeling in one word: _____

The following beatitude is a great help in knowing ourselves. "Blessed are you when men revile you and persecute you . . . on my account" (Mt. 5:11). These words uplifted the early Christians as they endured persecution and prejudice, but in today's world we are usually not persecuted for our Christian beliefs. Nevertheless, there is inner unrest that is a natural part of the spiritual journey.

Whenever we attempt to break a bad habit or rise above some limitation, there is negative momentum to overcome. Pushing a stalled car illustrates this principle. At first, we push and push, for great effort is required to get the car moving. Scientists speak of this as the law of inertia: A body at rest tends to stay at rest; a body in motion tends to remain in motion. When our life has been stalled and we attempt to get moving, there is a persecution of or resistance to this change. Herod is content with limitation. We begin to look for a new job and the inner persecution begins. "You'll never get a job. You've tried this before. You'd better stay where you are. At least you have a job."

Jesus stressed the fact that we are blessed when we experience this unrest. It is a good sign, for it signals our serious attempt to move forward in life. Therefore, we must persist until we get moving. Remember, a body in motion tends to remain in motion. Once we start to grow, the tendency is that the growth will continue.

Say to yourself: *I am blessed when I feel the inner unrest, for it means that I am beginning to move ahead. Herod is threatened, for a new me is being born.*

Describe a time in your life when you felt this "persecution":

281

Week 29
Day 198
continued

The truth will set me free.

There is a dialogue that goes on within the mind. Herod speaks his lies, and we listen. Sometimes we even believe without question the falsehoods which are presented to us. Notice that whenever Herod is on the phone, we feel limited and are at times overwhelmed by negative feelings. On these occasions, it is good to remember that the truth will set us free.

Enter into the dialogue and speak the highest and most ideal truth you know. For instance, if you are about to begin a new task and your lesser self tells you you will fail, you can reply, "I am engineered for success. With God nothing is impossible for me." The lesser self might reply, "If you're engineered for success, why has there been so much failure?" You might answer, "The past does not change the truth that I am engineered for success. Each day can be a new beginning, and this is my new beginning day."

Pay attention to the inner dialogue today. When it becomes obvious that Herod is on the phone, speak the truth, for it will set you free.

I refuse to turn stones to bread.

Before Jesus began His ministry, He went to the wilderness and faced three temptations. These same temptations are encountered by every human being and must be overcome if we are to live spiritual lives.

The devil Jesus encountered has many names—ego, lesser self, Herod, Satan, and others. Essentially, this adversary, as it is called in Job, is our human self that is opposed to the ways of Spirit. But we are spiritual beings, so the natural inclination of our souls is not to be ruled by our earthly appetites and urges. We are destined for greater things. However, we must first face ourselves and let the truth set us free.

Jesus' first temptation was to turn stones to bread (Mt. 4:3). There are two main parts to this encounter. First, there is hunger, or human appetite. We are not to be ruled by our senses and earthly urges whether they are hunger, thirst, lust, or whatever. Second, we are not to use our talents for selfish purposes. Jesus was capable of turning stones to bread, but He refused to use power for Himself. As a matter of fact, throughout Jesus' ministry, He never used power selfishly; it was always for humanity.

During this week's activities, you are becoming acquainted with your lower self and its ways. For today, acknowledge the appetites that tend to rule you.

In addition, make a list of your talents. How can these talents be used to benefit others?

I refuse to present God with choices.

Please read the account of Jesus' second temptation in Matthew 4:5-7. This temptation, like the previous one, has several ingredients. A historical perspective is helpful in understanding what Jesus faced while He was in the wilderness and what we, too, must face. The Jews of Jesus' day believed that if someone leaped from the highest point of the Temple and was not harmed, he was the Messiah. Jesus was the Messiah, but His vision of the Christ was different from most of the people's. They were looking for a warrior king. Jesus came to lead the people not to war, but to peace; not to establish a kingdom on earth, but to tell people the good news that the kingdom of heaven was within them.

This temptation, for us, is to ignore our inner knowing and to conform to mass human opinion. This happens to us whenever we enter into a discussion that turns negative, and we begin to gossip or speak negatively like others in the group. We have forsaken what we know is true and embraced the prevalent human opinion. A son or daughter can do a similar thing by, for example, becoming a doctor when they really want to become a journalist.

Another dimension of this temptation is that Jesus was told to leap off the Temple and God would save Him. Most people jumping from a great height would be severely injured. We must not present God with choices or expect the physical and spiritual laws to be put aside for us. Spirit is the same today and every day. The universe and our lives are ruled by divine law. We must not expect these principles to be put on hold because of us. Knowing the consistency of the universal laws is a great assistance to us as we seek to live spiritual lives.

Basically, we must live with the consequences of our consciousness. God will not rescue us from ourselves. If we experience unhappiness and limitation, we must come up higher. There is no way "out" aside from a higher

state of awareness. Let us not present God with choices. Let us respond to the choice that is perpetually before us—to come up higher.

Are you aware of a time in your life when you presented God with a choice? If yes, please describe the situation.

Are you aware of a time in your life when you conformed to the general human opinion instead of following your guidance? If yes, please describe the situation.

Notice that there is no condemnation because we have succumbed to this temptation. Remember, this is a week in which we are becoming acquainted with the ways of our lesser selves. This knowledge will prove helpful in the future.

I refuse to believe there are two powers in my life.

In Jesus' third temptation, the devil (the lesser self) offered Him the kingdoms and powers of the earth (Mt. 4:8-9). All Jesus had to do was fall down and worship, or give power to, His lesser self. The Man of Nazareth refused and re-established the truth of one power in His life.

The temptation to believe in more than one power is humankind's most persistent challenge. We not only succumb to the temptation, but we have come to believe in two powers. We have nothing to gain by this belief—certainly not the kingdoms of the earth. For Jesus, the truth was clear. "The earth is the Lord's and the fulness thereof, the world and those who dwell therein" (Ps. 24:1).

The words associated with this temptation as recorded in the Scripture are significant. Everything was offered to Jesus if He would *fall down* and worship the devil. It would have been a downfall of astronomical proportions had Jesus opted to rule the world instead of His own being. Let us refuse to give power to anything on earth or within us aside from the presence and power of God.

What do you worship other than God? (What do you believe has power over you?)

List those people or things that ask you to *fall down* and worship them:

Whenever the temptation comes, declare: *I refuse to believe there are two powers in my life.*

I resist not.

At this point in our growth it is important that we resist not. Notice in the Christmas story that Jesus, Mary, and Joseph did not resist Herod. They led no armed rebellion against the king. Instead the family followed the guidance of Spirit, and Herod did not harm the child.

Spiritually, the story is sound, for the Christ child is our true identity. We do not fully realize it yet, but the Christ *cannot* be harmed. Nothing of the earth has power and dominion over Spirit.

We are just beginning to awaken to who and what we really are. However, by resisting our lesser self we delay the time when our God self will assert itself and take its proper place in our lives. This we must not do.

We are being born spiritually, and newborns do not battle. They are too young and delicate. Therefore, let us not resist. Nonresistance has been an unspoken theme for this week. We are becoming more acquainted with Herod, our lesser self, which opposes the discovery of our spiritual identity. The indwelling Christ will assume its rightful "throne" more quickly if we do not resist the false person we have created. Therefore, this week we do not resist, but instead we become knowledgeable about Herod and his ways. In the future when he asserts himself, the result will be that we will be less prone to succumb to his temptations.

What are some of the ways you have been resisting Herod? (Here are several examples: A person has a sense of inadequacy, so he boasts of his accomplishments and is unwilling to admit his mistakes. Or perhaps an individual becomes defensive when shortcomings are pointed out.)

Week 29
Day 203
continued

Week Thirty

The Battle Is God's

Shortly after we embark upon any spiritual journey, there may be contention. Our lesser self, Herod, resists our spiritual birth, so a rebellion takes place. Please understand that the Christ, the truth of our being, does not contend. In fact, the upset and resistance we feel is the lesser self's fear and concern for the loss of its rule. During these times, it is good to know that the battle is not ours. It is God's.

This concept is found in the story of the Hebrews as they were fleeing Egypt and preparing to cross the Red Sea. Pharaoh's army was about to close in on the Hebrews, and they were fearful. In this situation, the comforting words came, "The Lord will fight for you, and you have only to be still" (Ex. 14:14). In a similar story of a siege on Jerusalem, God spoke through King Jehoshaphat and said, "The battle is not yours but God's" (2 Chron. 20:15). This is a figurative statement, for God does not war with what we have created—our ego or false identity.

Are you willing to call a truce in your battle with your lesser self? Are you willing to cease your attempt to solve the problem or make things better? Please realize that you may cease your actions, but most likely the ego will continue its attempts to have its way. Perhaps you remember the week entitled Stand Still. The truth is, who you really are does not contend with Herod, so you must cease your attempt to overcome your ego. There is another way.

I do not fight.

When Jesus was born, Herod thought he would lose his kingdom, and he sought to destroy the child. Fear generated this action. Remember that Jesus and His family did not try to defeat or destroy Herod. In fact, they were guided to go to Egypt and to wait until Herod died.

Who we are does not fight with the ego or lesser self. It waits, for the lesser self is its own enemy. It is self-destructive. For instance, an alcoholic's behavior is self-destructive. In most instances, even while the person is drinking, there is a desire for a new way of life. Certainly, this is the case on the morning after a night of drinking. This desire to start over is the beginning of the end for the lesser self.

Rather than attack the negative behavior and thinking that plagues us, let us open ourselves to know we are made in God's image. Let us discover we are spiritual beings. This new consciousness will then manifest itself by saying and doing specific things. Some of the limiting behavior of the past will cease because our beliefs have changed. Eventually, Herod will perish, and the Christ, our true identity, will begin its rule of love, peace, and joy.

List the limiting behaviors you want to change about yourself:

1. _____
2. _____
3. _____
4. _____
5. _____

From this day forth, do not try to change these things. You have admitted these limitations; now do a new thing. Your new purpose is to know yourself to be a spiritual being. As this discovery becomes more real for you, you will find that Herod's rule is ending.

For thousands of years, we have believed in two powers. The struggle between light and darkness dominates our world. It can be seen in our movies, read in our books, viewed on our television screens nightly. The promise has been given that eventually, in one great battle, good will have its way and evil will be no more. Humankind has believed this story since it first looked for a better way of life.

Now a new approach is introduced. People who live extraordinary lives do not participate in the war of light and darkness. When Jesus was before Pilate He refused to speak to the Roman procurator. Pilate responded by telling the rabbi of Nazareth that he had the power to kill Him. Jesus replied, "You would have no power over me unless it had been given you from above" (Jn. 19:11).

Jesus lived in a world where God, the power "from above," was the only power. We can speculate that Jesus did not talk to Pilate at first because, in the face of seeming power, Jesus was communing with His Father. He was rooted in the realization of one Presence and one Power. When God is the only power, there is no need to be threatened or to contend with people and things. Our purpose is contact with Spirit. We refuse to fight, not because we are cowards, but because God is the only power in our lives. Most would agree that this is a new approach to living.

It challenges us greatly because it is counter to our previous way of thinking. However, the truth is that it challenges our belief in a world of two powers.

As you begin to open yourself to this exciting possibility, let your word be the beginning. Three times during the course of this day, pause and ponder the following statement for at least ten minutes: *Where there is only God, there is no battle.* Also, be sure to practice monastic moments by declaring: *Where there is only God, there is no battle.*

There is no peace on earth.

There is no peace on earth. At this moment in history, most of human-kind would agree with this statement, but these six words are more far-reaching than they appear. It can be added that there will never be peace on earth. This is not the viewpoint of a doomsayer, but of one who has rede-fined the word *earth*. In this instance, earth is not the planet, but human consciousness.

There can be no peace in human consciousness, for peace is not its way. Peace exists in God, in spiritual consciousness; therefore, we must come up higher and experience the kingdom. Here and only here will we find true peace. Of course, there are other kinds of peace—the temporary peace created by treaties or the family truce that exists until the next fit of anger—but this is not the kind of peace Jesus spoke of when He said, "My peace I give to you; not as the world gives [a peace that comes and goes] do I give to you" (Jn. 14:27).

Consider the statement: *There is no peace on earth*, and let it give you the gift of knowing that peace rests not in conditions, but in knowing God. When this occurs, you will cease trying to make things happen which seem to bring peace of mind. This is important, for trying to make peace happen fills life with contention. Obviously, once there is inner peace, peace on earth is natural. People who are in spiritual consciousness *must* live on a planet of peace.

Coming up higher has a strange beginning—acceptance. It is almost unthinkable to believe that acceptance of a situation is the first step to a new way of life. However, acceptance is not defeatism, for not only are situations accepted, but so also is the truth that God is the power in our lives. The story of Meshach, Shadrach, and Abednego is a good example of how acceptance allows us to come up higher.

In the story recorded in the third chapter of Daniel, these three men were thrown into a fiery furnace because they refused to bow down to the king. Before they entered the furnace, the three men talked with the king, and he tried to intimidate them by making the fire seven times hotter than usual. It was so hot that those tending the fire died. To the king, who had asked how the men would be delivered from the furnace, the three men said, "O Nebuchadnezzar, we have no need to answer you in this matter. If it be so, our God whom we serve is able to deliver us from the burning fiery furnace; and he will deliver us out of your hand, O king. But if not, be it known to you, O king, that we will not serve your gods or worship the golden image which you have set up" (Dan. 3:16-18). Meshach, Shadrach, and Abednego accepted their fate, but they also accepted the truth that God was the only power in their lives.

The men were thrown into the furnace and were unharmed. The king and those who were with him then saw a fourth man walking in the flames. There are several interpretations of this fourth man, but essentially he was evidence of the Presence. The three men were released from the fire, and their clothes did not even smell of smoke.

What do you think allowed the men to accept their fate? On a purely human level, stepping into a fiery furnace results in death, but what if Meshach, Shadrach, and Abednego were able to accept their earthly fate because they viewed themselves from another level. What is this insight which allows them or you to say to a seeming power, "I am in God's hands"?

Please write your answer below:

What are you likely to encounter within the next week which you would best face through acceptance and the realization that you are a spiritual being?

The pattern is unfolding. First, we are nonresistant. Then we are accepting. Humanly, we know there are numerous problems and situations which can overcome us, but we are more than human. Being human is a condition, a part of the divine plan that enables us to discover who we are.

Remember from the story of the fiery furnace that the men accepted their human situation, but put their faith in God. Their focus was not upon the problem or in finding a solution. Attention was given to Spirit (to give attention to God is to come up higher), and the fourth man appeared.

Today is a day of acceptance, but first we must put aside resistance or the human inclination to try to find a solution to the problem. If some difficulty challenges you today, apply these three steps to your life:

1. Nonresistance: There is to be no attempt to change the condition or find a solution.

2. Acceptance: Let go as you accept your human situation. The following words might express this challenging step of the spiritual life. *If I lose my job, I lose my job. If my marriage ends, it ends.* These words may seem defeatist, but you will find them freeing, for they will help release from within you "the fourth man"—your true identity who never dies and cannot be defeated.

3. Faith in God: Give your attention to God in prayer and meditation rather than worrying about the problem.

Week 30
Day 209

My "protection" lies in knowing
who I am.

Human beings believe in protection. Weapons keep us safe, or so we believe. Doors are locked, and trained dogs guard us. Some people have bodyguards. Elaborate alarm systems are created. But in every instance there have been times when the system broke down, people were harmed, and their belongings were stolen or destroyed.

Actually, our protection lies in knowing who we are. As spiritual beings, we need no protection. What can harm the image of God? Our bodies can be harmed and in extreme situations the soul can flee the body, but the image of God remains untouched. In truth, nothing and no one on earth can harm a spiritual being.

Protection is a human need. Spirit needs no protection. *We* need no protection. Please remember that this last sentence is an expression of God's view of things.

List four things that can harm a human being:

1. _____

2. _____

3. _____

4. _____

Name one thing that can harm you when you are aware of who you are:

_____

I am a spiritual being.
Nothing can harm me.

There is no need to defend or protect ourselves. Our one need is to awaken to who we are. "Know thyself" is the call of the wise philosopher. When we fail to remember our spiritual identity, we are in harm's way.

There is a wonderful story about a man and a woman who lived in London during World War II. As the city was being bombed by the German Luftwaffe, this brave couple worked as fire watchers stationed on cathedral roofs and other high places. While some fled to underground shelters, this man and woman did their work for the common good of all. The amazing thing was that the couple were never harmed. There was destruction all around them, but their home was untouched. These God-centered people did not believe they were protected and others harmed. They lived in a consciousness of God's presence, and in God there was no destruction or chaos.

Please allow the following denials and affirmations to lift you up during your evening prayer and meditation time. And then wait. These ideas are shared with the hope that they will help you allow Spirit to reveal who you really are:

I breathe no air.
I drink no water.
I eat no food.
I am Spirit.
Wind and rain,
stone and harsh words
have never touched me.
I am not hot or cold.
I am not hurt or rejected.
I am Spirit.

Week Thirty-One
The Eternal Now

Ancient wisdom says that our contact with power is in the moment. To dwell upon the past, even the glorious past, is to be drained of power. To look to the future, even a better tomorrow, only inhibits our ability to experience the greater good that is present now. The vision that brings hope does not peer into the future. It sees the fullness of the moment. The vision of the future believes us empty now, but promises a time when our cup will be full. The vision of the moment tells us our cup is overflowing.

Perhaps you have felt a greater good was ahead for you. Even if the present moment was outstanding, you may not have fully experienced it because you wondered about the future. What lies ahead for me? you may have thought. The question *What next?* poisoned your present moment. Perhaps there was much to enjoy at the time, but you did not fully enjoy it because you were trying to see around the bend in the road, wondering what was going to happen. Let us never ask the question *What next?* when it comes to our spiritual lives, our professional lives, or our relationships. Strike from your vocabulary the question *What next?* These words poison the moment and also your future.

Now is the only moment I have.

There is a gift offered equally to everyone. What we do with the gift determines the course of our lives. It is more valuable than the most precious gem. It is irreplaceable, for once it is gone it is gone. Each day every individual is given 86,400 units of this "thing." We call these units seconds, this "thing" time. What we do with each fleeting moment determines the emotions we feel and the things that happen to us.

Now is the only moment we have. There is no discrimination with this offering, for every man, woman, and child receives the same quantity of the gift. It is for us to determine the quality of each moment.

Today's activity is a simple one, but detailed. Approximate how many seconds you spend on each of the following things:

1. Sleeping   _____ seconds

2. Eating   _____ seconds

3. Reading   _____ seconds

4. Prayer/Meditation   _____ seconds

5. Meaningful conversation   _____ seconds

6. Working   _____ seconds

In the moment, there is peace.

Once there was a monk who was being chased by two tigers. The man came to the edge of a cliff and slowly lowered himself down over the abyss by means of a vine that was hanging over the edge. After climbing down for a short time, the monk looked up to see one tiger peering over the edge. The man then looked down to see the second tiger waiting for him at the base of the cliff. Looking up again, the monk saw a mouse gnawing at the vine. It would not be long before the vine would be severed, and the monk would fall to his death. Then the monk looked at the wall of the cliff and noticed wild strawberries growing. He plucked one and ate it.

The ability to live in the moment is the greatest gift we receive when we fully accept the preciousness of each second. When we live in the eternal now, there is power and peace.

To be in the moment, no matter what it holds, is to use the gift of the moment wisely. Today you are asked to get a sense of how often you are conscious of the moment. There are many tasks that we do automatically. We are thinking about other things while we do them. Today you are asked to do three activities which you normally do, but they are to be performed consciously.

The three things are:

1. Wash your hands.
2. Get dressed.
3. Eat a meal.

How are these tasks different when you are conscious of doing them?

My five senses offer me the eternal now.

Being in the moment is not easy. Life seems so pressing that we do one thing while thinking of another. Often we are in the past or the future and because of this, the fullness of God's peace and power are unavailable to us. Also, our five senses provide us with continuous input, and we believe that these messages are a distraction from our spiritual journey. It is true that there are times when the senses can draw our attention away from the things of Spirit, but they also offer us the eternal now.

Perhaps you have noticed that the messages of the five senses are always received in the moment. Sounds, for instance, are never heard in the past or in the future. Sound is a now thing. The same is true of sight, smell, touch, and taste. As distracting as the senses seem to be, they are also the gateway to the moment.

Pause for five minutes during the day and listen. Be in the moment with the sounds you hear, and record them below:

During a meal, eat your favorite fruit and really taste it.

Finally, near dusk, sit and watch for five minutes. What do you see?

Because I live in the eternal now,

I am patient.

Patience is a virtue, and it is achieved when the moment is considered important and viewed as filled with wonders and possibilities. Impatience comes when we try to live even one second beyond the current time.

Waiting in line seems to cause impatience. This is not true. Lines are lines. They are neither good nor bad. However, long lines reveal to us the hurried lives we live. More importantly, they show us that we do not live in the moment, but are attempting to live in the future. No one has ever achieved this feat.

Hopefully, this day will contain at least one fairly long line. What do you usually do when you are in a line?

If you are blessed with a line to stand in today, please accept the opportunity to be in the moment. Use this time to commune with your God. Don't think about your next stop. Think about God.

May you find the eternal now and patience in the first long line you encounter!

 *Week 31*
Day 215

Through prayer and meditation,
I accept the gift of the eternal now.

Prayer, an experience of God's presence, knows no past or future. Only in the moment do we discover the Almighty, and then we are in a timeless state where there is only God.

However, in times of stillness this consciousness is not the first to dawn in us. During these times, our minds are often dominated by thoughts and images of the past or feelings of concern for tomorrow. But at least the thoughts, images, and feelings are experienced in the moment. We may not like their message or what they evoke in us, but they are our first encounter with the now. Because we are conscious of being in the moment, we are near the power God is—the power to heal.

Through prayer and meditation, we accept the gift of the eternal now. There will be oneness with Spirit, but first there is the past and the future. The way of healing is to return again and again to a moment filled with God.

During your time of prayer and meditation today, give conscious attention to your thoughts. Are they of the past or future? Do not resist the thoughts. Simply observe and identify them. Then return to Spirit with this or a similar statement: *I cannot find God in the past or future . . . only in the now.* Then rest and watch the movement of your thoughts again. Whenever there is mind drift, return to the statement.

The result of this practice is that we spend more time in the now. We are naturally patient, first with ourselves and then with others. This is a prelude to practicing the presence of God.

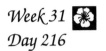
There are many things that we do during the course of a day. Sometimes we wander aimlessly. Other times we seem filled with purpose or are at least goal-directed. Something has to be accomplished, and we dedicate ourselves to the task at hand. Let us be active in these ways, but let us also remember the purpose of the moment. The moment is given so we can discover our oneness with our God.

Each moment, like life itself, is a gift. What you do with it will determine the quality of your life. Today's insight is immensely important, for it tells us the purpose of the gift of the moment—to discover our oneness with Spirit. Until this occurs, one moment will flow into the next. But eventually, we will awaken and the flow of time will cease. All that will remain is God.

Your mission today is to remember why you have been given the gift of each moment. Pause at three preset times during the day. For instance, you may choose to stop what you are doing at 10 a.m., 3 p.m., and 7 p.m. Write below what it appears you are doing. Then recall the true purpose of the moment.

For instance:

Time	Current Task	Purpose
10 a.m.	Project preparation	Oneness with God

I have presence.

To have presence is to have all that we need. When we talk to someone who has presence, we feel we have the total attention of the person who is talking to us. People who have presence are calm during stressful times. For these individuals, there is no past or future. Their moment is so filled with God that they do not look to a more favorable time.

The eternal now is the well from which you drink of the living presence of God. Today, review the lessons of this past week, and plan the activities that will help you have presence. Record the things you do and whether they work for you, for you may want to return again to this exercise. Please note that when a person has presence, the natural gift that emerges is a realization of the truth of being—who he or she really is!

Week Thirty-Two

Spiritual Strength

How can we be content until we know who and what we are? In the past, we may have given no thought to our true identity. It seemed obvious that we were human beings living on earth, working and trying to get ahead. Then because of some event or person, we began to wonder about our purpose and reason for being. Why are we here? Is it simply to live and to die? Is there nothing that endures? What are we? Who are we?

Divine discontent and questions start us on the spiritual journey. Intellectually we know we are spiritual beings living in a spiritual universe governed by spiritual laws; however, we realize that this kind of "knowing" is not enough. There must be revelation. This requires spiritual strength. We must persist with our work until who we are is revealed to us. It has happened to other people; a spiritual awakening is our destiny too. Spiritual forces are at work today to bring about the discovery of our true identity. Beyond this discovery is purpose.

May we persist until we are born anew!

I have a choice.
I can quit or I can go on.

Spiritual strength is the ability to persist and endure. We can persist in our efforts to attain a high school diploma or college degree or to achieve some other goal. However, we have choices. We can quit, but this misaligns us with the natural force and direction of the universe. Or we can go on. Our life is eternal and without end. Persistence and endurance are part of our identity.

When we give up, we deny who we really are, and yet, from the human perspective, we reach points where we feel we cannot go on. All of us have quit at some point in the past. There have been prisoners of war living under great duress, with the constant threat of reprisal, subjected to continuous torture. Seemingly, these unfortunate people failed to find the spiritual strength which was within them and quit. But this was not true. They may have quit for a time, but then the prisoners found the strength within them to go on.

The issue is not quitting. As human beings we experience hardships so great that we stop momentarily. This is normal, but let the *pattern* of our lives be persistence. In this way, spiritual strength is expressed, and we discover more of our inner resources.

God persists with us, and our persistence finds its highest expression when it is turned Godward. We will discover how challenging it is to give ourselves to the pursuit of the Infinite. The desire to know God and uncover our spiritual identity requires great persistence. On some days we will feel strong in this purpose, and on other days we will not even remember that we have made this commitment. However, let the general trend of our lives be this: We do not quit on God, for God does not quit on us.

On the next page, write a covenant that expresses your willingness to persist in all human matters as well as in your desire to know God.

Now condense your covenant into one sentence that you can memorize and use to assist you in "going on."

Persistence helps me
discover my inner resources.

Physical strength comes through human effort and repetition in which the muscles of the body are stressed. In order to meet the challenge, the muscles grow in power. Soon the individual is able to lift greater and greater weights and perform tasks that require more physical strength. Even in this earthly matter, inner resources are being discovered. It takes persistence to exercise so the muscles can grow.

By the same token, spiritual strength comes through exercising the spiritual "muscles." Spiritual strength opens the door of the kingdom of God.

Think of something you have wanted to achieve, but have not. Let it be an earthly matter like a diploma or learning some skill. Write it below:

Now begin again and persist with a new realization. The gift you are to receive far exceeds the achieving of the goal. Through your persistence, the door of the kingdom of God is opened, and you discover more of who and what you are. Return to this day in the near future, and write your discovery:

I take one more step.

Jim States, a mountaineer who stood atop Mount Everest, the highest peak in the world, tells the story of a high altitude climb in which he grew immensely tired. He would take a deep breath, affirm his faith in God, and take four steps. This process persisted for hours. Not only was the summit mounted, but Jim rose to new heights as he discovered a greater faith in God.

Remember the phrase: *I take one more step.* This is the way mountains are climbed, the way life is lived. As you persist, you can add another ingredient—faith in God. By approaching the things you do in this way, you are acknowledging that Spirit is the source of your strength. This aids in the revelation of who and what you are.

I do not persist through human will.

We do not persist through human will. We are determined to let Spirit do the work. Our persistence is in letting go and letting God. Human persistence results in exhaustion, while Spirit persisting through us leads to extraordinary happenings that give glory to God. These feats of strength and accomplishment are so dramatic that we shake our heads in disbelief, at the same time realizing that what has happened is possible for everyone.

For instance, nearly every year a story will appear in a newspaper about a woman who performed an extraordinary feat of strength. Her husband jacked up a vehicle and was working underneath it; the automobile slipped off the jack and pinned the man beneath it. The wife, working in the house, heard the muffled cries of her husband and went to see what had happened. She saw her husband pinned beneath the car. Without a moment's hesitation, she went to him and lifted the car. She had no concern for herself, and therefore, spiritual strength enabled her to do the "impossible."

Human will cannot achieve such things. Isn't it strange that a body-builder might not be able to lift the car, but a 90-pound woman is able to do it quickly and without taking thought? It is evidence of the resources that are within us and the importance of putting aside the human will.

Describe an extraordinary example such as the one given in today's lesson. If a story does not come to mind, be on the alert for one in the future, and when you discover it, return to this day and briefly describe what occurred. Perhaps it will be a story about you.

Spirit has endowed us with many talents, abilities, and resources. They can be used regardless of the state of consciousness in which we find ourselves. For instance, we can persist with great determination in athletic or artistic endeavors. A musician becomes an "overnight" success after twenty years of playing to small and often unappreciative audiences.

We can endure and persevere in having our own way, but this is willfulness. There comes a day when the gift of strength is willingly released and returned to Spirit. Our persistence finally turns from the earth to God. Earthly things may require us to go on, but the spiritual path and search for God call for an even greater persistence.

This is one of the great challenges of a spiritual life. If we have been successful in a human way and achieved many of our earthly goals, we usually think of ourselves as resourceful and able to "make it happen." It is possible to accomplish earthly goals and achieve many things without achieving God. Eventually, human methods must be put aside. Our persistence is no longer to have our way, but to let Spirit have its way with us.

Take this idea into prayer and meditation today: *I persist in letting Spirit have its way with me.*

Strength rests in Spirit,
not in me.

Spiritual strength, the ability to persist and go on, is innate to all of us. Two requirements met by us call forth spiritual strength. The first is that we must be willing to get up when we have fallen down; we must take one more step when we are tired and unable to see how we can reach the summit or achieve the goal. "One more step" is a key phrase when facing the challenges of life. Second, the effort we expend must not be for ourselves alone, but for the common good. Strength, like all qualities of Spirit, is expressed when it is in service to other people. As we enter into the consciousness of "one more step" and service to others, the gateway of the soul is opened, and strength which has always been a part of us is released into the world. When this occurs, we must not call it our own, for this will close the door. Let us remember, it is Spirit at work.

We are beginning to learn who we are. We are responding to the call to know ourselves. An illumined spiritual being is an open portal through which the Creator finds expression and is able to be a blessing. Obviously, when God is expressed through one of us, that person is blessed. We have a tendency to consider the person special and, in a way, he or she is remarkable, for God "appears" where that person stands. However, let us not praise the window through which we see the beauty of the universe; let us praise the beauty we behold. Spiritual strength is but one of the marvelous "sights" we can see.

What has today's lesson taught you about who and what you really are?

We need never fear the world and its trials and tribulations. There is in us the strength to bear all burdens. It is important to understand that the strength is present now. We do not receive it from other people or drugs or any earthly thing. Strength, the ability to persist and endure, is a part of who we are.

It is more than the ability to climb mountains or achieve goals, although it can be applied in these ways. In fact, that is how most of us become acquainted with strength. But the day comes when we persist in our quest to know our God. As we continue, we find strength to be one strand in the fabric of our being.

What will you do in order to assist the opening of the portal of your soul so that spiritual strength can be expressed? The process is similar to priming the pump that was in Grandpa's backyard. Water was poured down the well so that an abundance could rise from a deep, hidden source. In this case strength is exhibited by us, which provides an avenue for increased strength to do things we have not yet even dreamed of doing. So the question remains . . . what will you do to prime the pump?

Week Thirty-Three
I Am Whole

When we think of ourselves solely as human, there are many things we seem to lack. There is never enough money. We have love for a time, and then it is gone. Good health is ours, and then sickness comes.

The way we think of ourselves determines much of our lives' experiences. What would life be like if we believed we were made in God's image and after God's likeness? We would not be solely human beings limited by time and circumstance; we would be spiritual beings.

During this week, we will give our attention to the truth that we are spiritual beings. Not only will there be insights into our wholeness in God, but a call to live a week as if we were from above rather than below.

I lack nothing.

Is there anything that Spirit lacks? Does God have a need that is unfulfilled? No, the Creator is the fullness of every desire. As spiritual beings and offspring of the Creator, is there anything we lack? We may believe we are lacking, but it is not so. We are like the man who has enjoyed a good meal at a fine restaurant and discovers that his wallet is missing. Little does he realize that his money is in his overcoat pocket. God is whole and complete, and so are we.

Our basic problem is twofold. We think there are crucial things that we lack, and we think that the world can fulfill us. Money will bring us security and respect. Education will make us wise. People will confirm our importance, self-esteem, and worth. The truth is, security is not the result of employment and money. Many an expert in a particular field knows little about himself and other people. Some individuals are adored by thousands and still forfeit their lives.

What do you think you lack? List three things:

1. _____

2. _____

3. _____

It may seem that you lack these things, but are you willing to consider that you lack nothing? To carry this idea forward into tomorrow, abide with these words throughout the day: *What I think I lack, I am.*

I do not need to be healed.

Today we will examine a specific area of human need in which we think of ourselves as human and believe there is something we lack. May we come to know this is not true.

When we think of ourselves as merely human beings, we are subject to germs and viruses and a variety of human ills. Isn't it strange that something as small as a germ can assert power and dominion over us? Herein lies the key to our wholeness. God is never sick, and neither are we. In truth, we have never been ill and never can be. Bacteria and viruses do not have dominion over us. This is the viewpoint of a spiritual being.

Perhaps you are challenged by this way of thinking. This will be the case for many readers, but the current confusion is the beginning of revelation. If there is confusion and disbelief, it is because we believe we are human. We have a body for a time, but our ongoingness is spiritual.

Let us begin to think of ourselves as whole. Charles Fillmore, co-founder of the Unity movement, said, "There is nothing to heal, only something to know." There are many interpretations of this statement, but the central truth is that we are spiritual beings who are not ill and never can be. When Spirit reveals this to us, the world may say we are *healed*, but we are simply *expressing our wholeness.*

Do not judge by appearances. Wholeness is not a function of the body. In Spirit we are just as whole when we are near death as we were on the day we were born. The body does not determine our wholeness. We are whole, now and forevermore! May we awaken to this truth. As we enter into the consciousness of a spiritual being, earthly needs are fulfilled without making them the object of our existence or taking thought about them. Today's statement is: *I do not need to be healed.* Why is this statement true?

I breathe no air.

Let us continue to think of ourselves as spiritual beings. Consider the following series of statements:

I breathe no air.
I drink no water and eat no food.
I am never cold. Heat does not affect me.
No drug has ever moved within me.
The doctor's scalpel has never touched me and never will.

In an earthly sense you draw a breath each waking moment. You are fed. Perhaps your body has been operated on in the past. However, the statements above are still true from the vantage point of Spirit.

Let these words be seeds for your prayer and meditation today. Speak them, and then release them. Perhaps they will "prime the pump," and other insights will rise from within you. Also, as you move through your day, note how many of your statements reflect your belief that you are a spiritual being and how many are based on the belief that you are a human being.

For instance, if you speak of avoiding someone because he or she is sick, you are viewing yourself as a human being who can "catch" a cold from someone else. When you are in the consciousness of Spirit, no bacteria or virus can affect who you really are. How could an earthly thing affect Spirit? Please write down any thoughts, statements, or beliefs that become evident during the day:

I am whole.

If we are to live a spiritual life, we must cease looking outside ourselves as if we lack the resources and abilities needed to find happiness. The idea *I am whole* denies this lie and points us within ourselves to find all we need. The world is alluring and seems the place where needs can be fulfilled, but this is not true. We are vast and abundant beings because the kingdom of heaven is within us.

Our wholeness is to be revealed to us. Sometimes this occurs when we search for something in the world and even seem to achieve it, but finding it does not provide the joy we thought it would. For instance, we can marry the person of our dreams and have happiness for a time, but then discover that love is no longer a part of our lives even though we are still married to the person. The love we seek is actually within us.

Let us assume the following statement is true: We are whole. How, then, do we live our daily lives? When we are feeling unloved, insecure, ignorant, sickly . . . what do we do? In the past, our first response was to look to another person for love, try to make more money to feel secure, ask some wise one to tell us what to do, ingest a drug, or go to a doctor. These actions are predicated upon the assumption that we are missing what we desire. Now we have another premise. We are whole; therefore, our actions must be different. Our purpose is to open the gateway of the soul so that love, wisdom, security, and vitality can be expressed.

The splendor of the truth of our being is too great to intellectually comprehend. Only Spirit can reveal the wonders of our wholeness. Therefore, our first step is to stand still, open ourselves to God consciousness, prime the pump by speaking the truth of our wholeness, and wait. From the stillness will come the revelation of our wholeness and with it earthly things for us to do. The process is simple; the most challenging parts are shifting our motivation to a desire for Spirit and waiting.

This section of *A Daily Guide to Spiritual Living* is titled *"Know Thyself."* The prayer and meditation ideas you learned in the previous section, *"The Inner Journey,"* now become daily tools for transformation and revelation. Today, there is nothing specific for you to do, but you are issued a challenge. Remember, this is a daily guide for spiritual living. It is time to walk the talk. When you find yourself believing that you lack something, remember that you are whole, and venture within yourself in the way previously outlined. There you will find yourself a whole being, capable of many things.

I am Spirit.
———————

Make a list of what you believe Spirit is. The Bible says that God is love. It is obvious that God is also life. Be as inclusive as you can.

Simple logic coupled with the truth that we are made in God's image and likeness declares that what God is, we must be. Could there be any limitation to such a being? And yet, let us not become too enamored of ourselves, for without our God we can do nothing of importance.

I have no needs.

Children in our society quickly learn that money is necessary for human existence. By exchanging dollars and cents for goods, needs are met. When we view ourselves as merely human, we do have needs. However, when we realize we are spiritual beings, we have no needs. In fact, Thomas Merton, a twentieth-century monk, said that a rich man has no needs. Mr. Merton was not talking about financial wealth and the ability to buy anything a person desires. He was talking about a state of consciousness in which there are no desires and therefore no needs.

David, who wrote the Twenty-third Psalm, experienced the presence of God and entered into the state of being where there are no needs. "The Lord is my shepherd, I shall not want" (Ps. 23:1). Spiritual beings have no earthly needs. They are rich in spirit and without desires. Contentment rather than restlessness fills their souls.

If you were in the state of consciousness where "you did not want" but gradually lost this contentment and joy, what would be the likely reason for the loss and how would you return to the Shepherd? (Possible answers can be found on the next page.)

Week 33
Day 230
continued

Possible answers:

We gradually lose the richness of God's presence when we give our attention to the things and pleasures of the world. We are kept in perfect peace when our minds are stayed on God. "Thou dost keep him in perfect peace, whose mind is stayed on thee." (Is. 26:3).

We can begin our journey home to the Shepherd by "priming the pump" with the words: "The Lord is my shepherd, I shall not want." It is likewise important that we do not take earthly desires into our times of quiet. A desire for God is the only soul desire that will be fulfilled.

I best serve others

I best serve others
by knowing they are whole.

Week 33
Day 231

We may not appear whole, but this is because we do not have the eyes to see. Actually, wholeness cannot be seen through our eyes; the sight to see comes through Spirit's revelation. There is no image or form which can describe our wholeness. When we envision the lame walking, we are not seeing the person whole. Instead, we must know the person to be whole even if he never walks again. Wholeness is not about walking; it is a step deeper into the kingdom of God.

When we perceive the wholeness of other people, we accept them as they are. Jesus did this, and the masses loved Him. He did not try to fix them, but when people came to Him wanting to be healed, His consciousness of wholeness often manifested itself as a restored mind or body. This we must not forget. A consciousness of wholeness, like any state of mind, will manifest itself, and when it does, the lame walk and the blind see.

Actually, it is important that we do not try to do anything to the other person. Usually, what we try to do is fix the other person. If he or she is whole, is there anything that needs to be fixed? No. Let us maintain our consciousness of wholeness. In ways that we will investigate on another day, people will be helped.

Is there someone in your life who appears to need fixing? If you see the person in this way, you are not seeing him or her as whole. However, it is important that you do not try to share these ideas with the other person. Remember, the person is whole—NOW! You are the one with the clouded vision, so "put on your wings" and "prime the pump" so you can once again know the truth of being. This awareness of God will then do God's work. Do not try to direct it or focus it in any way.

329

Week Thirty-Four
I Do Not Judge by Appearances

How easy it is to judge by appearances. Let us be aware, however, that earthly events, physical things, and people do not change or alter God's creation. We see the happenings, the things, and the people, but it is what we perceive or believe that assigns meaning to what we see or hear. The five senses are servants. Servants do not rule the household and tell the master what to believe or what is true. Servants provide the facts. The master makes of them what he will.

Judging by appearances is not a matter of seeing and hearing. It is a matter of selecting whom we will listen to and who will be the authority in our lives. To the five senses, we say, "Thank you for doing your job and presenting the world to me, but I will determine what fact or event reflects the truth of being."

In much of comedy, the humor occurs because one thing is happening, but some people believe something entirely different is occurring. For instance, a husband overhears a conversation and assumes that he and his wife are going to have a child. He is overjoyed and waits for his wife to break the exciting news to him. While he waits, he begins to treat his wife differently. The truth is, she is not going to have a child and cannot understand why her husband is being so attentive. Imagine the fun a writer could have with this scenario.

Can you think of a situation in your life when, because of appearances, you assumed one thing was true or something was happening, but it was not so? Please give a brief description of the situation:

Week 34
continued

I have judged by appearances.

Anyone who has ever been entertained by a magician has judged by appearances. The magician shows the audience an empty box and asks a volunteer to confirm that it is empty. All agree, and the trick is on. The truth is, the box appears empty but it is not. It is one thing to be duped by a magician; we enjoy the surprise we feel when the rabbit appears. However, few people enjoy being duped by life.

Part of our judging is based on our five senses. Nearly every person who drives has stopped at a stoplight and suddenly jammed on the brakes because he believed the car was rolling into the intersection. Actually, the car next to his was rolling backward. There are many examples of our misinterpretations of sensory information.

Give an example of a time when you falsely judged by appearances:

What is seen is made out of that which does not appear.

It may seem that our senses provide us with false information, but the truth is that our interpretation of the data causes the problem. The senses are doing what they are designed to do. Let us do what we are engineered to do—judge rightly.

The world holds much beauty, but it is not a place in which to find meaning and wisdom. The direction is that we are to be in the world, but not of it. In Hebrews 11:3 it is written, "What is seen was made out of things which do not appear." Modern science confirms that this is true. Even school children learn that matter is made of unseen molecules and atoms. Charles Fillmore brought this one step closer to the Creator by writing in *Christian Healing*, "The starting point of every form in the universe is an idea." No one has ever seen an idea, but ideas move humankind to action.

If we are to know ourselves and live meaningful lives, we must get behind the form that we see and do our work in the realm of ideas. When we respond to ideas, then we are not duped by appearances.

The idea of freedom has been the motivating force throughout the history of humankind. List four examples of events that have come to be because someone has responded to this powerful idea:

1. _____

2. _____

3. _____

4. _____

The body can be seen and felt, but who can hold life in his or her hand? Soft, tender, loving words can be spoken, but can any sound carry the full wonder of love as its message? Students can know the wisdom of the ages and learn the insights that have transformed countless thousands of people and still remain untouched by ideas which move the person seated next to them.

It will be much easier to cease judging by appearances when we realize that the things of consequence are beyond our human grasp. When we begin our search of unseen things, we will more easily look beyond the appearances and be able to peer into the infinite.

No one can know himself or herself as long as the world and its appearances motivate the soul to action. Please consider the following statements, and begin to make them companions for the journey.

The reality of life cannot be seen.

I do not judge by what I see and hear and feel.

The world and its appearances hold no meaning for me.

What ideas do you think are "behind" the following happenings?

1. The American Revolution _____

2. Forgiveness _____

3. A healed body _____

4. A new job _____

Possible answers:

1. Freedom
2. Love and letting go or releasing
3. Life and wholeness
4. Security

I render unto Caesar.

It is true that the reality of life cannot be seen, heard, or felt. They are of Spirit and lie beyond the five senses. However, we must not be so heavenly that we are of no earthly good. In fact, we are to be of assistance here and to grow in understanding of the "things which do not appear." We live in a three-dimensional world, but we can live our earthly lives with the understanding and conviction of the reality of Spirit.

There is a wonderful episode in Jesus' life when the Pharisees (one of the religious groups of Jesus' time) posed to Him what they thought was an unanswerable question: "Is it lawful to pay taxes to Caesar, or not?" (Mk. 12:14) Undoubtedly, the people had asked their religious leaders the same question. If the Pharisees said no, then Roman soldiers would imprison or put them to death for encouraging the people to refuse to pay their taxes. If they said yes, the people would turn from the clerics because the Jews hated Roman domination.

When Jesus was asked the question, He asked to see a coin. A Roman coin was brought to Him and, after asking whose inscription was on the coin (it was Caesar's), Jesus said, "Render to Caesar the things that are Caesar's, and to God the things that are God's" (Mk. 12:17). Balance is necessary in one's life. The earth and people and events are part of human existence. We have been given five senses, so we can know what is happening around us, but we are also granted wisdom to understand the truth that sets us free.

A good question to ask when confronted with a difficult situation is: What is the truth about this? Things that appear can become like Goliath, but an unseen idea realized by us will release spiritual forces which will transform any earthly experience.

What situation in your life challenges you now?

What is the truth about this situation?

If there is illness, for instance, the truth is that you are pure divine life, whole and untouched by disease. If there is indecision, the reality is that you have the mind of the Christ, and you are engineered to know the truth and express it. When there are earthly things for you to do, render unto Caesar, but remember to render unto God the things that are God's. In nearly every human situation, there are Caesar things to do. What Caesar thing are you to do with your situation?

How will you render unto God the things that are God's?

May the one who has eyes to see, see.

From time to time Jesus would say to His listeners, "He who has ears to hear, let him hear" (Mt. 11:15). Perhaps this was a puzzling statement to many people. They were hearing what Jesus said; they were not deaf. The rabbi from Nazareth was not talking about the ability to hear sound, but to discern meaning. Language is an important part of the evolution of human-kind, and our language is becoming more and more refined and detailed in its expression. But words alone cannot convey the things of Spirit; they must be spiritually discerned.

Some people insist that the Bible is to be understood literally. The words say exactly what they mean. This is an absurd approach to this book of truth. Jesus said He was a door, and that we are to hate our fathers and mothers. Can we hold fast to literalism in the face of such statements? To such statements Jesus would say, "He who has ears to hear, let him hear."

The "ears" are actually the perceiving power of the mind. As this ability to perceive is developed, we are less prone to judge by appearances. An inner teacher, the spirit of truth, guides us in daily living.

Let's continue to develop ears with which to hear and eyes with which to see. There was a reference above to Jesus' statement that we must hate our fathers and mothers. Obviously, this is not to be taken literally, but has another meaning. Look up the verse in the Bible (Lk. 14:26), and read the adjacent passages. Then allow the mind of God in you to reveal the meaning. Please realize that the meaning cannot be forced. Through waiting and grace, the answer will come. As the powerful message dawns in you, know that you are less prone to judge by appearances. Also, in the space that follows, describe the insight you received:

The fields are white unto harvest.

The world is different than what we have believed. People experience altered states of consciousness and see people and other living things surrounded by light. Athletes see a ball that is moving at nearly one hundred miles an hour as if it were in slow motion.

Jesus saw the world in a unique way. There was a time in His life when He was with His disciples and said to them, "I tell you, lift up your eyes, and see how the fields are already white for harvest" (Jn. 4:35). In your imagination, see Jesus and the disciples in a place where they can see fields which ordinarily bear crops. But this is not the growing season, and the fields are brown and bare. Jesus looks at the disciples, stretches forth His hand over the fields, and says, "See how the fields are already white for harvest." How shocked the disciples are. One who judges by appearances could never utter these words.

People who judge by appearances see few possibilities; the world is only that which is before them. The one who expresses an unseen potential acknowledges the appearances, but entertains possibilities. This person is like the scientist who knows there is a cure for cancer or a way to put human beings on the moon. Known laws may say it is impossible, but the scientist insists there are other laws still to be discovered.

Memorize the statement, "The fields are white unto harvest." Let these words trigger in you the possibilities of a rich harvest, regardless of appearances. Whenever you seem stymied and blocked by life's circumstances, remember, even in winter the fields are white unto harvest.

I do not judge by appearances.

There comes a time in life when we are no longer to judge by appearances. That time is now! The world of manifestation has no power over the truth of our being and the reality of God. Circumstances may rise up like Goliath and seem unconquerable, but the only thing that is unconquerable is one's soul.

Our judgments and decisions are to be based on truth, and truth comes from within us, not from the world. Truth cannot be seen, but can be experienced. Our consciousness of truth manifests itself through the law of mind action, and a great light comes into the world. If this is to be our experience, two things must happen. First, we must not judge by appearances. Remember, nothing in the manifest realm has power and dominion over our unconquerable souls. Second, recall that the truth sets us free.

Quickly read through the days of this week, and write a short summary of what you have learned and how the insights will impact your life.

I Am Blessed When My Heart Is Pure, for Then I Shall See God

Our hearts are not pure, and therefore we judge by appearances. If we are to discover who and what we are, we must enter the cleansing stream of Spirit. God is willing to merge with and create a better world with humankind, but because our will is not aligned with Spirit's will, first we must become purified. Spirit is one with that which is like itself. Because our true identity is pure and cannot be touched by the purification process, let us not fear what we must release. Remember the promise: "Blessed are the pure in heart, for they shall see God" (Mt. 5:8). With a pure heart, we join William Blake in declaring: "To see the world in a grain of sand and heaven in a wild flower, hold infinity in the palm of your hand and eternity in an hour."

What is the one thing that is delaying your discovery of what you are?

Possible answer: Judging by appearances.

What symptom is telling you that you still have to release it?

The world is filled with God.

It is written that in the beginning there was God. Surely it is the same today. The world is filled with God. There is no place devoid of Spirit, and yet God seems hidden from our eyes. Some insist that Spirit is in hiding and reveals itself at certain times. Others say that they see the Almighty behind every bush and as part of the clouds and the red sky at sunrise.

We have been given eyes to see, but our vision is not clear. Clouds obscure God's beauty, even on sunny days. The problem is not in the world, and Spirit is not hiding. The problem is in us. We insist on seeing a world of scarcity, so we hoard our goods. We believe in contagious diseases and therefore fail to realize that no microbe can harm our spiritual essence. We want to be right and do not see the hand of friendship that has been extended to us.

Write what you see in the world that seems unlike God. Perhaps it is prejudice or famine or condemnation.

My heart is not pure.

"Blessed are the pure in heart, for they shall see God" is a simple prin-ciple that tells us something about ourselves. Whenever we see someone as less than an expression of Spirit, our hearts are not pure. Something in us is clouding our vision.

And yet there are times when we see clearly. A young student was walking in a field while prayerfully preparing for a class. There she spied a caterpillar resting atop a blade of grass. She watched the tiny green creature for a time, and then she realized that his stubby little antennae were probing the space above him. It was as if he were searching for something. She realized that in some way he had sensed her presence and was trying to "see" her. A strange thought crossed the student's mind: She was walking in the field in search of God and found a creature which she speculated was on the same search. They had found each other in their common quest.

Who knows if caterpillars search for God, but on that day the student was seeing the world differently. At another time, on another day, she would not have seen the caterpillar or even walked in the field.

The sight to see is not a matter of eyesight. It is a matter of conscious-ness. Anything that stands between us and this heavenly sight is an impurity and must be released.

Make a list of twelve impurities that can cloud our vision:

1. _____

2. _____

3. _____

4. _____

5. _____

Week 35
Day 240
continued

6. _____

7. _____

8. _____

9. _____

10. _____

11. _____

12. _____

Note: The chief impurity is unforgiveness of ourselves and others.

346

I am willing to be cleansed.

Impurities are part of our human consciousness. Unforgiveness, dishonesty, and fear of change are obstructions to our ability to see the world as it truly is. Let us be willing to be cleansed of the weaknesses that stand between us and the vision which "sees" God.

If we were camping and took water from a lake and found tiny dark particles floating in it, we would not drink it. We would strain it first. However, cleansing the water of the dark particles does not necessarily make the water pure. In many lakes, there are unseen substances which make the water unfit for drinking. In our own spiritual lives, there are obvious impurities that must be dealt with. But even though this is true, people often cling to those things which they know are limiting or harmful. We will not drink water filled with tiny dark particles, but we will hold grievances for years.

Just as water can contain impurities that we cannot see but which are still harmful to our physical bodies, the soul often contains beliefs which are hidden from our conscious minds. It is these impurities which we call to be released today. In most instances, we will never know the culprit, but our lives will be changed. Prayer and meditation are the cleansing stream which washes away that which is not like God.

May the following images be helpful to you as you invite the cleansing power of Spirit into your life.

I am deep in a forest. Silence has been my friend
for many minutes, but now I perceive, from a distance, the
roar of falling water. I am seeking a cleansing
waterfall. I expend effort to find this sacred
place, while knowing through years of trials that

the purification I seek cannot come through my effort.

I follow the sound and eventually find myself standing beside a pool of clear water. A silver stream falls from high above. It is strange, but in this place I hardly hear the sound of the water. The thunder of the falling water led me here, but now there is little sound.

I enter the water and stand beneath its purifying stream . . . I move forward, feeling the coolness of the water on my legs and sensing the silver thread of water calling me to a pure heart . . .

Why do some people see a situation in one way while others see it in an entirely different way? Thomas Edison, in his search for the proper filament for the light bulb, was unsuccessful over one thousand times. When asked about these "failures," Mr. Edison said that he had not failed; he had found one thousand ways that did not work. This is the vision of one who sees clearly.

The way we see the world tells us something about ourselves. Usually, we first grasp this standard of truth in an intellectual way. We are not able to demonstrate this truth, but we can talk about it. This is our beginning. When we use this truth on an intellectual level as a standard, comparing it with the life we live, we will constantly learn about ourselves.

As we adopt this process of comparison, let it be a healthy experience, free of condemnation. When we realize we are not living our lives according to the standard, or straight line, of truth, let this knowing turn us toward the cleansing stream once more. As we do this, we are quickened to constructive action rather than guilt and self-defeating behavior. We have a greater awareness of ourselves—our human nature as well as our spiritual nature.

As a result of engaging in this week's exercises, what new insight do you have about yourself?

What would God see?

"What would God see?" is a wonderful question to carry in our minds. In the book *In His Steps* by Charles Monroe Sheldon, a minister asked the townspeople to consider a question before they acted. "What would Jesus do?" This was done for one year. The town was transformed. Our question is a similar one and is consistent with *Week Thirty-Five*'s focus: What would God see?

Through prayer and meditation, rather than intellectual knowledge, answer the following questions. Your answers must be one sentence.

1. What would God see if you were sick?

2. What would God see if you were filled with hate?

3. What would God see if you were poor?

4. What does God see when God "looks" at you?

When our hearts are pure, not only do we see God in everyone and everything; God is also the eye with which we see.

For many years, a minister enjoyed leading people on a retreat experience called "A Closer Walk With God." Each participant spent at least an hour and a half in silence and followed a script which guided the individual on the closer walk. As the person returned to the place where the walk originated, he or she was instructed to continue in silence and to describe the experience through art, drawing, or the written word. After everyone had returned and shared the experience of the closer walk in silence, each person then shared the high points of the walk. Invariably, the experience was a closer walk with God, for the people found God in the forest, in the people they met as they walked, and in themselves. As the "Closer Walk With God" experience neared its completion, the minister always said, "Please remember, 'Only Spirit can see itself.' "

Express the sentence "Only Spirit can see itself" in your own words:

What is there to see but God?

What is there to see but God? Impure hearts and minds judge by appearances and fail to see the truth of being. A pure heart looks beyond the physical and sees Spirit.

How wonderful it is when someone sees something in us that we have not noted in ourselves. Parents, friends, and teachers often have a vision of us that causes us to search ourselves to determine what it is that they see in us. Through their vision of us, their respect for us, we are called to a potential that we have not seen.

Has there been someone in your life who saw in you a goodness and potential that you had not seen in yourself? If the answer is yes, please write the person's name and briefly describe a time when he or she saw the best in you. (If you have had this experience firsthand, you realize what a help you could be to other people by allowing yourself to see them differently, rather than by trying to "fix" them.)

Week Thirty-Six
Expression Equals Experience

The kingdom of heaven is within you. You are whole; nothing needs to be added to you. Instead, the wonders of God's presence must be released from within.

It is good to wait for the revelation, but it is also necessary to act as though you are whole, have the mind of the Christ, and are a child of God. Ultimately, the "imprisoned splendor" is released through *expression*. Remember: expression equals experience. For instance, love is our nature, and it is experienced by us when we are loving. We say that the only love we can truly experience is the love that is released from within us. A law of life is: As we give, so shall we receive. Another way of stating this great law is: *Expression equals experience.*

What aspect of God's presence do you want to experience?

Are you willing to allow this to be released from within you?

Today I experience love
by expressing love.

A legend is told of a person in search of love. By asking many questions, the seeker learned the identity of the most loving individual on earth. A map was purchased, and the one in search of love journeyed to a high place where an aged woman lived in simplicity. After greeting each other, the seeker said, "I am in search of love. Tell me how I can find it. Do you have love to give to me?" The woman tenderly answered, "Continue your journey and observe three loving acts—one by a man, one by a woman, and one by a child. Then return to me."

The traveler left and, after a time, returned to the woman. "I have witnessed three acts of love. Do you want to know what I saw?" The woman answered, "That is not necessary, but one thing is. Do the things you have witnessed, and you will experience love."

The most loving people in the world do not look to others for love. Those who have attempted this ill-fated practice have found it unrewarding. Eventually, people who become the lovers of humankind look to others not for love, but to discover how to be loving. Once this discovery is made, love pours from within them.

The world says that we experience love when someone loves us. We are like children hugging our stuffed animals, feeling loved, and telling our mothers how much our teddy loves us. The bear expresses no love, but as we hug the bear, love escapes from within us, and we are the first to experience it.

The most loving people in the world have found that when love is released from within them, they experience it. The genuine loving that occurs on this planet is not to fill the empty hearts of humankind, but to show human beings that their hearts are filled with the love they seek.

Today you will experience love by expressing it. Think of yourself as the wanderer in search of love. You have journeyed to the most loving person in all the world. You, like so many before you, ask this person how to find love. The wise one speaks and assigns you three tasks. When they are complete, you are told, you will know the mystery of love.

What are the three tasks you are assigned?

1.

2.

3.

 *Week 36*
Day 247

Today I experience peace
by expressing peace.

Peace is present now. Like all things we desire, it is part of our nature and is experienced through expression. Peace is not coming to the world. It is here in the world today and has always awaited our willingness to express it.

If you went to the most peaceful person on earth and asked for three tasks which would open your soul so its innate peacefulness could be expressed, what would those three tasks be?

1.

2.

3.

It may seem very important that particular events happen in our lives. It is during these times that we must remind ourselves that what we want to experience is already a part of us. Specific happenings are not common to us, but the essence of an event—love, peace, joy, security, and so on—is the common ground upon which all humans tread.

As we remember this truth, we cease trying to make it happen and begin to open the soul, so the experience can pour from within us into the world and into our experience. There are two things we must understand if we are to live life in this way. The first is the need to put aside the desire for specific outcomes. Our lives were born in mystery, and therefore a contrived existence, even one that appears fulfilling, is not our destiny. Second, let us remember that experience equals expression. When the expression comes from deep within us, it is of Spirit. It becomes our experience as it manifests itself *as* our life, but because of its divine origin, it is a blessing to everyone. Only spiritually mature individuals move beyond desiring specific things. They yearn for expression and become a blessing to many.

There are many possible experiences awaiting you. Which do you desire the most? Another way to write the question is: Of all the possibilities that are within you, what do you want to give expression to first?

I have found it difficult

to experience _____.

What is it that you have found difficult to experience? You want this experience, but it seems to be just beyond your grasp.

Reword the above question with the following formula as the foundation for what is written: Experience equals expression.

Possible answer:
What is it that you have found difficult to express?

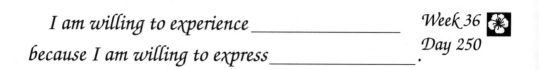

I am willing to experience _____ **Week 36**
because I am willing to express _____ . **Day 250**

Are you now willing to experience _____ ? (Please insert the "thing" you have found most difficult to experience/express.)

You realize the truth that experience and expression are one. For instance, by declaring your willingness to express love, you are preparing yourself to experience it.

Today is to be filled with action. How are you going to express whatever it is you want to experience? Formulate a plan of action, and write it in the space below. Then enact your plan. Remember that as you express that which is within you, you are doing what comes naturally. In reality, you were created to bear witness to the truth, to bear witness to what is within you.

*Today I experience life
by expressing life.*

Today experience life by expressing it. In what direction will your energies be directed? What would you do with your life if you knew you could not fail?

In many instances, it is a fear of failure that keeps us from fulfilling our destiny and using our God-given talents. We don't experience the fullness of life because we will not express what we feel inside. Today we do not wait for life to come to us; we express it.

How many people have waited for someone to love them when they were surrounded by people who needed a loving touch or kind word? Let us not wait for life to come to us.

There was once a man who was taking tennis lessons. He took an hour lesson from a professional teacher five days a week. This student was encouraged to play on his own, but he did not want to play until he was good enough. He never learned to play tennis. No sport is learned or enjoyed without full participation by the player. Watching the game being played does not make us a player. We must walk on the court and stumble like everyone who has gone before us. We experience tennis by expressing it. We experience life by expressing it.

The exercise from yesterday centered on your own preferences and human desires. Today give careful attention to allowing your spiritual identity to be expressed. A central characteristic is that the expression will be a blessing to others. Who you really are lives life in this way.

We come to know ourselves and experience who we are by expressing our spiritual identity. When we do not know who we are, it may seem unnatural to attempt to express anything. However, let us not forget our natural tendencies and divine guidance, which direct us in spite of ourselves.

In truth, there is no mystery as to what we are to do or how we should act. Let us not make life more difficult than it needs to be. If we pause for a short time, we will sense the guidance and spiritual forces which constantly move us on an ever ascending path toward union with God. This is why in yesterday's lesson the question was asked: What would you do if you knew you could not fail? Our imaginings and aspirations give us insight into the spiritual tendencies that are innate in us.

In a past decade, the theme was: If it feels good, do it. Some of the things that were done may have felt good to one person, but certainly not to the whole. There are natural, spiritual tendencies that seek expression from within each of us. Two criteria are important as we give expression to what seems natural. First, our actions must not harm our human selves or the humanity of others. Second, we are expressing our spiritual identity when we are serving others. We are then blessed because we are a blessing.

At the conclusion of this day, write about the expression of your spiritual identity.

Week 36
Day 252
continued

Week Thirty-Seven

I Am

Principles are individualized. For instance, a cook conceives of a new dish and writes the recipe. Other cooks take the recipe and individualize it as a sumptuous meal for family and friends. All games have rules, and when the game is played the rules become living things. They are individualized.

The great law and principle of the universe is God. God comes alive in each of us as the indwelling Christ is individualized. Moses stood before the burning bush and asked what to say to the imprisoned Hebrews when they asked who sent him to them. God answered, "Say this to the people of Israel, 'I am has sent me to you' " (Ex. 3:14). I AM is one of God's names.

Jesus is a living expression of Spirit's individuality. Paul discovered this principle and expressed it when he said that he did not live, but that Christ lived in him. The truth is that Spirit seeks expression through every human being, but we do not always allow it. God wants to be expressed through us as a loving, caring human being, but we sometimes say no. The deeds and lives of those who have said yes are recorded throughout history. We canonized these people and called them saints, but time and time again they have simply called us to more simple and useful lives in service to God and our fellow human beings.

During this week we will give much attention to the two words *I am*, for they are a bridge to the kingdom of God.

I stand on the bridge.

We stand on a bridge. In one direction is a land of light, love, peace, and joy. In the other direction is an alluring place filled with opposites—peace and war, health and sickness, love and hate. The bridge is called *I am.*

These two words are identity words. As we speak or think the phrase "I am," we attach ourselves to, or identify with, whatever we choose to connect to the words. For instance, we can say, "I am good for nothing." To speak in this way is to identify with limitation. However, when a person says, "I am good at listening," this person is identifying with good listening skills. By speaking and thinking the words *I am*, we attach ourselves to the world, to beliefs both helpful and harmful, and also to divine ideas like love and life.

Think of yourself standing on the midpoint of a bridge. On one side are limitless possibilities and a continuous awareness of God. On the other side are earthly things, some called good and others called bad. Every time you see yourself standing on the bridge, remember that through the words *I am*, you are able to identify with whatever you choose—limitlessness or limitation.

Watch your use of the words *I am*. List four "things" with which you have identified through the use of the phrase "I am":

1. _____

2. _____

3. _____

4. _____

I do not take God's name in vain.

As children, we were often taught that taking the Lord's name in vain meant cursing. As we mature, cursing ceases, but we may still take the Lord's name in vain. God's name is I AM. This was the name that Moses was given at the burning bush. "I am who I am" (Ex. 3:14).

When we first become conscious of ourselves, we receive the realization of *I am*. The Spirit of the universe has individualized itself as us. We are unlimited. Biblically, this is called the image of God. "God is love" (1 Jn. 4:8), and "God is spirit" (Jn. 4:24); therefore, our essence is likewise love and spirit.

This can be a challenging concept for people. Whenever you think of the words *I am*, substitute the phrase *God in me is . . .* or *God individualized as me is . . .* For instance, *I am* caring becomes *God in me is* caring or *God individualized as me is* caring.

We will discuss this in greater detail in a few days, but consider the inappropriateness of saying *I am* sick, which becomes *God in me is* sick or *God individualized as me is* sick. This cannot be. Therefore, we take the Lord's name in vain whenever we connect the I AM to anything but God.

Watch your use of the words *I am* again today. List three categories of things with which you have identified. For instance, you might identify with the opinions of others, the way you look, a certain emotion, and so on.

1. _____

2. _____

3. _____

Today I consciously choose that with which I identify.

We stand on the bridge giving our attention to the kingdom of God and then whirl and identify with something of the earth. Today let us consciously choose that with which we identify. During the last couple of days, we have caught a glimpse of the things with which we have identified in the past. We have joined to sickness by saying or thinking *I am sick*. We have identified with health by declaring or holding in mind *I am life*.

In some instances, our connectedness has lasted for years and has been unconscious. We have allowed ourselves to be joined to the past and have limited our current moment. Not today. Today we choose consciously that with which we identify.

Please indicate below that with which you have chosen to identify. It is best that the I AM be joined to that which is honorable, lovely, pure and just. Remember, to say "I am" is to say "God individualized as me is . . ."

1. _____

2. _____

3. _____

I choose to identify with that which is positive.

It is assumed that yesterday your focus was upon the positive. Today continue the exercise by imagining yourself standing on the bridge and identifying with the possibility of a wonderful human life. Choose three of the statements below. One is to be carried in your mind from the time you wake up until noon. The second is to be focused upon from 12 noon until 6 p.m., and the third shall be your companion until you go to sleep.

I am filled with infinite possibilities.
I am free; I am unlimited.
I am getting better and better in every way.
I am successful.
I am stress-free.
I am healthy, wealthy, and wise.
I am positive.
I am willing to change.
I am a good listener.
I am a good friend.
I am prospered.
I am caring.

I identify with God.

Your true identity is spiritual, for you are made in God's image and after Spirit's likeness. The call has gone out for you to know yourself. This has been the focus of the third quarter of this book. Obviously, if you are to discover who you are, you must identify with God.

There seems to be a rite of passage with regard to the discovery of our identity. We begin by identifying with the world around us. One of the first "objects" with which we identify is the body. We believe it to be who we are. This is not true. We have a body to use while we are on earth, but we are not the body. We identify with our parents' opinions about us. If they say we are worthless, there is a human tendency to believe it. Also, the mother and father may think of the child as the child's actions. This is not true. We are not what we do.

It takes years to understand that we are not the body or our actions or what other people say we are. When we look at the vast examples of human expression ranging from art and writing to athletic feats to people giving their lives for others, we begin to understand that we are incredible beings. This is because we are made in God's image. If the fullness of who we are is to be expressed, we must put aside thoughts of the body, the opinions of others, and what we do or what others have done to us and identify with God.

Today, identify with God. Do this in the way that seems right to you, but remember the theme of this week. Below, write the approach you took:

I am . . .

Jesus walked the bridge and entered the kingdom of heaven. He identified with God. Prior to dealing with a man born blind, Jesus identified with the Father and said, "I am the light of the world" (Jn. 8:12). Before He faced the crucifixion, He affirmed, "I am the resurrection and the life" (Jn. 11:25).

We can learn from the Master Teacher and identify with God. We do this by connecting the I AM to qualities of Spirit. The affirmations below will help anyone realize the truth of being:

I am light.

I am love.

I am joy.

I am peace.

I am life.

I am wisdom.

I am Spirit.

Add seven similar affirmations of your own:

1. _____

2. _____

3. _____

4. _____

5. _____

6. _____

7. _____

In order to experience the truth of your being, speak, sing, or think one of these affirmations as part of your prayer and meditation time. Then wait. If your mind drifts, bring it gently home again by speaking, singing, or thinking the affirmation, and then wait again.

Indicate the affirmation you used for this exercise:

_____

I am.

It is helpful to identify with the qualities and aspects of Spirit as we understand it, but God cannot be described with words or images. Spirit is too immense for human comprehension and explanation, too vast for measurement, and too transcendent to be contained. And yet we can know the truth of being. We may not be able to explain who we are, but we will be able to say what we are not. More importantly, we will live from the center that is our spiritual reality.

On a previous day, we connected our identity phrase with Spirit as we understood it. Therefore, we worked with statements like "I am love" and "I am peace." Now we make ourselves available to the purity of Spirit by working with the two words *I am*. Let us not connect this identity phrase to anything. If there is a joining, God must be the one who declares our oneness.

Take any tune and quietly sing "I am" to the song you have selected. Do this over and over again . . . and then wait. If you become distracted, sing again, and then wait again. *I am* is the first revelation we have when we become conscious. Record any feelings, thoughts, or images that come to you during this activity:

Halfway There

Many years ago during a period of prayer and meditation, an inner voice spoke to a young minister and said, "You are halfway there." How delightful. Self-congratulation was in order. One more step and it would be downhill from there. How "downhill" was soon discovered. The voice continued, "And you always will be." The prayer and meditation time was over, and confusion now filled a place where there had been peace.

Over a period of time we will realize the meaning of the phrase "halfway there." The spiritual journey is an infinite one. God cannot be known as we know our hometown or the house where we live. The mystery and wonder continue on and on . . . forever. You are always in the midst of life—right in the middle—for there is no end to God. Spiritual awakening, or being born again, is not a onetime experience. It is the experience of life.

To say that we are halfway there is to say that the inner journey will never end. It is to commit ourselves to a spiritual way of life and continuous exploration of the kingdom of God.

Listen for the inner voice saying to you, "You are halfway there, and you always will be." Write your reply in the space below:

There is no destination.

There is no destination, but there is a journey. There are no stopping places, but there are places to rest.

People tell us that we have to have goals. They say, "Vague goals yield vague results." Because most people aspire to material goods and follow earthly pursuits, this goal-setting approach seems helpful, and the person drives forward to success as conceived by the masses. But because we are spiritual beings, these successes do not fulfill us. We may create more earthly goals and spend a lifetime getting what we think we want, but never find contentment. In this way of life there is a destination, but little sense of a spiritual journey.

When we discover we are infinite spiritual beings, we realize that the only destination is God. Knowing God becomes the goal, but the Creator is vast beyond our comprehension. We cannot achieve God the way we close a business deal; in truth we cannot "achieve" God at all. There is only the journey, but it is filled with contentment and joy and life itself.

The question today is: Can you be content in knowing that the journey never ends, that no matter how conscious of God you become, there is always more? When it comes to certain skills and crafts, there are experts, people who are at the top of their profession. In the kingdom of God, we are all apprentices. The journey stretches before the novice just as far as it does before the master craftsman. Consider this example in stillness, and you will find humility and excitement for the journey.

I have no alpha and no omega.

As human beings we are conditioned to think in terms of beginnings and endings. Life on earth begins with birth and ends with death. School begins with orientation day and ends with graduation. Athletic events start and continue until the time runs out or the distance has been covered by the runners.

As we begin (there is that word again) to believe we are infinite spiritual beings, our minds are stretched by considering the idea that we have no beginning and no end. This idea of no alpha and no omega will continue to plague us until we put aside the concept of time. But how shall we ignore the rising and setting of the sun and the movement of the heavenly bodies? These are our standards for time, and they are with us each moment of our earthly lives. How can time stand still or no longer be a power in our lives? The answer is: When we give our full attention to our "halfway-there point"—our current moment—time is no longer a power in our lives.

Let the following statements be the foundation for a meditation that brings you to the halfway-there point:

The sun cannot set on my life.

I cannot cease to be.

On and on is my way.

Never stretching before me.

Always here.

In a state with no ending and no beginning.

Who I am was never born and can never die.

I have no alpha, no omega.

I am Spirit.

My life is not a line.

 *Week 38*
Day 261
continued

    It is a circle.
    My life has no seasons.
    Yet at the halfway-there point, seeds are sown and fruits are harvested.

I am content with the mystery.

To venture into the kingdom of heaven or the kingdom of God is to enter into mystery. God is the great unknown, and each step deeper into the kingdom must be mysterious.

What have you discovered about yourself since you began using this book that you did not know when you started?

When we are not content with the mystery, there are continuous attempts to direct the course of our lives. We know best. Goals are conceived, and we march toward them. Unpredictable things occur, but we resent them. They were not on the course we charted. Strange, but we entered into the unknown, uncharted territory of our lives and were taken aback when we came face-to-face with mystery. Could it be any other way?

When Lewis and Clark explored the Louisiana Purchase, they encountered mystery after mystery. They explored thousands of square miles of uncharted land, but found uncharted potentials within themselves.

Let us be explorers unafraid of mystery. There is no need to direct the course of our lives. In truth, we do not know our direction. Divine Wisdom and our consciousness will guide us on the journey.

Where there is mystery,
there is God.

When there is no mystery in our lives, we have no experience of God in our lives, for God is mystery. When mystery is a friend, we have faith, and through faith we find God.

Mystery is always with us, but we persist in thinking we know our tomorrows. If there is anything we do not know, it is tomorrow. It seems enough for us to understand our yesterday. How can we comprehend what has not yet come to be?

In today's busy world, many of us have schedules to keep. Even when we go on vacation, we schedule our lives and feel odd when we do not know what we are going to do next. We take away the mystery of our lives and wonder why we cannot find God.

Look ahead to a weekend when you can conduct an experiment. Perhaps there are certain things that you usually do during your weekends. List those things in the space below:

1. _____

2. _____

3. _____

4. _____

5. _____

6. _____

On the weekend when you are going to conduct your experiment, do not participate in these things. This is to be a weekend in which nothing is planned. Mystery shall abound and so shall God!

Write the date you are going to conduct your experiment:

Write any occurrences or significant insights that arise from your experiment:

In a few words, describe how the experiment felt:

I am mysterious.

Friendship is basically the result of discovery, for it develops as we get to know another person. Some of the mystery of who the other person is passes away, and friendship is born. But as a child must grow if he or she is to reach maturity, so friendship must also grow. This means that continued mystery is a requirement for friendship. We cannot know all there is about another person and expect the relationship to thrive, for when we know all, we come to a point of stagnation.

As we get to know ourselves and our God, there is discovery and continued mystery. Few people make the mistake of thinking they know all there is to know about God, but sometimes we think we know ourselves. If we probe the depths of self through prayer and meditation and wonder why we live life the way we do, we will find our mysterious self.

The mysterious self always points to needed growth. Its unspoken message is that we are halfway there. Let us not accept stagnation nor think of ourselves as knowing who we are. God is mystery, and we are made in the image of what cannot be fully known. We, too, must be mysterious. On what day will we say that our journey has ended and that we know ourselves fully? The day will never come, for Spirit is always willing to reveal more of our mysterious self.

Today identify with the mystery, and you will be identifying with God. As odd as it seems, this causes some of the mystery to vanish and more of God to be made known.

For most human beings there is a need to know. Mystery is the enemy. Hopefully, today you will discover it is a friend. The purpose of today's activity is to "get a feel" for the mystery. Your purpose is not to reveal some of the mystery, but to identify with it. When you do this, you will be identifying with God.

Another mystery for today is that you must determine how you will "get a feel for the mystery." Write what you decided to do:

Faith and mystery are joined in me.

We are discovering who we are. How strange it is that mystery is part of what we find when we look inside ourselves. But it is not mystery alone; there is faith. Faith peers into the unknown and finds the unseen rather than the seen to be the reality. In this way, faith and mystery are joined in us.

It is good to know and to understand, but no one knows the truth of being until mystery is as wondrous a discovery as uncharted islands and long forgotten artifacts. Knowledge comes to the mind and becomes experience and facts, or truths. Mystery envelops us, strengthens our faith, and grants us courage.

Are you beginning to realize the role mystery plays in self-discovery and spiritual growth? In your own words complete the following sentence:

Mystery is important to me because

I am halfway there,

and I always will be.

We are halfway there and always will be. "Halfway there" declares that the spiritual journey is infinite. The mystery always lies before us, but this is our unlimited potential and possibilities. This is an academic way of expressing a truth, but the soul on fire with God would say, "The best is yet to be!"

It is the way of God's universe. The force of the divine plan is an ascending spiral in which a greater good is always poised and ready to be expressed. The co-founders of the Unity movement, Charles and Myrtle Fillmore, were wonderful expressions of the Christ. They served the world and gave the gift of Unity, but they would be the first to say, "The best is yet to be!"

Jesus demonstrated the truth of being, but even He said that we would do the things that He did and greater. Only a few people are doing a fraction of what Jesus did, but the potential for greater things exists. Why? Because the journey and our potential are infinite.

Is Jesus halfway there? If your answer is yes, support your answer in the space provided. If your answer is no, why would Jesus be the great exception?

Week Thirty-Nine

Summary

In striving to know ourselves, God is a very good place to begin, for it has been written, "In the beginning God . . ." In this section of *A Daily Guide to Spiritual Living,* various statements have declared what we are, but more than intellectual understanding is required if we are to bear witness to the truth of being. Memorization changes our vocabulary, but not the lies we have believed about ourselves.

There must be revelation, a direct encounter with Spirit, a new look at ourselves from God's point of view. And so we open ourselves to this spiritual awakening, but in every person's true birth there is a part of us called Herod who does not want to see. This one resists and wants to fight. Thank God the battle is not ours, but God's. However, we can assist and ready ourselves for the revelation by entering into the eternal now. Only in the current instant can God be found. Patience and persistence are demanded.

The truth is, we are whole regardless of appearances. The image of God lacks nothing. The need is for purification, for as we are cleansed of error and no longer judge by appearances, who we are begins to appear. Experience and expression become one. The simplest thing to say about ourselves is also the truest—I am. We think we have finally arrived, but we are halfway there, and the journey continues.

Return to any day or combination of days that you have not understood or which you think need more work or review. Repeat the lesson(s) as *Week Thirty-Nine*'s work.

Resist the temptation to skip the review and continue with the next section, *"Finding Purpose."* The continuation of the spiritual journey can wait for one more week.

Week 39
Days 267- 273
    continued

In the spaces below write the lessons you chose to review:

Day 267   *Week* _____
                Day _____

Day 268   *Week* _____
                Day _____

Day 269   *Week* _____
                Day _____

Day 270   *Week* _____
                Day _____

Day 271   *Week* _____
                Day _____

Day 272   *Week* _____
                Day _____

Day 273   *Week* _____
                Day _____

Section Four
Finding Purpose

Week Forty
"In the Beginning God . . ."

When our lives were of the earth, everything began with us, with some outer condition, or with an event. But there was no satisfaction. So with divine discontent as our beginning, the spiritual journey began. At first we did not consciously desire a closer walk with God. We wanted solutions to our problems. That was enough for us, or so we thought. Gradually, God's desire for us became our desire for God. We walked the spiritual path consciously. Problems came to us, but so did solutions. Peace and many of the joys of human existence became ours, but one thing was missing—a sense of mission and purpose.

For everyone who knows God, there is purpose. With a meaningful mission to fulfill, there is passion for life and energy to do the work that is ours to do. This is the next step of our journey. It cannot be taken unless God is our beginning.

*I admit I have lived
a life without true purpose.*

Let us admit that we have lived a life without true purpose. The universe is vast, and we are creations of God, but our concern has been for ourselves. We have viewed ourselves as physical beings living in a physical world and have allowed ourselves to be driven to satisfy our base needs. Next we sought the respect of others and tried to find security through the accumulation of wealth. Even while we were pursuing these things, we wondered if this was all there was to life.

Most human beings, particularly as they enter the middle years, ask, "What is the purpose of existence?" Give several examples of what you have thought was your purpose. (Let these come from your past.)

You will discover that your purpose is directly related to what you value. Prioritize four "things" you value most.

1.

2.

3.

4.

I believe life has meaning.

The size of our world is important. If we are little people living in a little, limited world, life will hold little meaning for us. When our concerns are only for ourselves, how can we believe that we make a difference? The meaning of life expands in proportion to the size of our world and the things we value. As we begin to value our planet and the people around us, life becomes significant, and we entertain the possibility that we can make a difference.

If you had to draw a circle that was the size of your world, how many miles across would the circle be?

Who and what would be part of this world?

There is a reason for being.

"Why are we here?" is a question for which there is an answer. People who have a purpose are filled with energy and seem to be directed by an unseen hand. They are invigorated and become more productive as the years go by.

In our society, we tend to believe that we must have certain qualifications before we have purpose or can make a contribution to the common good. Education is valued and considered to be a prerequisite before we can make a difference. History records the accomplishments of the learned, but in some instances their knowledge was faulty. These educated ones had to put aside what they had learned so a discovery could be made. Often, many highly educated people wander aimlessly, for their knowledge has not provided them a reason for being.

Several of Jesus' disciples were educated men, but most of them were without learning. Paul was highly trained, but it was his ability to think and question what he had learned that led him to understand the role of faith in spiritual awakening. And many of the people who grasped the message which took so long for Paul to develop understood his words as soon as he spoke them. We do not have to be educated before we have purpose.

What do you believe to be your reason for being?

God is my beginning.

A wise creator must have a reason for creation. Human beings may believe they were created to live, work, raise children so the race can continue, and then die. If this were true, then our Creator would have little vision. There is a grander plan, and it is unfolding now. Spirit has purpose, and we are the center out of which the purpose unfolds. In truth, without us the divine plan remains only a possibility.

We cannot find our reason for being by giving our attention to the world. Our mission is directly tied to the Creator's reason for creation. Our work is something grand and wonderful beyond belief. Only by turning Godward can we discover our mission. It is best that as we turn to Spirit we do not ask God to tell us our reason for being or to give us some special work to do. Two things are important for us to do today.

First, we turn Godward in a prayerful way.

Second, we admit we do not know our purpose.

There once was a king who met with twelve people of his kingdom every day. These were not dignitaries, but people from tiny villages. The individuals would enter the king's chamber and sit quietly before the monarch. Their instruction was to speak only if the king addressed them. The people who left the presence of the ruler always found peace and a solution to their problems, even though the king never spoke to any of the people. What did the people discover to be their reason for sitting with the king?

(The answer can be found on the next page.)

Answer:

The people discovered that their purpose was to be in the presence of the king. If the king had spoken to the people, they would not have understood the importance of being in the king's presence. This is the way it is with God. Our first reason for being is to be aware that we are in the Presence. While in the Presence, we will find that God has a passion for us. Also, it is important to enter the Presence without an earthly purpose, for then we are more receptive to the God mission we will receive.

God has a passion for me.

Every child hears adults speaking of God. Because the child experiences much of life through sight or hearing, the little one wants to see God or hear God's voice. It must be difficult for children not to be able to see and hear the God that they hear so much about. Many years will pass before the children realize that the unseen Spirit becomes visible as it is expressed by human beings.

The truth is that God seeks expression through each of us. We are the hands, feet, and voice that the children long to hear. For this reason, God has a passion for us. This passion is for union and expression or creativity. We will know the union as love and the expression or creativity as purpose.

There is no specific activity for today other than to open yourself to experience God's passion for you.

I have a passion for God.

With God as our beginning, we discover God has a passion for us. I use the word *passion* to stress how great the Creator's desire for humankind is. Eventually we experience God's love for us as our love for God. In human relationships, the passion we feel for one another leads to union and creativity. Truly, our passion for God is actually God's passion for us surfacing in our souls. Ultimately, this unified desire results in what the mystics call the mystical marriage. From this union, a "child" is born, a God mission is given, and we become a cocreator with God.

The exercise for today is a meditative one. Simply consider the idea that God has a passion for you. Pause at least three times during the day for a ten-minute period and ponder this idea. Also, once every hour for a few brief seconds remind yourself that God loves you and desires the mystical marriage.

God has a mission for me.

There is a purpose and a mission for each of us. We can feel it when we are young. There is something we are to do, but often we do not know what it is. Many people die without knowing their mission. There is a sense of failure, a feeling of void. Life does not need to be this way.

The only reason a person dies without knowing the reason for being is that he or she has not begun with God. When God is the beginning, we say yes to God's love for us, we listen, and there is purpose and meaning. The only way we remain purposeless is to say no to love and to God's passion for us. Who could refuse such an offer?

What are possible reasons why we would say no to love and to God's passion for us?

With God Nothing Is Impossible

A human being, alone and apart from God, will find the simplest task to be impossible or devoid of meaning. A human being in union with God finds nothing impossible and the simplest task sacred. Impossible things are not accomplished by every human being, but throughout the course of history, things that supposedly cannot be done have been accomplished by at least one of us. The feat tells us that there is a way and challenges us not to do the thing, but to discover the way any seemingly impossible task is done.

**Week 41
Day 281**

*Impossible things are not accomplished until I
realize they are Spirit's offer to work with me.*

Is there an impossible task before you now? Has the doctor said you cannot be healed? Have you failed so often in the job market that you no longer believe success is possible? Has every relationship ended with so much anguish that you are afraid to try again?

There are many things that appear impossible to us. We try, but we fail. We seem cursed, but we are blessed. Blessed are those who feel they cannot achieve success, for they can become partners with God.

Impossible tasks are not accomplished by mere human beings, but by human beings who are conscious of their oneness with God. The things we cannot do are Spirit's offer to work with us. For some people a meaningful relationship is impossible, for others, public speaking or the healing of AIDS is impossible.

Perhaps it is true to say that some things are impossible for God. God cannot touch a person's face or kiss a cheek without a human hand. No wonder God has a passion for us. God is love, and love wants to be expressed. God must be loving. However, a person filled with hate cannot gently touch a person's face or tenderly kiss a cheek without a spiritual awakening. In truth, every genuine act of love is in union with Spirit.

If there is an "impossible" task before you, what is it?

If there is an impossible task before you, please know it is God's offer to work with you. Are you willing to join and do the work?

The principle is clear. When we are one with God, nothing is impossible for us. There is a sense of power, but it is not ours. We are the riverbed through which the river flows. We do not direct the course of the river, nor do we know its next bend or when it will rush over rocks and through narrow canyons.

It is said that water is the weakest of substances, but it erodes mountains. Rocks and boulders stand in the midst of rivers, but the water does not resist the stone. It rushes around and over it and eventually wears it smooth. Spirit does not contend. It flows through the channel of least resistance. Our work is to provide the channel. This does not mean we are to carve the riverbed through the canyon. Every mighty river carves its own bed. Sometime with rivers like the Mississippi the bed is enormous, and over the course of years it wanders through valleys that are miles across. However, there was a beginning, a tiny rivulet high in the mountains. If the river of Spirit is to flow through us and do its mighty work, we must be willing.

Our work is to desire union with God. This is a tiny beginning, but it is all that God needs. As Spirit expresses itself, our souls expand, and impossible tasks are done.

Your task for today is to be willing to be unified with God. How will you do this?

*Today I do something
I have never done before.*

Today, do something you have never done before. However, do not simply do the thing. Before you act, sit quietly in prayer and meditation and let God be the beginning. Beginning with God is not complicated. It is a matter of being willing to experience the Presence.

There is one more thing to know. A person may not consciously feel the Presence before beginning a task. Open yourself to union, and then act with courage and boldness. With the first step, realize God is with you.

What thing have you chosen to do today that you have never done before? Realize that because of your beginning you are inviting Spirit to work with you.

Your natural state is wholeness. No physical condition can change the truth that you are a spiritual being, whole and complete. This innate wholeness generates what we call a healing when we are one with God.

Our doctors may tell us a disease is incurable, but even as they speak, researchers are trying to find a cure, and eventually they will. One disease after another has succumbed to this method. However, there are people who cannot wait for a medical breakthrough. They need help now, and it is available.

With God nothing is impossible. Our natural state is wholeness. This breakthrough requires a willing soul rather than a team of researchers. God first, next a consciousness of wholeness, and then a healing happens.

Today, whether you are sick or not, let a consciousness of wholeness be your purpose. One thing must not get in your way as you open yourself to this discovery. Let there be no attempt to heal your body. Spiritual healing, the kind of healing Jesus shared with the world, may have resulted in bodily healing, but healing was not the issue. What was the issue?

Answer: A consciousness of wholeness was the issue.

With God,
love is possible.

Let us make a distinction between the two words *reason* and *purpose*. The *reason* for doing something comes from outside of us. For instance, pain motivates us to action. We want to be healed. The *purpose* for doing something comes from within us. Pain may be the reason we act, but our purpose is greater than wanting to be healed. We want to realize our spiritual wholeness.

With humans relationships are possible, but they may not be the kind we desire. With God love is possible, and powerful, peaceful, harmonious relationships naturally result.

Love is God's purpose. All the forces of the universe have been conceived in a way that promotes the expression of love. Love is natural for us, but first there must be God, then a consciousness of love, and finally, love's manifestation. The truth is that love is not possible without God, for God *is* love.

As you move through the fourth quarter of this book, you are moving toward your purpose or God mission. In order to discover your mission, your highest purpose and God's must be one. When it comes to love, what is your purpose?

There is a difference between what we want and what we need. A man made this distinction an opportunity of growth for his son. Whenever the boy expressed a desire for something, he was asked whether the "item" was a want or a need. By definition a toy would be a want, while a need was something necessary for life on the planet. What the boy discovered was that there were only a few things that he needed, but that life was filled with many wants.

We desire security, and it is as needful for the soul as air is for the body. When we are in human consciousness, we believe security comes from acquisition. We get a good job, and then we are secure. Next, we need to provide for our retirement, so we look for benefits and try to amass wealth in the form of securities, stocks, land, and so forth. Some people achieve these financial goals, but discover they have not achieved security. Security is one dimension of the gift of God's presence. Everyone who travels the spiritual path remembers a time when the outer world was bleak. We may have lost our job or experienced a loss in the stock market. Famine was in the land, but the soul was rich.

We felt secure, even though there was no apparent stability in our outer world. This is the kind of security that is possible with God. And it does not remain just a feeling, for through the law of mind action this consciousness manifests itself as a prospering idea, an opportunity, a new job, and so forth.

Have you ever experienced this kind of security? For an image that will give you insight into what it is like, read Psalm 23. In your opinion, which of the verses best expresses a security founded in Spirit?

With God, peace is possible.

A young woman was greatly troubled about a decision she had to make, for it would determine the direction of her life. She went to her mother for advice. Her mother told her of a secret garden in the mountains where wildflowers bloomed and pure waters flowed from an eternal spring. The young woman was told that what she desired could be found in that place. The daughter asked for directions to the garden, but her mother smiled and told her she did not know the way. The young woman then asked her mother to describe the garden, and as she did, the daughter saw it in her mind. There she found what she was seeking. Peace.

What does the garden represent? Please answer in five words or less.

(A good help in answering this question is to close your eyes and see in your mind's eye the mountain garden filled with wildflowers. Then ask it what it represents.)

Answer: The garden represents God's presence.

Week Forty-Two
What God Can Do . . .

People believe God can do anything. However, most people also believe that Spirit is not doing all it can do and must be spurred to action. Prayers must be offered, bargains struck, and promises fulfilled; then the Almighty will perform the miracle. This is not true.

Joel Goldsmith, world-renowned teacher and writer, said, "What God can do, God is doing." Spirit does not go on vacation, take days off, or decline to do its work. From the human perspective, there is so much that needs to be done. If God is doing all that can be done, we surmise, then we are in peril. We think we must find a way to make God act. There are diseases to cure, wars to end, and mouths to feed. We prod our reluctant God with bargains, praise, prayers, promises, and guilt trips.

Our methods seem endless and will not cease until we understand there is no disease, war, or famine in God. The need is not for us to spur God to action, but for us to discover what God is doing.

God is being . . .

God is being life, and when we know this, the blind see and the lame walk.

God is being love, and when we know this, guilt is no more, hatred ends, forgiveness abounds, and we obey the only commandment Jesus gave us: "Love one another" (Jn. 15:17).

God is being wisdom, and when we know this, our thinking is clear and our decisions are wise.

God is being supply, and when we know this, the deserts bloom, and those who thirst find eternal springs.

God is being peace, and when we know this, wars cease and the lion and the lamb lie down together.

God is being life.

Charles Fillmore said that God is more than alive or living; God is life itself and has many expressions. Spirit-life expresses itself as the great blue whale, the birds that fly, the seemingly ageless redwoods of California and the olive trees of Israel. Life's expression is all around us, some manifestations so small that they can only be seen with a microscope and others so large that we have to step back in order to see clearly.

The life that animates the plants and animals and us is divine and cannot be seen with the human eye, but must be perceived with a faith-filled mind. We are never without life. Even when the soul departs the body and our family and friends say we have died, we are alive. Actually, we are more than alive, we are life.

God is being life, and it is time we stop asking God to do more than this. Let us awaken to what God is "doing."

What will a walk in the woods be like when you awaken to the truth that all you witness is a manifestation of God being life?

If you are sick and awaken to the truth that God is being your life, what will happen?

If a loved one has died and you awaken to the truth that God remains the life of your dear one, what will be your experience?

411

God is being love.

Charles Fillmore said that God is more than loving; God is love itself and has many expressions. In some ways, a child's love of a pet or a stuffed animal is divine love moving through the little one. Certainly the oneness of two good friends has a divine origin. A man and a woman ideally are wed not so much because they love each other, but because they are allowing the love of God within them to be expressed.

God is being love, and it is time to stop asking God to be more than this. What could we ask that would improve upon God being love? A spiritual life is lived when we place demands upon ourselves rather than Spirit. God is doing all that God can do, but it is enough. We must become aware of the implications of what God is doing.

When you become aware that God is being love, how will this change your human relationships?

When you accept the idea that God is being love, how will this transform your view of yourself?

If you hold resentment toward another person will the truth that God is being love help you forgive? If you answer yes, how?

God is being wisdom.

Charles Fillmore said that God is more than wise; God is wisdom. Wherever there is any expression of intelligence, the mind of God is expressing itself. The whales and birds that migrate are guided by divine wisdom. The plants turn to the sun because of an inner light. Human beings think and decide upon matters, not because they are wise, but because God is being wisdom.

As human beings, we often ask God to tell us what to do or to give us the answer. Answers and guidance come, but it is not because God gives the answer. Giving answers and guidance is not what God does. Remember, God is being wisdom. As we awaken to the light of God, we experience a sense of guidance or an idea.

Please remember that when you awaken to the truth that God is being wisdom, there is nothing you cannot know.

Give five ways that a consciousness of God being wisdom can manifest itself in your life:

1.

2.

3.

Week 42
Day 291
continued

4.

5.

Possible answers:
1. As an idea
2. As a still small voice
3. As a thought
4. As a feeling or hunch
5. As knowledge that you are to go to someone or some place, and there you will find your answer

414

God is being the source.

Many people have the realization that God is more than the giver; God is the gift. This is true, but countless thousands of people ignore this truth. We are consistently wanting God to do something for us. We want Spirit to give us a job or provide a certain amount of money. God cannot do these things. Let this insight not cause us dismay but encourage us to act in a different way.

God is being our source. What else could we want? The wisdom of God has designed a universe so that when we become aware of our source, it manifests itself in our lives. The source does not need to do anything other than be what it is. We must find it. Let us not search the world for what is within us. A state of mind is not found in a distant land. It is part of us. This is the way of our source. The fountainhead of all good overflows into our lives when we are aware that God is our source. How it will manifest itself is none of our business. Our business is to continue to know that God is being the fountainhead.

When you first know that God is your source, how will this knowledge manifest itself in your life?

Answer: A consciousness of God as source first manifests itself as a sense of security. At this point nothing in the outer world will change. Ideas, opportunities, new jobs, and so forth come to be as we continue to give our attention to Spirit as source.

God is being peace.

For too long we have been looking for peace to come. World peace is "established" through war and maintained through "strength." Inner peace "comes" by our taking charge of our lives and having things conform to our vision of the way they should be. How correct this appears, but how incorrect it is.

Wars do not establish peace, nor do weapons maintain harmony. Peace is not coming, nor is the peace of God established when things go our way. Some people would argue with this, but the basis of the disagreement is that there are two kinds of peace. There is the peace of the world which comes and goes, and there is the peace of God which is and ever will be. "Peace I leave with you; my peace I give to you; not as the world gives do I give to you" (Jn. 14:27).

Something is being offered to us, but we have been unable to receive it. Let us assume that the gift has already been given. Peace is ours; it is part of us now.

How will you receive the gift of peace that is being offered to you?

God does not need to act;
I need to remember what God is doing.

There is peace in knowing that what God can do, God is doing. There is also new direction. God is being love, life, wisdom, peace, and our source. What else can we ask? This is enough, and this is evidence of Spirit's infinite wisdom.

However, the facts remain. Disease, famine, and war exist, and these are only some of the challenges that face humankind. The tendency is for us to do something about these problems. Sometimes they seem too great for us, and therefore we enlist God's aid. Now we know this method does not cure our diseases, feed hungry children, or bring peace, for what God can do, God is doing. Does this mean we are helpless?

We are far from helpless. We simply have a new mission. There is no war in the kingdom of heaven—no famine, sickness, or anxiety. Our mission is to remember what God is doing—being. As we allow ourselves to become aware of Spirit's work, *our earthly mission becomes apparent.* Spirit's way is always the same. We make contact with God, and then we are told what to do. Without a doubt, the God-directed things we do will help rid the world of its problems. Our earthly missions will be varied, but our work will be to remember what God is doing.

Do you have a difficulty in your life? If you do, how will you apply the principles above to the challenge?

Week Forty-Three
The Apprentice

Jesus said to them, "Truly, truly, I say to you, the Son can do nothing of his own accord, but only what he sees the Father doing; for whatever he does, that the Son does likewise. For the Father loves the Son, and shows him all that he himself is doing; and greater works than these will he show him" (Jn. 5:19-20). In these verses, Jesus is revealing an aspect of our relationship to God—that of apprentice to master craftsman. At first, an apprentice learns the basic principles of an art form, but eventually the more subtle and intricate skills are revealed by the master.

If we are to contribute creatively to humankind, we must learn the intricate, subtle, and seemingly mysterious ways of the "Master." We have thought the Creator's work was varied, doing this and that, but now we know that God's work is being. Likewise, this is what we must "do." Only through apprenticeship may we do the creative work of Spirit. We may want to act and try our hand at creating the masterpiece, but it is best that our first work be observation.

God's work is creation.

God's work is not maintenance. It is creation. The healing of the body is a good example of God's sacred work. Human beings see something to fix—a broken bone to mend or eyesight to restore. As a broken bone is mended or eyesight restored, there appears to be improvement, but this is not true. The spiritual integrity of the person is as it has always been. The individual is whole. Broken bones and physical blindness do not change the truth of our being. As we become aware of this truth, creative forces are loosed and a pattern of perfection is made manifest. This is not maintenance; it is creativity.

Our world is faced with many challenges. In the past, there was an energy crisis. Wise people declared there was no shortage of energy, only ideas. Disease calls us to creativity. The devastation of fire, wind, and earthquake calls us to creativity. Let us not think our work is restoration and maintenance. We, like our Creator, must be creative.

What have you thought God needed to fix in the world?

What have you thought God needed to fix in your life?

Remember, God's work is creation!

My work is creativity.

The work of all human beings is creativity. The apprentice must do what he or she sees the master doing. We are not to fix ourselves, others, or situations. Our work, like that of the Master, is creativity. As we enter into creation, we perceive ourselves, others, and situations differently.

Creativity calls for new thinking and actions never tried before. We can try harder at times, but on other occasions it is best to start over again. Thomas Carlyle wrote *The French Revolution* and asked his friend, John Stuart Mill, to read it for him and to give him his opinion of the work. Mr. Mill's maid thought the manuscript was worthless and used it to start a fire in the fireplace. Mr. Carlyle was distraught at first, but eventually he wrote the version of *The French Revolution* we have today. What would have happened if Thomas Carlyle had tried to reconstruct his work from the ashes? No amount of fixing would have restored the document.

When we think in terms of maintenance and fixing, we achieve ordinary results, but when we open ourselves to creativity, the results are extraordinary. This is the work of the master craftsman.

People and things I have tried to fix:

Isn't it interesting how they keep breaking down and needing to be fixed again?

I have much to learn.

Nearly everyone has been to a museum and walked through the modern art gallery thinking, "I could do this." Some have actually tried it, but when they stepped back from the canvas, their "masterpieces" were not what they hoped to see.

A true work of art evokes something deep in us. Our positive response to the piece comes when we consciously or unconsciously see something in the artist's work that is within us. Therefore, a part of ourselves must make its way to the canvas. All of this leads to the conclusion that we have much to learn. An apprentice who "knows it all" will not learn the master's secrets.

Become as a child and ask questions about the things that mystify you. For instance, how do birds fly? How can a seed beneath a sidewalk break the concrete and grow? List seven questions:

1.

2.

3.

4.

5.

6.

7.

Creativity comes from within me.

God works His art in a child as well as in a Michelangelo. Whenever something fresh and new comes from within us, there is creativity. It can be a child's drawing of a pet or a silly rhyming poem. Work is performed, but suddenly, in a flash, the revelation comes.

The wellspring of ideas and innovation available to us is beyond comprehension. Let us do our work so God's wisdom can be expressed in our lives and upon the planet. Not only will we be blessed, but others will benefit too. Creativity comes suddenly, but there is no overnight success. A man carrying a violin case asked a New York police officer how to get to Carnegie Hall. The policeman looked at the young man and his violin case and said, "Practice, practice, practice."

Years of practice are required to become competent in any skill. A composer first learns to play the piano. Later, this skill will become available to an indwelling wisdom so it can reveal to humankind the harmony and rhythm of the Infinite. The composer is willing to allow something new to come from within. This willingness and the learned skill of piano playing are joined so a new creation can come to be. As the "child is born," the composer begins to hear with an inner ear the notes that are placed on paper.

All that you need, and all that God can provide for you, will come from within you. This is the heart of the creative process. It is important that you allow this to happen. Your activity for today is to write a poem of at least twelve lines on a subject of your choice. Record it on the following page:

Week 43
Day 298
continued

Today I observe the Master at work.

The apprentice's work begins with observation. The student must see
what the master is doing. In the restored colonial town of Williamsburg,
Virginia, craftsmen carry on the creative works of the past as they were
performed hundreds of years ago. The people making furniture, pewter
mugs, and muskets and printing newspapers and books are willing to tell
the visitors how the work is done. A person could probably spend hours
watching and listening, but eventually that person would want to try his or
her hand at creation.

Become the apprentice today and observe one of God's simple acts of
creation. Find a restful place outside or sit by a window and watch carefully
what is occurring around you. Perhaps you will watch the weather, the
snow or rain falling. Maybe you will observe a butterfly emerging from a
cocoon, or study tiny insects in search of food. You will not duplicate these
tasks, but you will become aware of the fact that creation is around you.
This is enough for today, for the initial work of the apprentice is to observe
and appreciate creativity.

*Creativity is more
than the work of the hands.*

Let us remember that God's work is being. The world and our lives may be filled with activity, but creativity is not a matter of doing. Still, it is possible for simple, seemingly mundane tasks to be creative and sacred. The determining factor is contact with Spirit. When we are aware of God, what we do is sacred. We can be at rest or slicing bread and be brimming with creativity. Remember, God first, then action.

To our storehouse of understanding we can now add: Creativity comes from contact with God. How mistaken we are when we think that some forms of work are more noble than others. Work is neither noble nor unimportant. Work simply is, but the consciousness out of which any task is performed is important.

Every new religion has had God as its beginning. The first work is sacred, and there is much creativity. As the years go by, creativity can wane unless there is renewed contact with Spirit. Religions die because the followers do not make themselves available to God. Whenever there is contact with God, new ideas abound, and age-old religions are as fresh as the day they began.

Creativity is more than the work of our hands. We can create beautiful drawings or mold precious metals into jewelry, but there is no creativity without contact with Spirit.

What skills do you need to learn to be more available to Spirit?

Today is a sacred day.

Today can be a Sacred Day, and the work we perform, no matter what it is, can be God's work if we make contact with God. In fact, if we can maintain our conscious oneness with God, our work will be sacred and our day filled with meaning and joy.

How will you structure your day so you can maintain your availability to the Presence?

You may find the following things helpful in maintaining contact with God.

1. Begin your appointments with five minutes of silence.

2. Space appointments so there is ample time between them to become still and centered in God.

3. Pause throughout the day for times of prayer and meditation.

4. Enjoy monastic moments. (Please refer to the exercise given during *Week 20, Day 139.*)

Week Forty-Four
It Is Not I . . .

"Jesus answered them, 'My Father is working still, and I am working' " (Jn. 5:17). The Father's work is never done, and neither is ours. The desires we feel, traced to the core of our being, reveal that Spirit wants to express itself as each of us. This is God's work, and therefore it is natural. Spirit does not struggle to do its work, but our consent is required.

In most homes, water is always available. All we have to do is turn the faucet, and the water flows into the basin. We might live in perpetual thirst if we did not turn the handle and allow the water to flow. Spirit is always being ("My Father is working still"), but if Spirit is to express itself as us, we must do our work too ("and I am working").

I of myself can do nothing.

On the surface, there seems much that we can and do accomplish. Some people say we are powerful beings, others talk of empowerment. Let us not become too puffed up about what we can do. The truth is, we of ourselves can do nothing. Divine life and wisdom animate the body and the mind, and without the "assistance" of Spirit, we could not even pick up a piece of straw. From time to time we are injured and discover not our power, but our powerlessness.

If we are to discover our mission and purpose, let us not assume that it is our work. The revelation of the mission is God's work; the fulfillment of the mission is our work. This we can do if first there is contact with Spirit. Remember, God's work cannot be done without God.

List those things that you consider to be the major accomplishments of your life:

What qualities were necessary to accomplish each one? (For instance, writing a book might require wisdom and strength or persistence. Demonstrating forgiveness would require love and letting go of ill feelings.)

Aren't these qualities aspects of God? Could you have accomplished what "you" did without them?

When I exalt myself,
I am humbled.

There is a law of life stated by Jesus, "Every one who exalts himself will be humbled, but he who humbles himself will be exalted" (Lk. 18:14). The story of David and Goliath found in 1 Samuel 17 illustrates this principle.

Let us join David as he stands before Goliath and listens to the giant's thundering voice shout to him of how the birds will soon eat his flesh. David replies, "You come to me with a sword and with a spear and with a javelin; but I come to you in the name of the Lord of hosts, the God of the armies of Israel, whom you have defied. This day the Lord will deliver you into my hand" (1 Sam. 17:45-46).

Please note that as David stands before the Philistine champion, he does not rely upon his skill with the sling, although it is considerable. David's trust is in God. Goliath exalts himself and is rendered powerless. These are lessons we must learn.

Give an example from your life in which you exalted yourself and were humbled:

In the eighth chapter of John, there is an account of a woman caught in adultery who was brought to Jesus by the scribes and Pharisees. The Jewish law stated that the woman must be stoned to death, and the religious leaders were prepared to carry out the sentence. Their minds were filled with thoughts of death, and Jesus knew their intent.

Jesus made Himself small by bending down and writing on the ground. The physical act of stooping denotes humility. Obviously, it would not have been healthy to stand and argue with a group of men who intended to kill the woman. Jesus' exaltation came as wise words, "Let him who is without sin among you be the first to throw a stone at her" (Jn. 8:7).

Making ourselves small, or being nonresistant, is an act of humility. Whenever we act in this way, we invite the lifting, transforming, exalting power of God into our lives.

However, as one popular song goes, "It's hard to be humble." No one tries to be humble. The "it is not I" way of life grows out of an understanding that God is the one Presence and one Power. Also, there is a difference between being humbled and humbling ourselves. Basically, when we are humbled, we have exalted ourselves and reaped a bitter fruit. We have been brought to our knees and, oddly enough, from this position we usually see more clearly. When we have humbled ourselves, we are honest about our shortcomings and powerlessness and are aware of the one Presence and one Power.

The first step of the twelve steps of Alcoholics Anonymous stresses this idea. "We admitted that we were powerless over alcohol—that our lives had become unmanageable." The admission of powerlessness is the beginning of exaltation.

What is it that you are powerless over?

Week 44
Day 304
continued

Through Christ I can do all things.

Much is accomplished in partnership with God. We realize that God is the foreman of the project, and we are able co-workers. The work is immense and beyond our human comprehension. We will be asked to do things we never dreamed possible. The results will exceed what visionaries can foresee. The apostle Paul's work was this way.

The newness of Spirit can be endless when we remember who does the work and what is possible. With God, all things are possible. The primary requirement is that we allow the spirit of God to be individualized as us. The Christ appears once more in earthly form. Once again, the lame walk, the blind see, and stormy waters are calmed.

Is a sense of mission beginning to come from within you? If it is, describe what you feel and what is making itself known:

It is not I,
but the Christ within who does the work.

In the eleventh chapter of Matthew, Jesus says, "Take my yoke upon you, and learn from me; for I am gentle and lowly in heart, and you will find rest for your souls. For my yoke is easy, and my burden is light" (Mt. 11:29-30). The people to whom Jesus spoke understood the meaning of these words, for they had seen in their fields the yoke made easy. In the field there would be an ox or other beast of burden. A woman would be yoked to the animal as the field was being plowed. Most families could not afford two oxen, but the yoke was often for two animals. Therefore it was necessary for someone to be yoked to the animal for balance. The burden would be light, but the person yoked would be contributing much to the work being done.

This image can be expressed in these words, "It is not I, but the Christ within who does the work." Prayer is continuous in Silent Unity, Unity School of Christianity's worldwide prayer ministry. At the top of the prayer service these words are written: It is not I, but the Christ within who does the work.

Before you perform any task today, pause for a few moments and say to yourself: *It is not I, but the Christ within who does the work.* Then forge ahead with the task at hand.

Why do you call me good?

There was an event in Jesus' life in which a ruler called Him good. Jesus took exception to this and said to the man, "Why do you call me good? No one is good but God alone" (Lk. 18:19). This is an important point.

The qualities that we admire in a person are grounded in Spirit. They rise up and manifest themselves because the person experiences oneness with God. No one exhibits true peace and joy without contact with the Presence. These qualities are not our own. For instance, a large picture window allows us to look within and see the beauty and treasures of the household. We do not call the window beautiful or priceless. These words are reserved for what is within. Jesus' consciousness of God allowed humankind to see the beauty and pricelessness of Spirit which is within each of us.

When we are with someone we admire, let us be aware that the love or peace is not of the person; it is of God. The individual is the window through which we see what is within. Rejoice not in the person, but in the fact that God has made us so that the presence of God can be made known on earth.

Who do you know that is a clear window providing you a glimpse of the kingdom of heaven?

Realize that what you see is within you.

Without conscious oneness with Spirit,
the sacred work cannot be done.

Every human being is potentially able to do Spirit's sacred work. In truth, we are made so we can be the hands, feet, and mouthpiece of Spirit. However, Spirit does not force itself upon us. Spirit is willing, but we must be willing too.

Our fulfillment comes when we are consciously one with God. Then there is a mission for us which fulfills the divine will and gives our lives meaning. No longer do we take from the earth; we are a giver. Through our hands and mouths, Spirit gives itself to the world.

Are you willing to fulfill your destiny? Are you willing to be God's hands, feet, and mouthpiece? To say yes is to renew your commitment to become conscious of your oneness with Spirit. It is this simple and this complex. First there is contact with God, then there is your God mission and fulfillment. Write a statement that expresses your commitment:

Week Forty-Five
Here I Am, Lord

We of ourselves can do nothing that has enduring value. Only Spirit's work endures. All else will pass away.

God's work is being and so is ours, but as we enter into a consciousness of Spirit, the consciousness manifests itself in concrete, tangible ways. A God mission emerges for each of us, and when it does we find purpose and meaning. The lessons in this book, although focused upon many varied facets of life, have prepared you for your mission. *Week Forty-Five* is your final makeready before you discover your life's work. In many ways, you will cry out to God, "Here am I! Send me" (Is. 6:8).

My first purpose is conscious contact with Spirit.

As we move toward our God mission and the discovery of purpose, it cannot be stressed enough that our initial work is conscious contact with Spirit. The beginning is always God consciousness. Before the sacred work can be done, a spiritual being must be awake to his or her true nature and potential.

Our understanding of this principle is illustrated through action. There are times of daily prayer and meditation, periodic retreat times, monastic moments, and other activities that declare our practice of the presence of God. As we participate in these helpful practices, we discover that "things" within us rise up so they can be released. A suppressed anger or sense of guilt may emerge. A feeling of unworthiness may come into the light. This is part of our purification process, our letting go. These things have blocked our growth and Spirit's ability to use us fully.

What has come into your conscious mind that needs to be released since beginning the *"Finding Purpose"* section of this book?

I am willing to let go of
what I thought was my mission.

Many of us feel we know the purpose of our life, and we are pursuing it. Work is important to us and so is family. We want to succeed, make money, find security, raise and live in harmony with our family, help other people, and so forth. But no matter what our purpose or mission has been, let it now be released.

Declare: *I am willing to let go of what I thought was my mission.* In some instances, we will realize that our reason for being was shallow. Others may feel that their mission was noble and a true God mission. This may be true, but before something new can come, there must be no clinging to the past.

Declare: *As of this moment, I have no mission or purpose. If my life is to have meaning, I must do God's work.*

*Part of my current life-style stands
between me and my God mission.*

Many months ago when the journey just began, we called for change. Changes have occurred, and we have been in transition for months. Now if more change is required, it will be done. We have begun with God, and God will see us through. The changes that must be are now unfolding.

Part of our current life-style stands between us and our God mission. We are willing to let it go. This may cause dramatic change, but it is for God's glory and will ultimately be a blessing for us.

Is there anything about your life-style that stands between you and your God mission? (Perhaps some of your eating or drinking habits must change, or you must change the way you react to people or problems. Perhaps your challenges lie in compulsive work habits, human relationships, the area of forgiveness, or other areas of your life.) Use this space to explore this question.

As we draw near to the time when we will discover our purpose, let us not ask God what we are to do. God is not destined to serve us. God has not said to us, "Here I am, send me forth to do your bidding." It is we who will say, "Here we are, use us."

Our purpose is to make ourselves available to God. As we experience the Presence, what we are to do will become evident. Do not look initially for some grand work. Most likely, our guidance will be to do some simple thing that seems of little consequence.

Once there was an extremely gifted researcher. She had high marks in her training and was declared most likely to succeed by her peers. The faculty nodded their approval. This young woman went to her first research assignment at one of the great research centers in our nation. She was assigned to the senior research scientist who gave her mundane tasks to do. She was not assigned the problems for which there seemed to be no answer. She was distraught over this, and after a time the gifted researcher made an appointment with her advisor to talk about her feelings and concerns.

The advisor said that he had been waiting for this meeting. He had purposely assigned his gifted student mundane tasks because he wanted her to realize that although the answer to a problem can be a breakthrough for humankind, it usually is preceded by years of tedious and often mundane experiments and results. Unless she was comfortable with these things, she could not fulfill her potential.

It is helpful to understand that our current efforts or work are part of a greater whole which no one can envision. We have the capacity to do with joy and enthusiasm whatever it is we do. God missions are given to those individuals who can approach the mundane and challenging task in the same way.

What is your earthly work right now?

Is it mundane or challenging?

Are you approaching it with joy and enthusiasm?

There is usually much preparation before we begin our God mission and find our reason for being. Remember, Paul prepared for fourteen years before he embarked upon his missionary voyages. Jesus was thirty years old before He began His ministry. No one knows the preparation that Jesus and Paul went through, but there are always inner and sometimes outer skills to be learned before we can do Spirit's work.

Basically, our preparation is in the area of consciousness. In other words, we must allow our thoughts, attitudes, and feelings to be altered so that the work can be done. We can have sudden revelations of the Presence, but our souls evolve slowly, and hopefully steadily, over the course of our lives. To use an analogy we have used before: this is the cleansing of the window, so that the light can shine from within and others can see the Christ doing its work.

Along with this inner work, there are often earthly skills to be learned. Some people learn to speak, others to sing; some design buildings, counsel others, paint, inspire people, develop organizational skills, acquire education, write, and so forth. Spirit has utilized, for its glory and purpose, every skill that has ever been learned by a human being.

Is there some skill you feel you are to learn? If you feel there is, what is this skill?

What steps have you taken to acquire this skill?

It may be that you will be unable to fulfill your life's work until this skill is learned. If money is a factor, then your first step is not to acquire funds, but to unfold a consciousness of giving and security which will manifest itself as ideas or opportunities.

Preparation for our God mission extends beyond learning new skills and altering our life-styles. We are willing to grow and change in order to be a co-worker with God. If forgiveness is demanded of us, it will be done. If we must give up guilt and love ourselves, it will be done. We are willing to attempt new things and venture into territory we have avoided in the past. These things take time, so we are patient with ourselves. Like Paul, let us take fourteen years if that is what is required.

People who aspire to be ministers and to serve humankind in this unique way quickly find that before they can help others, they must be committed to the discovery of their own wholeness. In recent years, we have seen immensely gifted ministers who have helped thousands, but who have demonstrated their humanness and lost the respect of the public. In each instance, these wounded healers ignored their hurts until the pain became too great. Let us not condemn them. From a human perspective, their fault was a failure to allow themselves to be healed. From God's viewpoint, they refused Spirit's offer to reveal to them their wholeness.

We will not make this mistake. The God mission is too important. We are willing to be healed, willing to know our innate wholeness.

What is your healing need?

What steps are you willing to take to allow Spirit to reveal to you your wholeness?

"Here am I! Send me."

Through the activities of this week, you have come to the point where you can say, "Here am I! Send me" (Is. 6:8). This statement is more than words. It declares a state of readiness.

We are willing to put our faith in God.

We eagerly enter into the mystery.

We are able to do the simplest task with joy and enthusiasm.

We do what we do for God's glory.

We do what we do because we are guided to do it.

Please add four more lines in keeping with those written above:

Week Forty-Six
My God Mission

Our mission is to know God and to bear witness to the truth. But why? Is this the total of what we are to be and do? The answer is yes, but there is more. Any consciousness will manifest itself in our world. First, there will generally be feelings, thoughts, or images. Then there will be a corresponding change in the body. Finally, manifestation will take place in the earthly condition. This principle of manifestation is continuously at work in our lives. This week's insights and activities are an invitation for a *consciousness of God* to be made manifest in our lives. We will be blessed, but God is not given to one person. Wherever God appears, everyone can be blessed, for the one who is aware of God works for the common good.

A man whose livelihood is selling secondhand furniture and goods said that his store is a front for God. Beds and couches are sold, but this is not his real business. His work is God's work. It is being love, being peace, being joy . . . These are the greater goods that the people receive when they come to buy the used furniture. Undoubtedly, there are other people on earth who sell secondhand goods, but how many of these people see their store as a front for God?

Most likely you have a job, or at least your days are filled with activity. This can be more than it appears. A God mission is a potential part of everything you do.

God can use me right where I am.

God can use you right where you are. Where you are is more than a place; your "house" is a state of consciousness made up of beliefs, attitudes, and feelings. As your state of mind becomes a state of oneness with God, you find purpose. This purpose releases from within you hidden talents and energies. Resources pour forth, making possible God's work.

The first step in the God mission is finding meaning in your current work. It is true that as your consciousness develops, your life's direction may change drastically, but do not expect this at first. The people who are doing God's work are employed in every area of human endeavor. They are teachers, construction workers, truck drivers, administrators, and real estate agents. People who love God are everywhere.

You will know these people when you meet them. Have you ever met such a person? If you have, who was it, and what did he or she do for a living?

Today as you go about your activities, open yourself to meeting one of God's workers whom you have never met before. Remember to allow God to use you right where you are. Be a special influence in someone's life today.

Work does not cause me to lose sight of my first purpose.

Our daily work can be filled with an awareness of the Presence, but we can also give so much attention to our work that we are not aware of God. When this occurs, we have lost sight of our purpose. The job seems paramount, but it is not. No truly important work is done unless God is the beginning of what we do.

Thousands, if not millions, of people are trying to get ahead. Success as the world describes it has seduced them, and their sense of purpose is shallow: climb the corporate ladder, make money, or retire early. These things may be part of our quest, but they must have their proper place. Doing these things must not cause us to lose sight of who we are. Our life is a gift given so we can bear witness to the truth. When something else becomes all-consuming, our life is without meaning.

Was there a time in your life when work was everything? What was it like? How did it feel? What was your purpose at that time in your life?

What is your first purpose?

All work is simple to God.

It is said that we are challenged only with that which we can overcome. Likewise, we are given to do only that which we are capable of doing. To us one task seems more difficult and more important than another. This is not true. All work is simple to God.

Sir Christopher Wren was walking through a construction site. The workers did not know that this man was the force behind the cathedral which was being built. Mr. Wren asked one man what he was doing. He replied, "I am making a shilling a day." Another worker was asked the same question. "I am building a wall," he said. A third worker was asked the same question. He stood proudly and said, "I am helping Sir Christopher Wren build the greatest cathedral in the world." This man had purpose, and it transcended making money and building walls.

Spirit has the grand vision. All work is simple to God. It either contributes to the spiritual unfoldment of humankind, or it does not. The determining factor is not the nature of the work, but the vision of the worker.

Do the work that is before you with joy. As you do this, you will sense the true nature of the work you do. Then you are worthy of more responsibility.

What is your work? Please answer this question in twenty-five words or less.

What determines the value of your work?

We have two God missions: one is knowing God, and the other is doing our current work with joy and for God's glory. Even if we are unemployed, these missions can be fulfilled.

Please realize that it is natural for Spirit to individualize itself. If you open yourself to an expression of divine will, you will be given a sacred work to do. The two missions that have been outlined today are the prelude to a third mission.

What are you currently doing to fulfill your mission of knowing God?

What is the evidence that you are performing your current tasks with joy and for God's glory?

 **Week 46**
Day 320

I am becoming aware of my God-given talents and natural inclinations.

Spirit is always trying to communicate with us. The attempts are made in many ways. Our natural inclinations and heartfelt desires can be Spirit leading us to a God mission.

People often speak of a sense of aimlessness. They want to contribute and do some work with enthusiasm, but they do not know what to do. Usually, they feel limited. These people should put aside what they think is limitation by asking a question of themselves: "If I could do anything—with money, education, and skills being no problem—what would it be?"

As people answer this question, they get in touch with their natural talents and inclinations. In many instances, our talents and inclinations are trying to lead the way to fulfillment.

What are your God-given talents? Are you a good listener? Can you write or sing? Are you good with children or with your hands?

What are your natural inclinations? Do you like the out-of-doors? Children? Reading? Speaking? Listening? Are you drawn to the sea or the mountains?

What would you do if you could do anything?

I am willing to serve.

As we march toward our third God mission, let us add another key word—*service*. The things we do are not for us alone; they are for God's glory and the common good. We are not islands. We are connected to one another so closely that we are not totally free and fulfilled unless all of us are free.

Now is the time to be open to guidance. We do not ask God to tell us what to do, but by being receptive to Spirit and willing to serve, guidance comes. And the guidance becomes our mission. We will do what we are told. If it requires developing a talent, we will develop it. If it means pursuing our natural inclinations, we will do so.

Dear friend, today is a day of listening. Think of being with a friend high on a mountain overlooking a seaport. You are looking for a way down the mountain so that you can be with the people. You are going to serve them. Look carefully and you will see your friend point the way.

What directions were you given?

Once purpose and meaning come to our lives and our mission is clear, it can be lost. However, it need never be permanently lost. Most professional sports are also the games children play. When we are young, we play for fun. Winning is secondary to playing. Later, the joy of the child may leave us, and what was once fun can become work, something we do to support ourselves and our family.

During these times, it is good to become like a child again. Remember how natural it was when we began to make God consciousness the purpose of our lives? If we have lost sight of our mission, we must return to knowing God and performing our current task with joy. From this awareness will come renewed enthusiasm. The purpose and meaning that seemed so far away are actually close at hand. A Godward glance, and we are home again.

Remember today's lesson. You may need to return to it many years from now.

Week Forty-Seven
For God's Glory

Always remember that a God mission is for God's glory. People may heap praise upon us, but let us remember that what we do is for God's glory.

In Jesus' Sermon on the Mount, there is an interesting verse of Scripture, "Let your light so shine before men, that they may see your good works and give glory to your Father who is in heaven" (Mt. 5:16). The implications of this statement are far-reaching. Ideally, our God mission is performed in such a way that people know that it is God at work rather than us. They see us doing what we do, but they know that Spirit is at work. The reason for this is that a God mission is extraordinary in its outreach and ability to serve humankind. What is accomplished far exceeds what seems possible.

We have grand examples of this on our planet. Jesus' ministry spanned three years, but is still expanding two thousand years later. One person, Paul, inspired thousands of people to embrace Christianity. Mother Teresa founded a religious order dedicated to assisting the poor and dying; less than thirty years later, this work extends to eighty-seven countries. These are grand examples, but there are also numerous storefronts which are fronts for God. Nameless shopkeepers and good samaritans help thousands of people realize that they are loved, special, and important.

I have worked
for my own glory.

Most of us have worked for our own glory. Our world is small, and its center is us. In our insecurity, we try to ensure our place in the world. We believe we are people of worth when we win the praise of others and earthly awards. Who we are needs the confirmation of other people. This is because we do not know ourselves and our potential role in the universe.

Write an award you have received:

What has been your primary means of securing the praise of others?

When we work for our own glory, two things happen. The first is exhaustion. When we are not in touch with a power greater than ourselves, we become depleted. Second, no matter how much praise we receive, it is never enough because the emptiness we feel inside cannot be filled from the outside. Only Spirit can reveal to us our rightful role in the world and give to us a sense of worth and security.

I have worked

in order to receive the love of others.

Week 47

Day 324

Glory from the human perspective takes many forms. For some, it is awards. For others, it is education. For most people, it is the praise and love of others, for we fail to know the love that is within us. We are an empty cup held out to the world in the hope that we can be filled.

We want others to love and respect us, so we try to get their approval. We remain silent when we really want to speak because we are concerned someone may disagree with us or think us stupid. We may nod our head in approval when we actually disagree. We may go places we do not want to go or do things we do not want to do.

What are some of the "techniques" you have used in trying to get people to love you?

I want to work for God's glory.

It is natural that we reach a point where we want to work for God's glory. Working for our glory has not fulfilled us. How alone and forsaken we sometimes feel when our work is for ourselves. The world seems against us.

Over the course of the last year, our souls have gradually filled to a point of overflowing. Now it is time to give, to share, and to serve humankind. It is wonderful to experience our cup being filled. There is great joy as this occurs, but the greater, more abundant joy occurs when the truth of who we are overflows like a mighty river onto a parched land.

"The earth is the Lord's and the fulness thereof, the world and those who dwell therein" (Ps. 24:1). Let us never be without a God mission. There is much work to be done, but the laborers are few. Our earth, God's earth, is in need of those who will nurture it. People in need are everywhere. The homeless now include families. Children need the attention of loving adults. People addicted to drugs want to be free.

List possible things you could do or are doing for God's glory:

I do simple things
for God's glory.

When we think of God, we usually think in grand terms, and therefore, it is natural to believe that work for God's glory must be grand. How tempting it is to want to do something big. A minister does not want a "small" church of two hundred, he wants to speak to thousands. If it is for God's glory, it has to be immense, he thinks.

Can simple things in life be for God's glory? Can any human endeavor that seeks to serve humankind be for God's glory? Is it possible to do seemingly mundane things for God's glory? We may think, "Well, no one will know." Why does anyone have to know? Is the work for God's glory or our own?

Consider the following idea: anything done *from* an awareness of God's presence is done for God's glory. Other people may or may not become aware of it. Worldly attention or praise is not the issue.

Choose a simple task that you do every day, and do it for God's glory. Perform the task from an awareness of God. What did you choose to do?

 *Week 47*
Day 327

I do whatever I do
for God's glory.

It is possible to do all things for God's glory. In the course of the day, we perform many tasks. Most of them are mundane, but they are tasks we must do.

Before we do the many mundane tasks we do today, let us silently repeat to ourselves: *I do it for God's glory*, and then act.

Also, as an exercise today, do something anonymously for another person. What did you do?

There is a treasure in heaven
when work is for God's glory.

Week 47
Day 328

Work which is for God's glory requires much from us. Spirit will utilize any natural talents we have, but more than earthly abilities are necessary if God's work is going to be fulfilled. For instance, a person may be a gifted speaker, but more than oratory must be expressed before God's glory is made manifest.

There is basically one gift that Spirit gives—itself. In the individual, this becomes a consciousness of the Almighty; the person can feel the Presence. If this occurs in the life of one who communicates Truth, the listener receives more than the words spoken. The audience has a sense of God's presence. This is more valuable than any spoken word.

Humankind manifests many talents, but those who are doing God's work experience and express the Presence.

Mother Teresa of the Missionaries of Charity possesses earthly talents, but what quality of Spirit is she allowing to be expressed from within her?

Gandhi of India freed his nation from British rule. What quality of Spirit do you think expressed itself through him?

When you are with someone who works for God's glory, you will have a sense of the Presence. Do you know anyone like this? Who?

465

*The treasure of heaven
is for God's glory.*

When the things we do are for God's glory, we are given the treasure of heaven. We experience the Presence. We feel blessed, as if we have received something special. We may even feel undeserving of so great a gift, but let us realize that the treasure is not given solely to us. It is given for God's glory and thus to all humankind.

As we lose ourselves in the things we do and declare before every task: *It is for God's glory*, we are given the treasure. Not only may we feel a deep peace, but we speak and act with authority. Jesus amazed the people because He spoke as one having authority. This is the sign that we have been given the treasure.

After Jesus' crucifixion, the disciples hid themselves. But after their experience at Pentecost when they received the treasure of the Holy Spirit, they became bold and without fear. Peter, the one who had denied knowing Jesus, spoke openly to the people.

People who work for God's glory are not timid. They have been given a commission; therefore, they speak and act with conviction.

How do you think a person acts or speaks when he or she has received the treasure?

Week Forty-Eight
Sacred Work

No task is more important than another. What we do is not as important as the consciousness out of which it is done. Religious work is not necessarily sacred; sacred work does not have to be "religious." Sacred work rises from an awareness of Spirit. If we are aware of God as we prepare the evening meal for the family, the work is sacred. Works rising out of an awareness of God are like God, and they penetrate our beings and find the heart of us. Words, even words that are technically true, fail to move beyond our memories when they originate in human consciousness.

May this week be filled with sacred work.

I can tell when my work
is not sacred.

We can tell when our work is not sacred. It stands alone and is not a part of something greater. There seems to be no purpose to the work other than making ends meet. We do the thing because we have to. We retire from work like this. Sacred work, however, becomes part of our lives. It is fun, for it energizes us and lifts us up. Work that is not sacred seems never to end; it is drudgery.

What do you regularly do that is not sacred work?

Why do you do it?

All work can be sacred.

All work can be sacred if its beginning is a consciousness of God. A minister visited a prisoner in a maximum security prison. He had never met the man he was going to see, but had become aware of him through correspondence. The man had committed murder when he was eighteen years old and received a life prison term. Their time of sharing was meaningful, not because of what they said to each other, but because it was a sacred happening. When their time was up the minister stood and placed his hand against the glass that separated them. His new friend placed his hand up also, and the friendship was formed.

Whenever a sacred happening occurs, it is helpful to determine how the event became so meaningful. In this instance, the treasure of God consciousness was received because during the visit the minister gave complete attention to the man. It was discussed during the past week that whenever we are fully in the present moment, we are candidates for spiritual awareness. Work becomes sacred and the treasure is given when we give our full attention to it.

Choose some simple task you will do today, and give it your full attention. It will become sacred work.

Silence can be sacred work.

Silence can be sacred work when it is an experience of the Presence. The word *work* generally denotes activity. This is the human way of viewing life. Most of Spirit's work is done in silence.

The silence can be listening to someone, and sacred work is done. All that is required is that we give our full attention to the one who is talking. The sacred work can be done as we sit in silence at a dear one's bedside. Attention and a receptivity to God improve the possibility that the work can be sacred.

Discover this principle for yourself today. How will you test the idea that silence can be sacred work?

I prepare

to do a sacred work.

Today is a special day. Prepare yourself to do a sacred work. In performing this task, you will find that mundane things come alive with joy and purpose when they are done from an awareness of the Presence.

Today or during a remaining day of this week, prepare a meal in total silence while giving full attention to the simple things you do. Washing vegetables, for instance, should be done with reverence. Your movements should be slow and deliberate so you can sense the Presence. Perhaps you might want to ponder the life essence which is the nourishing life-force of the food you are preparing. Describe your experience:

When work is sacred,
it is filled with joy.

When we are aware of God, we are highly productive. Creativity pours from within us. We work with ease. *Effortless* is the word we use to describe what we have done. In fact, we may even look at what has been accomplished and wonder if we really did it.

Let us remember that the true reward is not the accomplishment itself, but the consciousness which produced the work. It is easy to think of the work as completed, but this only taints our experience. We will eventually become sidetracked and task-oriented. Our way of life is to become God-oriented. The sign we are looking for is not a feeling of accomplishment, but a sense of joy. We can have this feeling while we chop wood, plant a garden, or groom our pet. Remember, we are in the world, but not of it. Joy is within us. What is accomplished is of the earth.

Simple, sacred work prepares me for the God mission.

When we are competent and content in simple, sacred work, we are prepared for our God mission. Spirit's work is too important to be entrusted to someone who will not carry it through.

Sometimes we have the feeling that we are destined for some special work, but we do not know what it is. We search and wonder and wander. Undoubtedly there are people who die still searching or wondering what might have been. Most likely, there was something simple they were to do before their life's work was given to them, but many people look for the grand mission and miss the work that is at hand.

In the human work environment, no one is hired as the president of the company out of college or business school. The graduate must "pay his or her dues" before the opportunity for leadership is granted. In the kingdom of God, soul development is the prerequisite before a God mission is given.

What simple, sacred work is at hand for you today?

My life is sacred
when I am doing the sacred work.

Our lives are sacred when we are doing the sacred work. There are things to be done, but our true emphasis is upon being. Being comes first, then doing. Life, the gift of God, appears meaningless when we ignore this principle.

Our lives are precious. Not one life is to be wasted. The fields are white unto harvest, and laborers are needed to harvest the field and present the promise of love, peace, and joy.

In your mind's eye, see a vast field of grain moving with the wind. The potential harvest is great. The backward and forward movement of the grain is calling you to come and do the sacred work. In your vision, when you are prepared and aware of the Presence, enter the field.

Week Forty-Nine
Fulfillment

There is a way to tell if we are experiencing our oneness with God. We are fulfilled. When this is the state of our soul, there is nothing we need. Naturally, we do not ask for anything. We are rich in Spirit. Our God has us; we have our God. This is enough.

If we have much, but are compelled to have more, we are not rich. We are poor because there is something we feel we must acquire. We are rich not because we can buy anything we want, but because our contentment is so great that there is nothing we need. Most of all, what our soul requires is a mission—a reason for being. When we have this, we are fulfilled. We have moved beyond the human needs of shelter, food, water, and clothing, through our more intangible desire for companionship and a sense of worth, to the desire to make a contribution for the common good.

Let our richness extend beyond what the world can give us. Let us enter the kingdom of heaven, experience God, and find a fulfillment so complete that asking ceases.

I want to be fulfilled.

We want to be fulfilled, to feel a security so great that we lack nothing or, at least, there is nothing we cannot have. Therefore, we try to either acquire the things we believe will fulfill us or discover the means to have whatever we believe will make us happy. For those people who are of the earth, money is thought to provide for all our wishes. As we grow, we begin to expand our list of things needed for fulfillment.

What do you believe is necessary for your fulfillment?

Which of these things do you not have?

In the past,
I have asked for much.

We think we know what will bring us fulfillment. We look at our lives and acknowledge that we do not have what we think is necessary for happiness. We turn to the promise given by Jesus, "Ask, and it will be given you" (Mt. 7:7). How easy it seems. The problem is that we want this promise to fulfill our earthly needs. Don't we realize that it is not our world that is lacking? It is the soul that feels empty.

In the last five years, what have you asked to receive?

Please circle those "items" that are earthly.

Do you believe Jesus' promise about asking and receiving?

I thought fulfillment
was in the world.

Whether we were aware of Jesus' promise or not, we have asked and asked and asked. In many instances, we either have not received, or we have received what we asked for but it did not fulfill us. Children feel they must have a certain gift at Christmas. They ask and receive, and in a short time, the thing is forgotten. Usually, something else becomes important, and the child asks again.

Basically, we have believed that fulfillment was in the world. It does not take long to realize that this belief is a lie. In fact, after a time we will either reject Jesus' promise about asking and receiving or look at the law in a new way. Let us not forget that Jesus was a man of God. He did not try to find His fulfillment in the world. His joy was the fulfillment of God's will. Jesus must have asked often, but not for the things of the earth. He asked for something else!

When Jesus asked, what did He receive?

What I ask for must change.

Fulfillment and asking are one, but what we ask for must change. In this section of the book, we have opened ourselves to our God mission and asked for God. We have become sensitive to the Presence as part of the simple things we do.

To ask is to be willing. This is the consciousness of the servant. It is strange, but we think that servants are unfulfilled. No. Slaves are bound; servants are not. Servants of God are lifted up. They humble themselves, but humankind praises them, looks to them for leadership, and holds these individuals up to the children as examples.

Ask today, but let the asking be different than it has ever been before. Allow the purity of your soul to ask so that it can be fulfilled. What is the soul's desire?

I ask for God.

Today let us ask for God, not so that God will come to us, but so that we might know that God is with us. This gift will be freely given. In truth, Spirit has already given itself to us, but it waits for our asking.

Today ask with every faculty of your being.

With your mind, ask by silently thinking: *I ask for God.*

With your voice, ask by speaking aloud: *I ask for God.*

With your hands, ask by turning your palms upward as a gesture of openness.

With your imagination, ask by seeing yourself holding an empty vessel waiting to be filled.

Today we come to the central insight of this week's work. When we are conscious of our oneness with God, asking ends. In the first five days of the week, we reviewed the state of our asking. How refreshing it is to reduce our many desires to the soul's yearning for its Creator. Fulfillment comes as we ask for God and receive the spiritual awareness we are prepared to receive. In this moment of unity with our God, fulfillment reigns. The sign that this is so is that all asking ceases.

We are fulfilled and cannot ask for anything. It is this state of consciousness that is described in the early verses of the Twenty-third Psalm. "The Lord is my shepherd, I shall not want; he makes me lie down in green pastures. He leads me beside still waters; he restores my soul" (Ps. 23:1-3).

People who are one with God are fulfilled. When they return to an awareness of the earth around them, they do not ask. They are about God's business. From the fulfillment of a few moments in unity with God, a purpose is born.

Today I will not ask.

When our lives are filled with many needs, it is difficult to consider a way of life in which we do not ask for anything but God. However, common sense indicates that when we are consciously one with God, there must be a state of fulfillment. There can be no substitute for this experience, but we can begin to move in this direction.

We can prime the pump by not asking for anything during the course of the day. Or if a need arises and we are tempted to ask, we can declare: *Today I will not ask.* We let these words be our companion for the next twenty-four hours.

As many times as possible today, enter into a state of prayer and meditation. Prime the pump by saying within the quiet recesses of your soul: *Today I will not ask.* Be willing to experience your oneness with God. Then observe the number of times you want to ask for something. Remember, asking is a sign that you are losing your sense of oneness. In summary, let this be a day of alternating times of prayer and meditation as well as consistent observation. This practice can be repeated throughout any day. Eventually, there will be less asking and more fulfillment.

I Am God's Responsibility

When the human journey is in progress, we are irresponsible. Someone or something is the reason for our woes, and if good things happen, we are lucky, but wonder when they will end. The inner journey begins when we become responsible. We realize that our thoughts and feelings manifest themselves as our experience. We change the way we think, and our lives are transformed.

With this understanding, there is also guilt. We have done it to ourselves. Given time and forgiveness of self, self-acceptance follows, and guilt passes away. Now we are ready to become God's responsibility.

When we realize our oneness with God, we are God's responsibility. The things we think and say rise from within us. We cannot call them our own. Their origin is God. We are the mouthpiece of Spirit. The mind fills with ideas, and they overflow into the world. We do not act because we think something should be done, but because we feel a sense of guidance. The work we do is directed from within and is for God's glory. This is a powerful realization, but let there also be caution. Through the ages, many people have attributed their actions to God. They have claimed that God was responsible for what they have said and done. In some instances, atrocities have been committed and attributed to God. Such things are not God's responsibility, nor have they been ordained by the Creator. They are human acts, for they have not come from a realization of oneness with God and, therefore, they do not express the love and gentleness of Spirit.

When we are not in tune with the Infinite, we are our own responsibility. We can choose whether to be consciously responsible or not. If our choice is conscious responsibility, we are empowered. But if we deny the ability of our thoughts and beliefs to impact our experience, we will be tossed to and

fro by events and conditions. Obviously, the best life can offer occurs when we are God's responsibility. Please realize that the prerequisite for this way of life is an awareness of our oneness with God. Then Spirit can express itself through the voice, hand, and heart of humankind. It is for God's glory, but we are blessed and made aware of the truth that God and humankind are destined to be joined in creative acts that lead all who are willing to follow to a life of love, peace, and joy.

When we realize our oneness with God, the mind of the Christ is activated in us. Thoughts unlike any others we have ever entertained move within us. These thoughts are destined to stir us up and invigorate others. Our minds are not solely for us; they are for the wisdom of God. They are wicks for Spirit's light. What comes forth is not our responsibility; it is God's. We must not claim ownership, but we must assume our responsibility by being willing followers of the light.

Our primary responsibility is to be as available to Spirit as we possibly can. We do not have to concern ourselves with the thoughts and ideas that will move within us when the mind is open to God. This is God's responsibility. Rest assured that Spirit will do its job. We will be stimulated and thrilled with the thoughts and ideas.

Make yourself available to Spirit today through extended periods of prayer and meditation. As you become aware of your oneness with God, your mind will become God's responsibility. Let it free you and take you to new heights of awareness and creativity. Write below any new ideas or thoughts that come to you:

Week 50
Day 345

When I realize my oneness with God,
God is responsible for what I say.

When we are aware of our oneness with God, the words we speak are given to us. In our society, there are people who make their living as speech writers. They are the faceless and nameless people who write the speeches for many of our politicians and public figures. In this profession, the speech writer tries to become one with the speechmaker so as to capture the essence of the person's beliefs and thoughts.

When we are God's responsibility, we have allowed ourselves to become aware of the divine ideas that move within the mind of God, and we become the mouthpiece of Spirit.

There are times in our lives when we say things and wonder where the thoughts originated. At other times, we do not even remember saying something, but find later that it helped another person. The truth is that every human being is capable of allowing Spirit to speak through him or her.

The minister or spiritual counselor speaks to many people whose problems are so grave that he or she can think of nothing helpful to say. At such times it is common to say within, "God, I don't know what to say. You are going to have to speak through me." Our willingness to speak and our admission that we do not know what to say invite God's wisdom to be expressed.

Let there be extended periods of prayer and meditation today as you make yourself available to Spirit. As you become attuned to your oneness with God, your words will become God's responsibility. Let them be a force for good in the world, and listen carefully, for not only will you be the speaker, but the listener.

In the space that follows, write what you hear "yourself" saying:

Week 50
Day 346

When I realize my oneness with God,
God is responsible for what I imagine.

When we are aware of our oneness with God, our imagination becomes the tool of Spirit. Our dreams and the images which form in our minds are divine illuminations.

During a time of prayer and meditation, a powerful image can become a friend and a symbol of God's caring love.

When we realize our oneness with God, the dreams, images, and visions are God's responsibility. They are given to us and to the world.

Let there be extended periods of prayer and meditation today as you make yourself available to Spirit. In your oneness with God, your imagination faculty will be God's responsibility. Be still and watch carefully. Record any significant dreams, images, or visions which you receive. Do not try to force any imagery.

When we are aware of our oneness with God, our actions are not solely our own. We are directed in the way that we should go. The Bible is filled with examples of people following the guidance of Spirit. Abram, who became Abraham, left Haran and traveled to the Promised Land because of divine guidance. Jesus endured the Cross because of the guidance He received in the garden of Gethsemane. Paul carried the Christian message to distant lands when he felt the guiding hand of God.

These people followed instructions and went forth, not knowing what was before them. They had become God's responsibility, and they were willing to place themselves in Spirit's care. When we are in touch with our oneness with God, we receive guidance and should follow it. If we allow ourselves to be guided daily, we have nothing to fear, for we are God's responsibility.

Give another example from the Bible of someone who became God's responsibility because of the guidance received and followed. Also, give an example of this principle at work in your life.

When I realize my oneness with God, all my needs are met.

When we are aware of our oneness with God, we are God's responsibility. Our souls' needs and our earthly needs are no longer our business. The prophet Elijah was fed by the raven. He was one with God, and all his needs were met.

This same process can unfold in our lives if we are aware of our oneness with God. As we continue to dedicate ourselves to an experience of the Presence, we do not need to concern ourselves with earthly needs—what we shall eat or drink or wear. Our attention can rest in God. Daily bread is the experience of all who are one with Spirit.

What do you think was the responsibility of the Hebrews who received the manna in the wilderness?

Possible answer: The Hebrews' responsibility was to make themselves available to Spirit and to collect the manna that fell each evening.

When I realize my oneness with God, nothing can harm me.

When we are aware of our oneness with God, there is nothing to fear, for we are God's responsibility. In God's presence, there is no harm or hurt. This is the message of Psalm 91:

He who dwells in the shelter of the Most High,
who abides in the shadow of the Almighty,
will say to the Lord, "My refuge and my fortress;
my God, in whom I trust."
For he will deliver you from the snare of the fowler
and from the deadly pestilence . . . .
You will not fear the terror of the night,
nor the arrow that flies by day.

The key words for us are "He who dwells in the shelter of the Most High." This is our responsibility—awareness of our oneness with God. Then we become God's responsibility, and we fear nothing.

Read Psalm 91 today and rest quietly with many of the verses. It will help you know the caring love of God and how secure you are when you are God's responsibility.

I am God's responsibility.

Let us now declare that we are God's responsibility. This means that we are aware of our oneness with God. There is no other way to relinquish our responsibility and rest in the care of Spirit. This truth frees us from earthly concerns. It takes the burden out of doing God's work. Even the work we do and the fulfillment of the mission become God's responsibility. Our responsibility is to remain conscious of our oneness with God and to be willing to follow our guidance. We watch the thoughts moving in our minds; speak the words we hear within us; give thanks for the dreams, images, and visions we see; and do the tasks we are given to do.

Let this be a day when you totally fulfill your responsibility of giving yourself to Spirit. All that happens is then God's responsibility. Bring together all the things you have learned in this book and become God's responsibility. Pray and meditate, practice the presence, pause for monastic moments, and do everything else that will make you available to your God.

Week Fifty-One
Finally . . . Contentment

Our journey began with divine discontent. Now we have come full circle and can say with Paul, "I have learned, in whatever state I am, to be content" (Phil. 4:11). For so long, for too long, our contentment required that other people behave in certain ways and that the world conform to our vision of what it should be. How interesting that there was always someone who did the thing we dreaded most and that the world seemed to have a mind of its own. Eventually, we learned how fruitless and unproductive it was to depend upon people and earthly events for our peace of mind.

Jesus suggested that there is a peace that passes understanding. This is the peace that comes, for instance, after the death of a loved one. There is no logical reason for peace to reside in our souls, but often it does. In crisis, we sometimes think clearly and act swiftly, with courage and daring. This is the normal state of the soul. We always rest in the Presence, but when we know it, there is contentment.

 ## *Divine discontent was my beginning.*

Divine discontent was our beginning nearly a year ago. It is usually the beginning for everyone who seeks a spiritual life. So many things have happened since the first day we began using this book. What seemed so pressing and difficult is now seen in a new light.

From this day forth, we have no guarantee that we will not be discontent again, but if we are, we now know that it is only a beginning leading to joy and peace.

Can you recall the divine discontent that filled your soul a year ago? If yes, what was it?

Give thanks for the discontent from the past, for it caused your first step on this phase of your spiritual journey.

I thought contentment
depended upon people.

Week 51
Day 352

We once believed that our contentment depended upon other people. There was a time when people and their words and actions seemed to cause our peace to flee. Now we know this is not true. Other people are not the cause of contentment or our discontent.

List the people you once thought determined your contentment:

When did you last allow another person to determine your state of mind?

What is the key to your being able to maintain Paul's stance, "I have learned, in whatever state I am, to be content"?

495

I have chosen contentment.

We have chosen contentment by choosing God rather than the world. The truth is, there is no contentment in the world, only contention. The "world" is defined as a state of consciousness that knows nothing of the spiritual principles that govern our lives.

There is a choice we must make each day. People and situations will be presented to us, and we will have to choose contentment or contention.

Let this be your answer: *I choose contentment rather than contention. I choose God rather than the world.*

My contentment passes understanding.

The contentment which rests in God passes understanding. People in crisis have experienced a great calm. There is no logic to the peace that they experienced, for it passed understanding, and yet it was present. The story is told of Ralph Waldo Emerson standing outside his home, watching his house burn. Inside was a vast library of valuable books. Louisa May Alcott tried to console him, and Mr. Emerson purportedly answered, "Yes, Louisa, they are all gone, but let's enjoy the blaze now."

When contentment passes understanding, we can enjoy the moment. That is the way it must be for us. Our joy cannot depend upon logic. There will be times when we are greatly challenged by life. Peace is still present and can be experienced by us. Let it be so today.

My experience of oneness with God
is the source of my contentment.

"Nothing can disturb the calm peace of my soul" is a statement that has assisted many people in becoming relaxed and calm during times of crisis. However, saying this statement is not enough. Many people have said these words and felt no degree of calm. Words are never enough. There must be revelation. But before there can be revelation, there must be the experience of oneness with God.

Oneness with Spirit is the source of contentment. Spirit is a peaceful calm; the quiet of the evening; the still of the night. During your time of prayer and meditation today, form an image of the most peaceful and calm scene you can image. In this place, nothing disturbs the calm peace of your soul. Rest in this place, and let the peace of God that transcends all images come upon you.

It is wonderful to find the peace of God, but as quickly as it is found it can be lost. Actually, it is not contentment that is lost, but something even greater. We lose conscious contact with God. This is the connection we must re-establish.

Electricity is useful when it moves in a circuit. When we turn on the lights in our home, the circuit is completed (it becomes a circle), and the electricity can do its work. Contentment can be our experience, but a circuit must be completed. We must make contact with God. Contact with God and contentment are part of the same circle.

Let today be dedicated to the circle which is contact with Spirit and contentment. If the circle is broken, you know what to do so it can be re-established.

Week 51
Day 357

I have learned,
in whatever state I am, to be content.

We have come full circle and learned that we can be content regardless of the conditions of life. But there is much more to this than contentment. Our purpose remains before us, for no condition can hide from us what we are destined to do. It is clear that when there is discontentment, the issue is not the situation but the state of our relationship with God. When a problem looms and fills the screen of life, we have forgotten our relationship with God.

We have learned that, no matter what state we are in, the most vital thing is an awareness of God. Not only have we learned this truth, but we know what we must do to rediscover the Presence that is always with us.

Carry with you today and always this truth: I have learned, in whatever state I am in, that the most important thing is my awareness of God.

Week Fifty-Two
Summary

The Bible begins with God and so must a spiritual life, for with God nothing is impossible. Humankind has hoped for thousands of years that this is true. We have asked God to perform the impossible, to do what we have been unable to do. However, we have discovered that God can only do what God has been doing. Primarily God is being . . . being life, love, wisdom, peace, and so forth. This is enough, for when we awaken to the Master's handiwork, all is well.

No more do we ask the Almighty to repair our world. Spirit's work is creativity, not maintenance. We have our role to fulfill in God's acts of creativity, but our mission is not given to us until we realize that it is not we who do the work. For too long, we have tried to make God our servant. Now we realize we are to be servants of the Most High. Each of us must declare, "Here I am Lord, use me."

As we do this, our God mission begins to emerge. We are blessed by the mission, but it is for God's glory, not ours. We begin with simple things and the knowing that any work done from an awareness of Spirit is sacred work. And so we work, and there is fulfillment in which our cup is so full that we cannot ask for anything. We are one with God and therefore God's responsibility. The things we think, say, imagine, and do come from our awareness of God. They are not ours, but God's. We have returned to God and what God has given us—our lives. We have come full circle. First there was divine discontent. Now there is a contentment whose center is God. No matter the state of the world, we are content.

Return to any day or combination of days that you have not understood or that you think need more work or review. Repeat the lesson(s) as *Week Fifty-Two*'s work.

In the spaces below write the lessons which you chose to review:

Day 358   *Week* _____

            Day _____

Day 359   *Week* _____

            Day _____

Day 360   *Week* _____

            Day _____

Day 361   *Week* _____

            Day _____

Day 362   *Week* _____

            Day _____

Day 363   *Week* _____

            Day _____

Day 364   *Week* _____

            Day _____

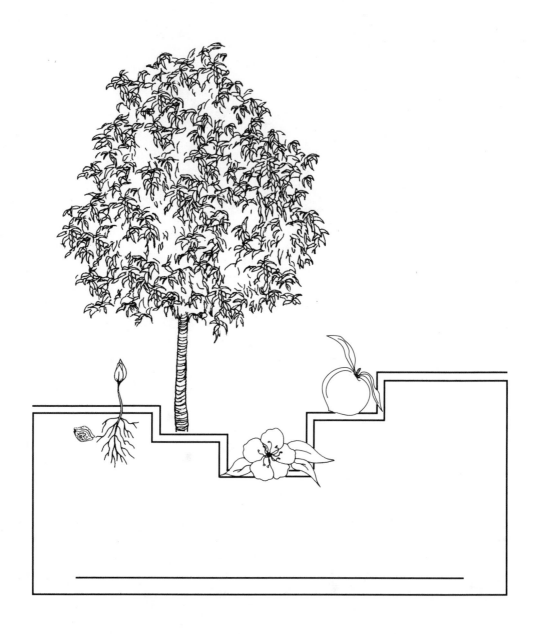

Day 365
The journey continues . . .

You, dear friend, are to be praised. *A Daily Guide to Spiritual Living* required commitment and persistence. There were most likely times when you did not want to continue with the exercises, but you have persevered. Your inner being was stirred, and you felt resistance to the change which was taking place in you, but you knew that without change, there would be no new life.

You have done more than change. Your why, your motivation, has been transformed, and because of this, you are new. Let there be great expectation now, for there is a new movement in your life.

I do not know your life circumstances or where you are now as you read the final words of this book. (Perhaps you are sitting in your favorite chair in your apartment, or on a park bench enjoying the fragrances and freshness of spring.) But I know where you are in consciousness. You are on the summit of a mountain, a high place where you can see the world and your life in a new way. And yet your journey has not ended. Look around you, and become aware of other mountains you are destined to climb. Close your eyes, and let Spirit reveal even more of the kingdom of God. "Stretch forth your wings" and allow the wind of Spirit to take you higher.

The gate through which we enter the kingdom of God may be narrow, but the road of life meanders endlessly. It is filled with eternal turns. The unknown greets us daily. When we are dedicated to living a spiritual life, there is nothing to fear, for we are not alone. Spirit is with us, closer than hands and feet and breathing. We, Spirit and all of humankind, are joined together in an eternal quest. We may not know one another's names, but together, with joyous confidence, we walk the road named Life. Godspeed, dear friend, and always know you are not alone. There are unseen friends around the world who journey in love with you.

Also by Jim Rosemergy

Books

A Recent Revelation
Living the Mystical Life Today
The Watcher
Trancendence Through Humility

Audiocassette Albums

What Unity Teaches
Raising Children or Raising
  Consciousness, Which?
The Science of Prayer
From Metaphysics to Mysticism
How to Win the Human Race:
  Lessons in Unconditional Love
The Cornerstone of a New World:
  Personal and Planetary Change
Awakening Spiritual Consciousness
Famous Bible Stories From the
  Old Testament: A Mystical View
Living the Mystical Life Today

About the Author

Jim Rosemergy is executive vice president of Unity School of Christianity, with responsibilities in the areas of world outreach, facilities, publishing, human resources, and education.

An ordained Unity minister, Jim pioneered his first ministry in Raleigh, North Carolina, in 1976. With a deep devotion to prayer as a foundation, he inspired that ministry to grow from eighteen people to over three hundred in seven years. He has since served the Unity Church of Truth in Spokane, Washington, and the Unity Temple on the Plaza in Kansas City, Missouri, the founders' church. A strong emphasis on spiritual awakening has been the focus of his ministry. For the year 1987-88 he was elected by his peers to serve as president of the Association of Unity Churches.

Jim is the author of four books; his articles and poetry have appeared in a variety of spiritually based magazines, including *Unity* magazine and *Daily Word*. Unity School produces many of his Sunday lesson series on audiocassette albums.

Jim and Nancy, his wife of over twenty years, have two sons, Jamie and Ben. Jim enjoys spending time with his family, taking long walks, and playing tennis and golf.

Printed U.S.A.

87-4660-15M-11-92